BLACK WOMEN, WRITING AND IDENTITY

Black Women, Writing and Identity is an exciting new work by one of the most imaginative and acute writers around. The book explores a complex and fascinating set of interrelated issues, establishing the significance of such wide-ranging subjects as:

- re-mapping, re-naming and cultural crossings
- migration and the re-negotiation of identities
- the discourse of uprisings and constructions of Empire
- African women's writing and resistance to domination
- creativity, theorizing and critical relationality
- gender, language and the politics of location

Carole Boyce Davies is at the forefront of attempts to broaden the discourse surrounding the representation of and by Black women and women of colour. *Black Women, Writing and Identity* represents an extraordinary achievement in this field, taking our understanding of identity, location and representation to new levels.

Carole Boyce Davies is Associate Professor in the Departments of English, African and African-American Studies and Comparative Literature at the State University of New York at Binghamton.

BLACK WOMEN, WRITING AND IDENTITY

Migrations of the subject

Carole Boyce Davies

London and New York

First published 1994
by Routledge
11 New Fetter Lane, London EC4P 4EE

Simultaneously published in the USA and Canada
by Routledge
29 West 35th Street, New York, NY 10001

Typeset in Bembo by
Florencetype Ltd, Kewstoke, Avon
Printed and bound in Great Britain by
Clays Ltd, St. Ives PLC

British Library Cataloguing in Publication Data
A catalogue record for this book is available from the British Library

Library of Congress Cataloging in Publication Data
Davies, Carole Boyce.
Black women, writing and identity : migrations of the subject /
Carole Boyce Davies.
p.   cm.
Includes bibliographical references and index.
1. American literature – Afro-American authors – History and
criticism. 2. English literature – Foreign countries – History and
criticism. 3. American literature – Women authors – History and
criticism. 4. English literature – Black authors – History and
criticism. 5. English literature – Women authors – History and
criticism. 6. Identity (Psychology) in literature. 7. Afro-
Americans in literature. 8. Authorship – Sex differences.
9. Blacks in literature. 10. Women and literature.   I. Title.
PS153.N5D32 1994
810.9′ 9287′ 08996073 – dc20 93-44335

ISBN 0-415-10086-0 (hbk)
0-415-10087-9 (pbk)

For my mother, Mary Boyce Joseph,
my first teacher,
who taught me all that she knew
and then gave me the space to explore the world.

CONTENTS

ACKNOWLEDGMENTS

A number of friends, colleagues, students and relatives offered support, love, words of encouragement and interest in the development of my ideas, during the tedious days of writing this manuscript. I would like to identify the wonderful students I have worked with over the years at Binghamton, who have always supported me as I have supported them. In particular those in my various Black Women's Writing classes who have participated in a variety of transformations of knowledge and consciousness, among them, Vinnie Cuccia, Donnette Dunbar, Julia Fernandez, Nicole Gaskins, Joel Haynes, Thekla Holder, Marie Soto and others too numerous to mention. Leo Wilton, Francisco Reyes, constantly made sure I was on track by constantly asking the "how is the book coming?" question. Erica Braxton, Kim Hall, Siga Jagne, Gladys Jimenez-Muñoz, Greg Thomas were wonderful graduate students and friends who often offered helpful references and read or listened to various bits and pieces of this work. A number of colleagues especially Elsa Barkley Brown, Deborah Britzman, Marilynn Desmond, Monica Jardine, Velma Pollard, Juanita Ramos-Diaz and Kelvin Santiago-Vallès read, listened to and/or offered advice on various versions of chapters at different times. Special thanks to Susan Strehle who read the final manuscript and offered important affirming and helpful words. Arlene Norwalk of the English Department, and Lisa Fegley-Schmidt and Jim Wolff of Binghamton University, helped with word-processing advice at critical moments. My high-school friend, Sheila Henry, has always been there to listen and sometimes seems to enjoy my journeys and their stories as much as I do. Above all, she has helped me to see the need for balance and I thank her for that. *Aché*!

The NEH-Brazil, 1992 group, particularly Chuck Martin,

Charles Rowell and Clyde Taylor, offered companionship, listening ears and great advice, reflective observations, during a time of transition for me. Special thanks to Michael Hanchard and Bob Stam who read chapters and offered wonderful suggestions and references, but above all offered faith in my work and the kind of encouragement which pushed me to finish this manuscript. Anne Adams, Abena Busia, Beverly Guy-Sheftall, bell hooks, Janis Mayes, 'Molara Ogundipe-Leslie have been wonderful sisters-in-struggle. Aṣẹ. The London Black Women Writers who welcomed me and made me feel at home during my five-month stay in 1992: in particular, Merle Collins, Beryl Gilroy (Mrs G), Isha McKenzie Mavinga, Susheila Nasta, Netifa, Grace Nichols, Joan Riley, Janice Shinebourne, Dorothea Smartt, Frances Anne Solomon, Storme Webber, Claudette Williams . . . A big Aché. Anna Davin, Elizabeth Gunner, Murray Last, Anne McClintock, Rob Nixon and particularly Amon Saba Sakaana encouraged my efforts. My daughters, Jonelle Ashaki Davies and Dalia Abayomi Davies have been their beautiful selves, strong and wise in their own right. Axè!

The following are offered sincere thanks for permission to quote from or include the following: Joyoti Grech for "In Answer to Some Questions"; Kamila Zahno for "Ethnic Monitoring or a Geography Lesson"; Maya Chowdhry for "Birth Certificate" all of which appeared in Feminist Art News vol. 3, no. 10, 1991 and Maya Chowdhry for "Diary of Home"; Netifa Masimba for "We Are Revolting" from A Woman Determined (London, Research Associates School Time Publications, 1987); Nancy Berreano for Cheryl Clarke's "Living as a Lesbian Underground: A Futuristic Fantasy" from her Living as a Lesbian (Ithaca, NY, Firebrand Books, 1986); Marlene Philip for She Tries Her Tongue. Her Silence Softly Breaks, Karnak House for Grace Nichols's "The Return" and "Epilogue" from her I Is A Long Memoried Woman (London, Karnak House, 1983).

A different version of Chapter 5 appeared in Carole Boyce Davies and Elaine Savory Fido, eds, Out of the Kumbla. Caribbean Women and Literature (Trenton, NJ, Africa World Press, 1990, pp. 59–73). A portion of Chapter 6 appeared in Brenda O. Daly and Maureen T. Reddy, eds, Narrating Mothers. Theorizing Maternal Subjectivities (Knoxville, Tenn., University of Tennessee Press, 1991, pp. 44–57).

1

INTRODUCTION:
MIGRATORY SUBJECTIVITIES

Black women's writing and the re-negotiation of identities

I had realized that the origin of my presence on the island –
my ancestral history – was the result of a foul deed. . . .
(Jamaica Kincaid, *Lucy*, p. 135)

Opening migration narrative

My mother's journeys redefine space.[1] Her annual migrations,
between the Caribbean and the United States, are ones of persistent
re-membering and re-connection. She lives in the Caribbean; she
lives in the United States; she lives in America. She also lives in that
in-between space that is neither here nor there, locating herself in
the communities where her children, grandchildren, family and
friends reside. Hers is a deliberate and fundamental migration that
defies the sense of specific location that even her children would
want to force on her. In each home place, she sets up a network of
relationships based on kin, community, spirituality and a fundamental presence organized around service and disruption of the
very specific norms of that community. Northern New York is
home for her only when there is warmth. Her sojourns in these
parts defy the false constructions of specific US suburban patterns
and their noted absence of neighborliness. In the US, she calls on
family members scattered in the various cities, and re-calls others.
What ever happened to Cousin Vi (the spiritual/shouter Baptist
mother-healer who moved to Brooklyn with the migration of her
spiritual and biological children)? Isn't it a shame that after Cousin
Laura worked domestic and brought all those children up to the
States, they don't even go over and see her on a Sunday afternoon!
Everybody is too busy! Of the Caribbean set at home, she says,

1

"They only come to visit when they want something. How people get so selfish? Nobody drops by to see if you are dead or alive anymore." Still, in the Caribbean, she calls on neighbors, friends and church members to announce that she is back home, cleans out her house, decorates it with the material acquisitions, stories and pains of her North American encounters. In suburban New York or Baltimore, Maryland, she announces to friends and neighbors that she is back home, paints rich hibiscus flowers in bright colors for her grandchildren, comments on the stench from the local sewage plant which no experts can seem to fix. "Imagine that, in a place with all this money!" In the Caribbean, she asserts in an exaggerated manner the accomplishments of her children and offers cogent critiques about the specific nature of US culture. She reflects with amazement and recognition on the vastness of homelessness in the US. She telephones from home with dreams which signify in multiple ways.

*

My mother belongs to a generation of women who migrated in search of opportunity.[2] She is one of that group of women who migrated to the US in the 1960s and worked to ensure that their children had space for growth and access to more resources than they had at home. She is also a member of a number of overlapping communities which, with each departure, are instantly hurled into a movement of exile and return which is so fundamentally inscribed in "New World" post-/modern identities.

I locate myself in the context of migrations, my mother's experience and in the midst of this work as a necessary strategy of concretizing the question of identities. My own path has included migrations to North America, various African and Caribbean countries, Europe and Brazil. Each place shifted, re-defined and re-constituted my identities.

*

I resent not being able to drive
an automobile more than I resent having
to wear a veil.

This quote from a Saudi woman interviewed on US national TV during the Gulf War, February 1991, identified for me issues of movement, freedom and circumscribed or flattened identities. I begin with these words, the epigraph from Jamaica Kincaid and my mother's migratory history as generating thoughts. For this unnamed Saudi woman, in the midst of multiple struggles of imperialist and patriarchal domination, movement was located within the politics of desire. Hers was an identification of the need for physical movement as fundamental. "Being able to drive an automobile" assumes some form of modern mobility as opposed to being frozen in space and time. The wearing of a veil takes second place in the chain of resentments, for one can be veiled and yet mobile. Besides, the veil in historical context has multiple significations of self-presentation and self-effacement which allow motion between identities to take place.[3] Still, in the context of this double-voicedness, the veil is also resented for the ways it is used to highlight the self-presenting woman as an illegal external position. So in effect there is a layering of resentments, issues to be struggled with, one assuming – for the moment – primacy over the other.

The re-negotiating of identities is fundamental to migration as it is fundamental to Black women's writing in cross-cultural contexts. It is the convergence of multiple places and cultures that re-negotiates the terms of Black women's experience that in turn negotiates and re-negotiates their identities. I propose to locate this discussion at the sites of those convergences. Throughout this book, I will pursue analyses of the construction of female subjectivity through literary and cultural texts. I will explore the ways in which Black women's writing re-negotiates the questions of identity. I will also demonstrate how, once Black women's experience is accounted for, assumptions about identity, community and theory have to be reconsidered.

This introductory chapter is organized around five central concepts, all of which concern the relations between identity and place. The section, "Re-Mapping and Re-Naming: On the Ideologies of Terminologies," begins by unpacking the terminologies and meanings implicit in terms and identities such as "Black," "Women," "American." Another section "Crossings: Re-connections and Invasions," addresses some of the implications of studying literature cross-culturally. "Redefining Our Geography" examines how received geography limits our understanding of identities. "Tourist Ideology or 'Playful World Travelling'" is a play on the constructions of "tourist" and "native" in cross-cultural relationships. "Black Women's Writing and Critical Movements" examines some of the movements and developments of critical responses to Black women's writing.

3

Interspersed in different ways in this introduction is a series of "migration horror stories." These narratives have their own separate textualities, and are deliberate attempts to break through the tiredness, fake linearity and posturing of academic discourse. Horror disrupts seamless narratives of people and place.[4] These anecdotal breaks, deliberately written into the text, are also an attempt to mirror my own patterns of writing, which never run as unbroken, linear, discursive expositions, but are actually produced through a series of interruptions – my younger daughter Dalia's need for a hug in the midst of a complicated thought I am trying to express, errands I have to run, teaching responsibilities, pots boiling over, washer completing cycles, my older daughter Jonelle's impassioned inquiries about the meaning of some term, friends' phone calls, my need to get out of the house and walk, or go to the gym or to a rap, reggae or jazz concert or poetry performance or reading.

Black women's writing, I am proposing, should be read as a series of boundary crossings and not as a fixed, geographical, ethnically or nationally bound category of writing. In cross-cultural, transnational, translocal,[5] diasporic perspectives, this reworking of the grounds of "Black Women's Writing" redefines identity away from exclusion and marginality. Black women's writing/existence, marginalized in the terms of majority-minority discourses, within the Euro-American male or female canon or Black male canon, as I have shown in "Writing Off Marginality, Minoring and Efface-ment,"[6] redefines its identity as it re-connects and re-members, brings together black women dis-located by space and time.

The writings and cross-cultural genealogy and experience of many writers represent well the inanity of limiting the understanding of Black women's writing to United States experience or any one geographical location.[7] In other words, there are Black women writers everywhere.[8] Thus to identify Black women's writing primarily with United States writing is to identify with US hegemony. If we see Black women's subjectivity as a migratory subjectivity existing in multiple locations, then we can see how their work, their presences traverse all of the geographical/national boundaries instituted to keep our dislocations in place. This ability to locate in a variety of geographical and literary constituencies is peculiar to the migration that is fundamental to African experience as it is specific to the human experience as a whole.[9] It is with this consciousness of expansiveness and the dialogics of movement and community that I pursue Black women's writing.

4

Migration horror story 1

In the summer of 1992, in Brazil, I began a project on Afro-Brazilian Women's Writing.[10] It became a bit of an exercise in futility for me to enter bookstores or libraries and ask for Black women's writing. On each occasion, I was taken to the section that housed the works of Toni Morrison and Alice Walker or directed to mainstream Brazilian writers like Jorge Amado. I was often told that there was no Black Brazilian or Afro-Brazilian writing, much less Afro-Brazilian *women*'s writing. This remained consistent until I met the (women) writers themselves and found out the reasons why this was so. This experience has repeated itself many times for those of us working on various versions of Black women's writing.

RE-MAPPING AND RE-NAMING: ON THE IDEOLOGIES OF TERMINOLOGIES

People often protest any attempts to get rid of misnomers like "Third World" and "First World" because, they claim, the alternatives are too much of a mouthful. This view clearly adds insult to injury. Because it insists that in order for some people to easily identify some other people the latter should agree to have their identities truncated.

Ama Ata Aidoo[11]

The terms that we use to name ourselves (Black, African, African-American, Black British, Minority, Latina/o, West Indian, Caribbean, Hispanic, People of Color, Women of Color, Afro-Caribbean, Third World and so on) carry their strings of echoes and inscriptions. Each represents an original misnaming and the simultaneous constant striving of the dispossessed for full representation. Each therefore must be used provisionally; each must be subject to new analyses, new questions and new understandings if we are to unlock some of the narrow terms of the discourses in which we are inscribed. In other words, at each arrival at a definition, we begin a new analysis, a new departure, a new interrogation of meaning, new contradictions. Let us begin with the term "Black" to illustrate this point. Black "Black" as a descriptive adjective for people of African origin and descent, came into popular usage during the period of the Black power movements in the US, the UK, the English-speaking Caribbean and in South Africa during the 1960s and 1970s. At that

5

historical juncture, there was also a political imperative to articulate African existences in relation to white/Anglo cultures. While there was some relationship between these movements, each carried its own specificity based on geographical and political realities. What was consistent, however, was the assertion and definition of a "Black identity" globally. In most contexts, the term "Black" resonated unabashed acceptance of African identity, located in history and culture ("blackness") as powerful or as beautiful in a world of cloying, annihilating whiteness. Black was deliberately removed from its moorings in pathology and inferiority and located in power as the Carmichael and Hamilton work *Black Power*[12] indicates. By contrast, in Black British contexts, the term, similarly produced by racism and resistance, has more to do with the political and racial positioning and activism of a variety of groups, and did not reside solely in African identity. Instead it incorporated that broader category of Asians, Caribbean and Latin American peoples and Africans who in the United States are often called "people of color."[13]

Zora Neale Hurston, in "How It Feels to Be Colored Me,"[14] says that her identity as a "colored" person came alive when she was thrown against a sharp white background. It is that sharp, white background or "whiteness", then, that mandates, in African-American (US) or other sharply-polarized, racially-defined contexts, the tactical assertion of Blackness. Paradoxically, the tactical assertion of Blackness in US contexts has been equated with Black manhood and therefore has been at the expense of, but also with the participation of Black women.

In parallel, in many cases, the self-assertions of Black women were often attacks on white women's racism as in Hazel Carby's early piece, "White Woman Listen!"[15] which so self-consciously emulated the earlier "White Man, Listen" of Black nationalist formulations. In other words, the audience for Black assertion, within the conventions of the protest tradition, was initially largely white society and secondarily Black communities as in "let us assert ourselves against whiteness." Whiteness is conceptualized, then, not primarily in skin color but in the conjunction of Caucasian racial characteristics with the acceptance of and participation in the domination of others.

But it is also here that one begins to find a construction of Black female specificity and the critique of the multiple oppression of Black women, as in Pratibha Parmar's piece, "Gender, Race and

6

Class. Asian Women in Resistance", in the same collection as the Carby piece, and earlier works like Toni Cade Bambara's *The Black Woman* which identified the "double jeopardy" issue of Black female subjectivity. Other helpful work by US Black feminists (as reflected in the collection *All the Women Are White, All the Blacks are Men, But Some of Us Are Brave*; the work of Michelle Wallace, *Black Macho and the Myth of the Superwoman*; and, later, bell hooks', *Ain't I A Woman. Black Women and Feminism* plus her more recent contributions) identified the gap between feminist assertion and Black nationalist assertion into which Black women disappeared and, paradoxically, out of which Black female specificity had to articulate itself.

Politically, the term "Black" is linked essentially and primarily with a vision of a (Pan-Africanist) Black World which exists both in Africa and in the diaspora. But "Blackness" is a color-coded, politically-based term of marking and definition which only has meaning when questions of racial difference and, in particular, white supremacy are deployed. One might, for example, compare the ways in which racism works on the Irish in England and how some of the same language, separations, criminalizations and social constructions are applied. A very important eye-opener for me has been the booklet, *Nothing But the Same Old Story*,[16] which provides historical information on the representations of Irish in racialized contexts and how those links are sustained by identification of the Irish with negativities associated with Africans.

In Africa, colonialism, with its emphasis on assimilation and expropriation, asserted Euro-American culture to the African peoples it sought to conquer. And in South Africa and the United States, the ideology of white supremacy reached the dangerous levels of apartheid and racial segregation. Senghor, one of the founders of the Negritude movement, asserted a certain Blackness in the context of French colonialism and deracination. Within the same context, Leon Damas in *Pigments* caricatured the associative pathologies of behavior identified with whiteness and colonization, and Césaire in his *Cahier* used *nègre* in multiple ways.[17] Yet, ideologies, even resistant ones, based on biology or nationality's "imagined community" also become a kind of flirting with danger as they too have the potential of being totalizing discourses. So, Negritude, itself, becomes a "nativist discourse" when approached uncritically.[18] Similarly, certain versions of African nationalism, Pan-Africanism and Afrocentrism become discourses which turn on the concept of a uni-centricity and imply the exclusion or subordination of women's issues or questions of sexual identity or difference within.

We therefore have to insist consistently that non–Westernized African peoples negotiate the terms of their identities in ways other than only "representing" Blackness, even within the umbrella of a homogeneous "African" identity. Blackness or Africanness, then, in operational terms, has more to do with a sometimes essentialized, tactical assertion as a counterpoint to overwhelming "whiteness" or Eurocentricity, which tries to pose itself as unmarked but is historically linked to technologies of destruction.

For these reasons, I want to activate the term "Black"[19] relationally, provisionally and based on location or position. The term "Black," oppositional, resisting, necessarily emerges as whiteness seeks to depoliticize and normalize itself. Still "Black" is only provisionally used as we continue to interrogate its meaning and in the ongoing search to find the language to articulate ourselves.

In locating identity within the context of assailment, interrogation and belatedness, Homi Bhabha cites Fanon's "The Fact of Blackness"[20] in which Blackness activates itself as a response to these three. Blackness, marginalized, overdetermined and made stereotypic stands in for the human figure which is located and disrupted. But what of Black femaleness or Black womanness? For it is the additional identity of femaleness which interferes with seamless Black identity and is therefore either ignored, erased or "spoken for." One still finds some women trying to say that they want to speak only as an African or as a "Black," and not as a woman,[21] as if it were possible to divest oneself of one's gender and stand as neutered within the context of palpable and visible historical, gendered and racialized identities. Black men have often claimed the space of speaking only in terms of their race with the assumption that their gender remains unmarked. But their manhood is often frontally identified in these assertions.

It is at this point "when we enter"[22] that one gets the convergence (at least of race and gender) and hence the challenging of specific identities. If following Judith Butler,[23] the category of woman is one of performance of gender, then the category Black woman, or woman of color, exists as multiple performances of gender and race and sexuality based on the particular cultural, historical, geopolitical, class communities in which Black women

8

exist. Those complicating locations of these multiple and variable subject positions are what I propose to explore in this study.

A similar interrogation of the term African-American explodes its often synonymous identification with "United Staters" of African descent ("Black Americans"). It is also significant that in the United States, the term "Black" does not include other "Third World" peoples (Asians, Arabs, Latino/as) as it does in the United Kingdom. For in the United States, the historical convergence between "race" and "nationality" has kept separate, for the most part, all the possibilities of organizing around related agendas and has operated in terms of polarizations of various races. It has also either sublimated racial differences or reified them in essential ways. Interrogating "African-American" as a defining terminology first mandates moving beyond the limited definition of what is "American."[24] In this way, "African-American" could correctly refer to the African peoples of the Americas: North America, the Caribbean and South America. Yet, since the term "American" has become synonymous with United States imperialistic identity, would the "other Americas" being colonized (both internally and externally) by the United States of America want to claim such a monolithic identification? Perhaps not, especially since the term "America" is also identified with European "discovery" and the destruction of native communities and nations. But perhaps yes, for tactical self-assertive reasons as Canadians or South Americans and Caribbeans sometimes do. Nancy Morejon would suggest that the term "America" is insufficient to discuss the entire spectrum of socio-historical interactions. She therefore uses the interesting formulation, for example, of "Amerindia" which embraces the continent extending from north to south geographically and which captures the extent to which the First People (Amerindians) made possible the emergence of Afro-America.[25]

The other half of the claimed "African-American" identity, "African," is a term based on another misnaming and an attempt to create a monolithic construction out of a diverse continent of peoples, cultures, nations and experiences. "Africa" becomes important as a defining term only in opposition to what is European or what is American. African historians indicate, for example, that the term "African" (derived from the terms Afri, Afriqui or Afrigi) was originally the name of a small Tunisian ethnic group which then began to be applied to a larger geographical area ranging from what is now eastern Morocco to Libya. For the Romans, "Africa *proconsularis*" was an administrative, territorial category.[26] Unpacking the archeology and genealogy of the term "Africa" is an important exercise in our understanding of how the politics of conquest and domination are so fundamentally linked to naming. The origin of the term "Africa" for colonialist, administrative reasons and its subsequent application to an entire continent (again for administrative, colonialist reasons), has implications for how African peoples (particularly in the diaspora) begin to activate monolithic categories of heritage and identity, as, for example, "Afrocentricity." The political basis of identity formation is a central issue in all of these interrogations. For, again, in the diaspora, under Pan-Africanist ideologies, the reconstruction of "Africa" as homeland occurred, also for management of reality. As resistance to European domination, monolithic constructions of Africa posed an alternative identity and did duty against the European deployment of its reality and its attempt to redefine the identities of large numbers of people taken from their native homelands.

So, we come back to America. Juan Flores and George Yudice, in "Living Borders/Buscando America. Languages of Latino Self-Formation,"[27] argue that since the "discovery" of America transformed the ocean into a frontier on whose other side lay a "new world" for European immigrants, then the reconceptualization of America by Latinos is as a "cultural map which is all border." For Flores and Yudice, "America" is a "living border," a site of "continual crossover," in terms of language, identity, space, geopolitical boundaries (p. 59), a "trans-creation" (p. 72). They say, for example, that:

> The view from the border enables us to apprehend the ultimate arbitrariness of the border itself, of forced separations and inferiorizations. Latino expression forces the issue which tops the agenda of American culture, the issue of geography and nomenclature. . . . For the search for "America," the inclusive, multicultural society of the continent, has to do with nothing less than the imaginative ethos of re-mapping and re-naming in the service not only of Latinos but all claimants.
>
> (p. 80)

It is in this context of refusing to surrender to US hegemony, which includes its blanket claim of the word "America," that we place the interrogation of West Indian or Caribbean identity. At the same time, we already accept that the term "America" itself has origins of definition and conquest. We similarly recognize that the term West Indian is one of the products of Columbus's error of naming – the West Indies. The complexity of the renaming *vis-à-vis* the Carib Indians elides the presence of the Arawaks and other native groups who populated that region.[28] According to Retamar,[29] even Carib is not necessarily the name the native peoples gave to themselves. Similarly, "Indian" is a European designation for a variety of nations of people who inhabited this area of the world. Rigoberta Menchu makes a similar point, suggesting that new terms for identification will be given by the people themselves.[30] And, "Latin American" has similar implications in terms of language, geography and identity. Still, as Morejon correctly identifies, all of these more recent namings take place at the expense of the First People populations.[31]

Other conceptions of the Caribbean as the "islands in between" (Louis James) or as "fragmented" (Livingston)[32] have to be jettisoned. Instead, a dramatic re-imagining of the Caribbean would allow us to see and explore the land/space dichotomies in different ways. Thus, the inability to see repetitions, traces, convergences, trans-Caribbean migrations, can be called into question within the captured definition of the term "American" by the United States or via the various European colonizations which had "separations" as a primary agenda. The language of "backyarding" or "basining" to which the Caribbean is often relegated can be similarly addressed.

The forced national constructions that Ernest Renan talks about in "What is a Nation?"[33] offer significant understandings of our current separations and dislocations. Renan argues that the creation of the concept of the "nation" is fairly new in history, that antiquity was unfamiliar with it, that what existed were republics, kingdoms, confederations of local republics and empires. Renan similarly talks about geography or "natural frontiers" in the formation of a nation or the division of nations. He continues, saying that "people talk about strategic grounds" but that many concessions have to be made. However, these should not be taken too far, otherwise we will have unceasing war:

> A nation is therefore a large-scale solidarity, constituted by the feeling of the sacrifices that one has made in the past and of those that one is prepared to make in the future . . . A

11

nation's existence is a daily plebiscite, just as an individual's existence is a perpetual affirmation of life.

(p. 19)

The interrogation of the philosophical underpinnings of much of our current consciousness in Western languages and thought is a necessary undertaking. Ideas like nation, nationalism and national consciousness, even when deployed by the oppressed groups (Black nation, Black nationalism, queer nation, etc.), allow us to understand all the varieties of nationalism be they Caribbean, African, American, European or more specific to individual smaller nation-states and countries. The recent disintegration of a variety of European geographic identities which were mapped as nations brings us forcibly to the recognition that nationalism was a management "trap" within which the growing independence movements in the Caribbean were interpellated. We may want to go further and ask, as a number of feminist scholars are beginning to do, if the concept of "nation" has not been a male formulation. This may explain why nationalism thus far seems to exist primarily as a male activity with women distinctly left out or peripheralized in the various national constructs. Thus, the feminine was deployed at the symbolic level, as in "Mother Africa" or "Mother India,"[34] and women functioned as primary workers for a number of nationalist struggles but ended up not being empowered political figures or equal partners.

For the Caribbean, the separations based on language, colonial political and economic structures, land and the treacherous sea allow us to understand and question the formation of nations based only on island boundaries. Also, the multiple peoples and languages of this part of the world offer us interesting postmodernist ways of seeing identity. Further, the Caribbean understood (within the context of the Americas) as the history of genocide, slavery, physical brutality, as in the Kincaid recognition with which I began, demands some sort of understanding of culture either as oppositional or as resistance, and further as transformational if we are to recoup any identities beyond the ones imposed. Edouard Glissant describes the Caribbean as "the other America"[35] (p. 4) and proceeds to offer thoughtful understandings of the ways we can construct and deconstruct Caribbean identities. Nancy Morejon sees the Caribbean as a primary source in understanding what we know as "African-America," for it is from this that the "invisible center" resonates into "diaspora."[36] The Caribbean Sea is therefore a site of dissemination of a variety of socio-cultural processes, a site of continuous change and the ongoing questioning of self, origin, direction.

Caribbean identities then are products of numerous processes of migration. As a result, many conclude that the Caribbean is not so much a geographical location but a cultural construction based on a series of mixtures, languages, communities of people. Thus some speak of "creolization" or "métissage" as a fundamental defining feature of the Caribbean. Still, "creole" and "mestizo" carry their own negativities and associations with positions in racial hierarchy, if used in relation to Black populations in certain countries like Brazil.

In this context the identities of various ethnic/national communities based in Canada, the United States, Great Britain, France, Holland, Israel, African nations and South America exist as challenges to the very specific definition of what constitutes a "nation" in terms of geography and place. The identification of "Third World" carries its own problematic, even as it becomes a necessary tactical assertion.[37] Perhaps Benedict Anderson's formulation of "imagined communities" is helpful in understanding the ways we identify in groups. For the enforcement of very specific national identities and the policing of these at the various immigration posts and in everyday life (neighborhoods, schools, workplaces, the law, the political arena)[38] become an unnecessary encumbrance once we begin to redefine identity. Still, the need to understand transnationally the various resistances to Eurocentric domination and to create an "elsewhere" is embedded in the diaspora formulation. Paul Gilroy, in his revision of Benedict Anderson, sees the diaspora framework as "an alternative to the different varieties of absolutism which would confine culture in 'racial', ethnic or national essences" (p. 155).[39] Michael Hanchard argues that:

> Embedded in the tale of the diaspora is a symbolic revolt against the nation-state, and for this reason the diaspora holds a dual significance. It suggests a transnational dimension to black identity, for if the notion of an African diaspora is anything it is a human necklace strung together by a thread known as the slave trade, a thread which made its way across a path of America with little regard for national boundaries.[40]
>
> (p. 40)

13

Stuart Hall similarly talks of "diaspora-ization," (p. 30) and Kobena Mercer identifies the interaction of "diaspora culture and the dialogic imagination."[41] For Hanchard it is the "elsewhere" embedded in the diaspora formulation which has palpable meaning as a working formulation. For elsewhere means "consciousness . . . as a combination of knowing the condition of one's existence, imagining alternatives and striving to actualize them" (p. 99).[42]

Migration horror story 2

A Costa Rican woman has several children by a Barbadian man on a work assignment in her country. After some years, he decides to return home and take the children to his family. They remain there until they are teenage. All this time, they are immigrants and their papers for Barbadian citizenship are being processed. Meanwhile, he moves to the US for economic improvement and subsequently takes on US citizenship. He brings the children to the US as visitors intending to keep them there and sponsor them but discovers he cannot do so unless he marries the mother whom he has not seen in years, or legally adopts them. By the time he is aware of this latter possibility, the age of legal adoption has passed. The children cannot get US residence nor can they go back to either of the places they originally came from. They have not maintained communications with family in Costa Rica and have lived too many years away. What/who is an illegal alien? Where is the silenced mother in all of this?

*

A mere look at the boundaries of our discourse reveals that we are operating, in a limited way, out of a reality that is more complex than is presented. Thus, terms like "minority," when used to refer to people of color in the US, or "Black," in Great Britain, "alien" or "immigrant" have power only when one accepts the constraints of dominating societies or when one chooses tactical reappropriation for resistance. As soon as one moves out of those contexts to see what "Black" conveys in geopolitical scope (embracing North, Central and South America and the Caribbean) or the more expansive implications of the category "African-American" or "Caribbean" (reaching to New Orleans and Columbia in some formulations), then we are talking in a transnational or global context which eschews localized minority status and recognizes

14

these as attempts to place nation–state/binding identity status on transnational identities. The dynamics of location and re-connection offer a new and more contradictory set of questions and responses.

Kobena Mercer, in "Black Art and the Burden of Representation,"[43] shares my position when he sees a signifying chain in each community in which this "struggle–in–language entails an interminable discursive antagonism in which subjectivity and identity are at stake" (p. 76). For him this "struggle over the sign does not come to a full stop. There is no definitive 'answer-word' to the master discourses of racism and ethnocentrism, because our Other can also re-appropriate what we have ourselves appropriated" (p. 77). The ongoing inquiry into meaning has to resist closure as it holds itself open to new meanings and contests over meaning.

*

The implications of United States and European imperialism and other oppressive constructions *vis-à-vis* "majority" people of color and any other subordinate groups, take on important implications in these global battles. Cheryl Clarke puts it succinctly in "living as a lesbian underground: a futuristic fantasy":

> Don't be no fool, now, cool.
> Imperialism by any other name
> is imperialism.
> Even Vietnam was finally over.
> It's all the same –
> *a*-rabs, gooks, wogs, queers –
> a nigger by any other name . . .
> Johannesburg is Jamesburg, New Jersey.
> Apartheid is the board of education
> in Carnasie . . .[44]

The reality of imperialism mandates specific anti–imperialist alliances and discourses that eschew the trap of prescribed local/national/identity boundaries.

CROSSINGS:
RE-CONNECTIONS AND INVASIONS

Gloria Anzaldua in *Borderlands/La Frontera. The New Mestiza*[45] talks about border spaces as locations or sites of contest, of flux, of change. The new mestiza consciousness is one of "crossing over," "perpetual transition," plural personality which resists unitary paradigms and dualistic thinking (pp. 77–91). Thus, borders are those places where different cultures, identities, sexualities, classes, geographies, races, genders and so on collide or interchange. For Anzaldua, mestiza politics and poetics allow one to create a new story to explain the world. This formulation is an important way for me to enter the idea of the meaning of cultures in multiple contexts, and in particular the identification of the dynamics of the experience and writing of Black women/women of color. Still, I am conscious of the way in which "mestizo" or "mestiza" can be used as oppressive separation in Latin American communities in order to distance one from darker-skinned peoples and others who identify as "African," "Afro-" or "Black." The point is that all of these terms carry their internal contradictions. For Anzaldua, home is not necessarily a comfortable or safe place: "Woman does not feel safe when her own culture, and white culture, are critical of her; when the males of all races hunt her as prey" (p. 20). For her, "homophobia" can be read as "fear of going home" (pp. 19–20). Still, "homeplace," as bell hooks would term it, can be a site of resistance[46] if one understands some of the historical roots of oppression. And in this context, movement or crossing-over is a necessary antidote to the paralysis of oppression and depression which Anzaldua calls the Coatlicue state:

> It is her reluctance to cross over, to make a hole in the fence and walk across, to cross the river, to take that flying leap into the dark, that drives her to escape, that forces her into the fecund cave of her imagination where she is cradled in the arms of Coatlicue, who will never let her go. If she doesn't change her ways, she will remain a stone forever. *No hay mas que cambiar.*[47]
>
> (p. 49)

The new consciousness that she proposes is the borderland consciousness which supports "perpetual transition" (p. 78).

One of the final moves of conquerors, after conquest, is the dividing up of territories, creating unnatural boundaries and thus ushering in perpetual struggle over space and place. In that context, invasions take on complex meaning. On the one hand, there is the need to reconstruct destroyed historical consciousness and the hierarchies of meaning bestowed there. On the other hand, there is the recognition that once these borders are created and change is instituted, we have entered a stage in which the meaning of location and ownership is already defined and almost irredeemable outside migratory consciousness.

All of these issues relate to literature in a cross-cultural perspective. Because we were/are products of separations and dislocations and dis-memberings, people of African descent in the Americas historically have sought reconnection. From the "flying back" stories which originated in slavery to the "Back to Africa" movements of Garvey and those before him, to the Pan-Africanist activity of people like Dubois and C.L.R. James, this need to reconnect and re-member, as Morrison would term it, has been a central impulse in the structuring of Black thought. Thus, Toni Morrison in *Beloved*[48] makes re-memory central to the experience of that novel; the recalling of what she calls the "unspeakable thoughts, unspoken" and the re-membering or the bringing back together of the disparate members of the family in painful recall. Morrison is clearly talking here about crossing the boundaries of space, time, history, place, language, corporeality and restricted consciousness in order to make reconnections and mark or name gaps and absences. In *Beloved*, the duality of reconnection and occupation provides some of the dynamics for our discussion of crossing the boundaries. Beloved's presence/absence heightens the contradictions of the home and allows for the crossing and re-crossing of a variety of boundaries as it becomes at once invasion, at once re-connection. This we have established is not specific to African-American experience, but to a number of identities disrupted with the coming of the Anglos or others under bourgeois, Western European hegemony. Paula Gunn Allen in *The Sacred Hoop*[49] talks about re-membering within the context of the destruction and devastation of native Americans/First People. For her, remembering is what heals; the oral tradition is what mends and gathers the tribes back together. Remembering or the function of memory means re-membering or bringing back all the parts together. Trinh Minh-ha in *Woman Native Other*[50] also talks about the story that similarly links women and storytelling in the experience of people of color. The process of re-membering is therefore one of boundary crossing.

It is in this more unbounded context that I want to locate Black Women's Writing. Still, problems remain and we must take Bernice Johnson Reagon's intervention seriously when she states that any crossing of boundaries can mean occupying space belonging to someone else.[51]

Often it is the inability to cross boundaries for reconnection which causes distancings, misunderstandings. Audre Lorde in "I Am Your Sister. Black Women Organizing Across Sexualities"[52] shows how lesbophobia and heterosexism get in the way of sisterhood even among Black women who want to claim the site of most multiplied dispossession. Lorde's "I am your sister" affirms her many connections and re-connections. Women can communicate, work together with multiple languages. For this reason, Lorde's revision of the term "lesbian" of Greek origin with the term "Zami" of Caribbean/creole origin is an important attempt at redefinition which has not entered the critical language in any significant way. Lorde was talking in her 'biomythography" about the way Carriacou women work together as friends and lovers. Similarly Gloria Anzaldua in "To(o) Queer the Writer – Loca, escritora y chicana,"[53] speaks of the way in which her various identities converge, but also of how European language and definition do not capture her identities.

Cultural theorizing is often done by those with the power to disseminate, generally male scholars (more recently white women and Black men). Because of heterosexism and male dominance, the language and concepts of male scholars gain easy currency. The ways in which Black women/women of color theorize themselves often remains outside of the boundaries of the academic context, or "elsewhere." For the Caribbean, Brathwaite,[54] for example, sees creole cultures as occupying a certain prismatic conceptual plane in which "all resident cultures are equal and contiguous, despite the accidents of political history, each developing its own life-style from the spirit of its ancestors, but modified – and increasingly so – through interaction within the environment and other cultures of the environment" (p. 42). He also talks about the process of nativization at which point creolization begins. At this point all begin to share a style, even though that style will retain vestiges of their original/ancestral heritage. Brathwaite's metaphors, however, are heavily male-gendered, yet his claims are to represent all of Caribbean creole culture.

The advancing of our understanding of creoleness has become an important undertaking in the process of understanding the negotiating of identities. In another contribution, "In Praise of Creoleness,"[55] Bernabé, Chamoiseau and Confiant advance this discussion by their insistence that: "creoleness is an open specificity. It escapes, therefore, perceptions which are not themselves open. Expressing it is not expressing a synthesis, not just expressing a crossing of any other unicity. It is expressing a kaleidoscopic totality" (p. 892). Importantly, the writers also assert that there are different versions of creoleness which link with each other in interesting ways. The sharing of this creoleness offers a disruption of a variety of metanarratives.

In various ways, all of these reinterpretations or reinterrogations of questions of identity offer opportunities to rethink a variety of categories with which we work and which we identify as "automatic" categories, as if meaning remains constant and understandings of identities never change.

While I find some of the theorizing on culture to be valuable, I propose to find some of those "elsewhere" modes and open space for other questions. I propose to read Black women's writing within the context of cultural critical theory and a variety of new forms of knowledge, but also to see what the texts themselves offer, theoretically, on the questions with which we are grappling. Studying Black women's writing in more expansive terms and relationally offers ways of responding to some of these discourses of borderlands, creolizations and the critique of nationalist identities. We can also address dialogically the negative marking of invasion and the positive possibilities of recovery.

REDEFINING OUR GEOGRAPHY

"Ethnic Monitoring or a Geography Lesson"
Black, Asian, White, FAR EASTERN, Other!
The boxes on the tear-off slip remain blank.
I never thought there'd be a space for Indo-Swiss!
but my mind turns its attention
To the mind behind the confusion
Behind those mixed-up boxes.

Is there a line between middle east and far east?
And where's nearly east?
And can't someone be black, asian, *and* far eastern?
In my colonial style geography books
With whole areas coloured empire pink
There was a line . . .

The rest of this poem by Kamila Zahno,[56] a Black British woman writer of Asian descent, goes on to problematize the ways of geography in which the maps, produced by the colonizers, continue to maintain artificial separations. She ends by defining herself as "black of course what else/Not their terms/But my terms."

We are talking of necessity of the politics of location and geography. Chandra Mohanty, in "Cartographies of Struggle. Third World Women and the Politics of Feminism,"[57] suggests that we are operating out of redefined geographies in which, "while such imagined communities are historically and geographically concrete, their boundaries are necessarily fluid" (p. 5).

Pan-African scholars seem unified on the issue that the export of Africans to the "New World" unified Africans across their ethnic differences as it cut them off from their past. So too did a range of other migrations. The Pan-African community thus created the conditions for another "imagined community", on the one hand a unified homeland, on the other a diaspora. Similarly, the migrations of many peoples from homelands for economic or other political reasons, create conditions of exile and demand the creation of new communities with new relationships to those homelands. Keya Ganguly speaks of "Migrant Identities"[58] in the context of understanding how gender, migration and racial oppression create a sense of a unified culture as they create difference. Divergences of thought surround the modes of identifications. So, discourses of home and exile are central to any understanding of the politics of location. But it is the way both home and exile are constructed as flat, monolithic categories that demands the multiple articulations of class, race, gender, sexuality and other categories and identities.

For the many Black women writers whom we read in English or French or Portuguese, a variety of boundary crossings must occur. English or French or Spanish or Portuguese become indispensable for the writer who wants to reach a larger community. And for the women who tell their stories orally and want them told to a world community, boundaries of orality and writing, of geography and space, engender fundamental crossings and re-crossings. For the readers as well, a variety of languages, creoles, cultural nuances, history have to be learned before the texts can have meaning.[59]

Geography is linked deliberately to culture, language, the ability to hear and a variety of modes of articulation. It is where one speaks from and who is able to understand, to interpret that gives actuality to one's expression. Many women speak, have spoken, are speaking but are rarely heard. From the many narratives in which peasant and working-class women tell of sexual and physical abuse and exploitation or their joys to audiences which do not want to hear them to the 1991 case of a law professor testifying about sexual harassment to the US Senate, the reality that women are not seen as credible speakers or have no authority to speak their experience is an issue which is immediately implicated in this discussion. So it is not solely a question of physical geography, but location or subject position in their wider senses in terms of race, class, gender, sexuality, access, education and so on.

In her provocative essay, "Can the Subaltern Speak?",[60] Gayatri Spivak addressed the way the "subaltern" woman as subject is already positioned, represented, spoken for or constructed as absent or silent or not listened to in a variety of discourses. Her speech is already represented as non-speech. Spivak's meanings were forcibly clarified and activated for many by witnessing the way Anita Hill's speech and Lani Guinier's writings (other Black women speakers) were mis-characterized, ignored, distorted, erased.

The question that begs to be asked is: if Black women are not credible speakers, what then is the reception of Black women's writing, or is it already constructed and specifically located even as it speaks its critique of dominance? The success, then, of a Maya Angelou as inaugural poet for the Clinton administration in 1993 as well as the popular media reception ought to be the subject of detailed analysis within what I call elsewhere the "discourse of the prize."[61] Speech, then, is as much an issue of audience receptivity, the fundamentals of listening, as it is of articulation.[62]

The autobiographical subjectivity of Black women is one of the ways in which speech is articulated and geography redefined. Issues of home and exile are addressed. Home is often portrayed as a place of alienation and displacement in autobiographical writing. The family is sometimes situated as a site of oppression for women. The mystified notions of home and family are removed from their romantic, idealized moorings, to speak of pain, movement, difficulty, learning and love in complex ways. Thus, the complicated notion of home mirrors the problematizing of community/nation/identity that one finds in Black women's writing from a variety of communities. In Nafissatou Diallo's *A Dakar Childhood*,[63] for example, home is linked to the closing in of worlds and the enforced domesticity for the girlchild; the reverse of the *bildungsroman* or the novel of male coming of age. For Angelou in

I Know Why the Caged Bird Sings, particularly, home is migratory, sometimes joyful but generally a difficult space which she must eventually leave in order to grow, as is Africa for her in a subsequent work.[64] And speech and silence are central to these texts and to the writers coming to voice as Black woman writers. For, in many homes, the silence that is demanded of the young girl child becomes the speech of the young girl child (Angelou), or, as bell hooks would say, the "right speech of womanhood" (*Talking Back*, p. 6). Siu Won Ng, a woman writer in England, tries to voice the quiet pain that many women suffer in their homes:

> Papa said don't
> so I don't tell
> I keep it all
> dug deep in my head . . .
> I try to scream
> I scream inside
> it hurts too much
> to silent cry –
> my throat is choked
> I hurt it so
> from silent moans
> deep down my throat.[65]

So home is often a place of exile for the woman, as are, sometimes, community and nation.

The dismantling of received geography is an important step in approaching women's writing relationally. Observing the ways a variety of women are able to challenge these constructions offers a more developed reading of the many directions that women take in writing of their experiences. Questions of power and speech, language and authority and locationality are also addressed by Marlene Nourbese Philip in "The Absence of Writing or How I Almost Became a Spy":[66]

> I see the issue as being one of power and so one of control. Writing entails in many areas: control of the word, control of the image, control of information, and, perhaps as important, control in the production of the final product. For a female and a Black living in a colonial society, control was absent in each of these areas, and hence the lack of recognition of writing as a possible vocation or profession.
>
> (p. 278)

Yet, this is the reality out of which one must reacquire the "power to create" and re-create. Black women writers are engaged in all kinds of processes of reacquisition of the "tongue." And these, I assert, are movements of re-connection and, at times, of re-evaluation.

Crossing the boundaries as a critic has multiple implications. It means listening to the "polyrhythms,"[67] the polyvocality of Black women's creative and critical speech. It means rejecting some of the category maintenance which generic constraints demand. It involves examining questions of sexuality, of gender, of race, age, class, of language and location. The kind of critical work I envisage moves to redefine our geography, to re-create and remove the lines of impossibility in which we exist. In the process, one must recognize power and dominance and the ways in which sometimes critical or creative work can assume colonizing postures and invasiveness in relation to the materials with which one works.

In redefining the critical and creative landscape, it is necessary to foreground whether one's work is for reconnection, invasion or exploitation.

TOURIST IDEOLOGY OR "PLAYFUL WORLD TRAVELLING"

In "Playfulness, World Travelling and Loving Perception,"[68] Maria Lugones makes a necessary distinction between arrogant perception linked to racism, conquest and disrespect and loving perception allied with caring and identification. She speaks of exploring other cultural locations in a respectful way. Yet, even as I understand her arguments, even as I accept the necessity of engaging other cultures, I still find the language "playful world travelling" troubling. The Caribbean child that I was witnessed many tourists who seemed to be "playful world travellers" in my Caribbean city. We became the backdrop for their encounters. We were never fully thinking, acting beings. The Caribbean is too easily identified as the place of playful world travelling for us to engage that formulation without caution.

Migration horror story 3

I am having dinner with a well-known poet, a colleague whose work I respect and his wife and a few of their friends. Immediately upon learning that I was from Trinidad, the wife, also an academic, began to go on about taking a cruise through the Caribbean and about being so welcomed in all the places except in Trinidad where people seemed to go about their business and act indifferently to or completely ignore her presence. I asserted bravely, conscious of her construction of me in the process and my parallel potential to speak out of a narrow, nationalist island patriotism, that I found it a benefit for her as it allowed her to see the country unencumbered by tourist constrictions and I elaborated on some Caribbean economic information which underpinned relations of tourism to certain countries and not to others. Even after my well-informed and impassioned explanation, she retained much of her earlier position. All subsequent interactions with her have been strained.

*

Visions of Tourist Annie of my childhood surface and I remember now how she costumed herself exaggeratedly in stereotypical Caribbean folk-dress, with big colorful skirts, bright make-up, large earrings and several necklaces, shack-shacks, baskets with fruit and dolls which she sold to tourists as she welcomed them to the Caribbean. Hers was an elaborate mask, a performance which allowed mostly white tourists to photograph themselves with her in the Caribbean, to see her dance for them. Her costume, based both on Afro-Caribbean historical dress and tourist constructions, subsequently became part of what is often exported with Caribbean dance. Now I reconstruct the meaning of Tourist Annie in Port-of-Spain, a bustling business-oriented city with a sometimes healthy GNP. Yet we must inevitably deal with both arrogant and playful world travellers who want us to step back into their fantasies and be photographed again.

The question I raise, then, about any cross-cultural movement is the extent to which it is tourism or serious engagement based on mutual respect. After the Gulf War, former US President, George Bush, in one of the biggest commercials for the Caribbean tourist industry and parallel assertion of US hegemony, flew to the Caribbean to rest. There, he met and talked with his ally Mitterrand who occupied a similar position in relation to the Francophone Caribbean as did George Bush to the Caribbean as a whole. The symbolic meeting of these two on Caribbean shores highlighted the implications of tourist ideology in the perception of the Caribbean as "prostitute," as source of pleasure and relaxation, and the link to economic and political domination and exploitation.

Critical thinkers have been slow to acknowledge that, in the latter half of this century, it is the United States of America which is the colonial power, not Europe as a generation of writers had alleged.[69] Indeed, the writers tied to the British and/or French colonial agony model, mostly male and writing in the 1950s and 1960s, missed the articulation of United States interests in the Caribbean as more consolidated than was the visible political apparatus of the European colonial powers. Bush's visit to Martinique and his discussion with Mitterrand was his tacit acknowledgment that, in the face of French colonialism, the US master remained present, assertive and dominant.

If we see Black women's writing only as gender- and race-based, peripheral, then we miss a major understanding of the very specific critique of imperialism that many of these writers are offering. For postures of dominance, of the policing of boundaries and categories are almost always linked to another anti-hegemonic reassertion. Tourist ideology and manners, United States domination and its impact, are being addressed by a number of Black women writers. For example, Jamaica Kincaid, in *A Small Place*, attacks the construction of both the tourist and the "native." It is a hard critique which links various forms of colonial domination to tourism and internal exploitation. Audre Lorde similarly poses the question of US dominance in her essay, "Grenada Revisited," which attempts to come to terms with the meaning of the invasion of Grenada by the United States. Merle Collins in a poem from her collection, *Rotten Pomerac*, simultaneously criticizes the US imperialists and scrutinizes the internal power dynamics of the men in the New Jewel Movement. Paule Marshall in *Praisesong for the Widow* in particular, but also in all of her other works, has a similar engagement.

In this connection, African-American constructions of "Black" subjectivity or African-American identity have to be subjected to the same scrutiny because they participate so heavily in United States constructions of itself, as Michael Hanchard shows. W.E.B. Dubois's discussion of double consciousness speaks of the need for the African-American to understand the conflict s/he feels as both "American" and Black. But this conflict, or worse its absence, can be dangerous for other people around the world, as African-American participation in the United States military reveals. It is that conflict that is central to the critique that Lorde launches in her "Equal Opportunity" poem:[70]

The american deputy assistant secretary of defense
for Equal Opportunity
and safety
is a homegirl . . .
pauses in her speech licks her dry lips
"as you can see the Department has
a very good record
of equal opportunity for our women"
swims toward safety
through a lake of her own blood.

(p. 18)

How do African-Americans participate in this major recolonizing project and US imperialism? Further, how do United
States Black women/women of color, often the most dispossessed
on the ladder of social and economic resources, pursue their own
liberation? Is it through alliance with oppression or in resistance?
And, similarly, does Black feminist criticism and politics have the
potential of occupying a similar position with respect to a variety of
related discourses, other Black women's literatures and subordinated identities (as does mainstream feminism in relation to Black
feminism, for example)?

I believe it is exactly at that intersection of discourses and their
critiques that a book like Jamaica Kincaid's *Lucy* and a whole genre
of Black women's cross-cultural writing resides. As Kincaid pursues her critique of United States values, questions her homelessness and coldness as an immigrant in a white household, she
repeatedly asks "How does a person get to be that way?" (pp. 17,
20), "How do you get to be the sort of victor who can claim to be
vanquished also?"(p. 41).

The Grenada invasion was also blatantly a tourist trip. United
States soldiers used old tourist maps as guides to the terrain. So, if
we are clear that tourism never really brings economic prosperity,
that multinational corporations who own the industries take their
made-money away, that tourist installations often destroy the environment and displace many people, that people are denied some
of the most beautiful areas of their countries because of tourism,
that the local people are constructed perpetually in positions of
service, then the link between tourism and invasion is not far-
fetched.

Migration horror story 4

A young African-American woman in the US army has Caribbean parents. During the Gulf War, her mother supported her presence in the Middle East to fight the Iraqis, because in her words, "it is better than being in the war-on-the-streets in the drug infested Bronx." Her mother simultaneously recognized that if there is another revolution of some sort taking place in the Caribbean, or an invasion of the order of Panama or Grenada, technically, her children (she also has a son in the army) could be in a position of invading and killing their own kin, perhaps their own grandmother who still resides there, in the interest of some larger imperialistic goal.

BLACK WOMEN'S WRITING AND CRITICAL MOVEMENTS

Black feminist politics has the potential of truly being an oppositional, transformational, revolutionary discourse, but has not yet become so for a variety of reasons. Black feminist politics can only become transformational if it is sharper in its opposition and critique of systems of domination and able to activate its principles in more practical ways.[71] It would therefore have to be more deliberately and practically located at sites of resistance to, and struggle against, multiple oppression: whiteness, maleness, bourgeois culture, heterosexuality, Anglo-centeredness and so on. Black feminist politics can only be transformational if it seeks to challenge social conditions and processes and give value to existences often rendered silent or invisible in current patterns of social ordering. Consequently, it is important at this point to differentiate between activist Black feminists and conservative Black women scholars (even when they are working on women), between those who are committed to social change and those who want fuller participation in systems as they exist. And, further, within the category of "Black feminist" one must continue to make sharper distinctions for purposes of clarity and alliances.

Problems of definition still exist. But for me, these are not as critical as a commitment to a critique of dominant discourses and some movement to transform these. In effect, we have to move to recognize those Black women who do not see the validity in any feminist politics of any sort as an indication of where they are

27

located *vis-à-vis* social movements, class position, privilege, etc. In effect, then, not all Black women automatically are sisters-in-struggle. The primary resistance by many Black women to feminism because of the identification between feminism and white women has been ameliorated by the understanding of the numerous women from other parts of the world and from the US who were not white or bourgeois but who felt the need to struggle around women's issues and for social change. The need for qualification of the term with specific descriptive adjectives is already accepted as a given.

Feminist discourse has itself been a politics directed at changing existing power relations between men and women and in society as a whole. These are power relations which structure all areas of life: the family, education, the household, political systems, leisure, culture, economics, sexual intercourse, sexuality and so on. In short, feminism questions and seeks to transform what it is to be a woman in society, to understand how the categories woman and the feminine are defined, structured and produced. The range has moved from Kristeva's "Woman Can Never Be Defined"[72] to ways of understanding how gender – the normative movements of the masculine and the feminine – is constructed in society. The notion that woman is constructed as living the gift or donation of her*self* to the fulfillment of all others' desires and needs – i.e., to making everyone else happy – is an originary myth that is still in need of deconstruction.[73] For example, what does this unconditional donation of self by the woman mean in economic terms? What does it mean, as Patricia Williams says, to be legally defined as the object of property?[74] Also, how is sexuality defined and normalized (heterosexualized)? How are Black women's bodies seen and represented under the Western, male, patriarchal "gaze"? What is the relationship of medical machinery and science to (Black) women's bodies? And, how do these constructs relate to other colonizations? What about (Black) women's legal status in marriage? Do Black women have rights, if so what are they? What does it mean to be a wife in heterosexist society? There are still too many questions to be held open, even as answers are offered, before we accept arbitrary closure, dismissal or *post*ings. Feminist politics, in my understanding, is a resistance to objectification of women in society, in literature, art and culture. It is also the articulation of a critical and an intellectual practice which challenges all patriarchal

28

assumptions and norms. It is also a politics of possible transformation.

At the same time as we articulate some general principles, projects and questions, we recognize that within current postmodern understandings, metanarratives of feminism have to be challenged. This moves us to the understanding of the multiplicity of feminist theories and practices. I find Karen Offen's article, "Defining Feminism. A Comparative Historical Approach,"[75] helpful. Offen pursues some of the history of feminisms, identifying the "Anglo-American individualist tradition of feminism" (p. 137) as the model on which much discussion of feminism has been based but sees it as only

> one important band, one significant possibility on the broad spectrum of feminist thought. Focusing on it alone blinds us to the range of effective arguments used to combat male privilege in the Western world during the past few centuries, and even to arguments put forth today by women and men in less-privileged countries, where women's aspirations to self-sovereignty are often subordinated to pressing short-term political and socioeconomic necessities.

> (p. 138)

Linda Alcoff's "Cultural Feminism Versus Post-Structuralism. The Identity Question in Feminist Theory"[76] also offers important ways of reading female subjectivity and the debates about whether gender is nature or construction. Alcoff's contribution has nevertheless been challenged on the question of its delimiting of female agency.[77]

But how does this all shift once Black women are introduced into the discussion? I believe that questions of Black female subjectivity bring a more complex and heightened awareness to all theoretics and feminist concerns rather than an escape from them. In other words, if we take any feminist issue[78] and run it up the scale to its most radical possibility, its most clarifying illustration will be the experience of Black women. Where are the women of color in decision-making, in medicine and its technologies? Who speaks for us in the media? When are we seen as credible speakers? In all situations of state power globally, we are generally absent. And these are some of the questions that Black women's writing addresses. We can of course look at demographics, placement, location for some concrete information. But, for literature, the

29

affective responses and creative articulations speak in ways the statistics cannot.

The "mythical norm" as Audre Lorde calls it,[79] or the "standard," is defined as white male, monied, propertied, middle or upper class, thin, young, blonde, Christian, heterosexual. The more one can check off in these categories the better off one is in society. These standards are given positive value in society and the rest of us it seems must strive to emulate them or be defined as "strange" or "mad." Anytime we pose Black women and women of color against these, generally we note the oppositional or negative marking inscribed.

So far, it has been extremely difficult to fully articulate Black feminist positions in a racist society such as the US because the politics of race is so ubiquitous, so overt and overwhelming that they shift and subsume all other discourses. Still, the combined politics of gender/race oppression are perhaps the most insidious. Thus, gender oppression seems best overturned within the context of movements to transform various societies. Black women (and men) everywhere can be victimized by both the system and the men, their children and others in their lives, precisely because of their race and gender combination. Societies still have to struggle with social reconstruction as was attempted in Eritrea and link questions of gender to new modes of being in these societies.

One has, therefore, even in doing literary criticism, to identify a politics which articulates multiply and not singly because there are all sorts of interests and identities being submerged and which demand voice. The recognition of as many identities as exist (or the inherently plural character of identity) ensures that one is not placing oneself in the oppressive position. Black feminist politics by its very nature exists right at the intersection of several issues that are located in Black women's experiences. And since experience is also ideologically produced, and Black women's experience is what Black women's writing purports to express, we are also simultaneously examining ideological, discursive positions of some Black women who are writers.

Migration horror story 5

One night I had a dream that I was attending a secular function in a church at which were presiding five bishops, of various races, sitting in panel fashion, dressed in pastoral surplices of green and yellow on white robes and with faces that were familiar to me. They were speaking on autobiography, a subject on which I was working and had a great deal of information available. There were several omissions and gaps as they spoke. I raised my hand to say something but at each point was told to wait, that they would recognize me later. Eventually, I got up and walked out and strolled around the building which seemed like one of those gigantic cathedrals, and, as it turned out, out of that nightmare of silencing.

★

Black feminist criticism began as a subversion and counter-articulation to the terms of both Black and feminist criticism. But its limitation, so far, is that it is almost wholly located in African-American women's experiences. People, of course, begin to work with the information at their disposal, and as their ideas and consciousness grow, there is an expansion of the range of possibility. Much can be learned, for example, from how Black women, even as they noted difference, allied with the feminist movement in certain major cities in Brazil, such as São Paulo, to effect legal changes which empowered women constitutionally. The ideas of Black Brazilian women, as expressed in their creative works, carry some specific identifications of their politics. However, because Black women's writing is located principally within United States experience, there has been no major attempt to study the range of Black feminist writing or to redefine its meaning.

A brief look at some of the movements so far will help to locate this present contribution. Black feminist criticism in the United States began by naming exclusions and omissions, excuses and afterthoughts and token, singular identifications. The essays in *All the Women Are White, All the Blacks are Men, But Some of Us Are Brave*[80] pursue some of these angles and identify the specificity of Black female subjectivity.

Still, Black feminism, even as it named and identified itself, already had within it the potential of excluding a range of experiences, and this it did. In a similar way, so do *Black Feminist Thought*[81] and *Talking Back. Thinking Feminist. Thinking Black.*[82] The exclusionary nature of US constructions of Black feminisms[83] has to be identified or it forces Black women from other parts of the world to locate their identities within the context of US hegemony.

In my own undertaking, I have discovered that the field is vast and humbling, and that the more one begins to explore the dynamics of Black women writing anywhere, the more one becomes conscious of not knowing. Moreover, it is difficult work in multiple languages and places. A consciousness of tentativeness and incompletion has to be at the center of any work of this period.

Textual criticism so far has moved in a few directions. One early and important stage was the identification of Black women's representation in the works of Black and white men and women. It appeared first in a rudimentary way as "image of women criticism" and subsequently as representations of women or gender in specific works. For example, while it was specific to the continental African experience, *Ngambika. Studies of Women in African Literature*[84] identified some of the movements in this issue as they pertained to African literature. A number of essays showed that when women are represented they appear in a stereotypical series of flat images, based primarily on the ways in which they identified with or supported men.

Other major movements have been the reclaiming of hidden writers, the identifying of new writers and the re-reading women writers defined through the politics of canonization as marginal. With this came a recognition that there were many writers "lost" in the traditions in which we participated. We recognized the major absence of Black women from the picture and sought to challenge that absence. A number of collections of interviews with Black women writers appeared. These include, for example, Claudia Tate's *Black Women Writers at Work* and, more recently, Adeola James's *African Women Writers Talk*.[85] Anne Adams's forthcoming collection *Seventy African and Caribbean Women Writers*[86] includes bio-bibliographical studies of a variety of Black women writers. A variety of interviews and conversations with Black women writers, a growing body of essays in popular magazines, textual criticism in academic journals and a variety of critical anthologies continue to make this writing accessible.

In-depth analyses of the ways these writers represent their Black and female realities have been important. In the US, the work of Mary Helen Washington, especially her introductions to *Black Eyed Susans* and *Midnight Birds* and the more recent *Invented Lives*,[87] was significant. Work of individual scholars like Deborah McDowell, Hortense Spillers, Valerie Smith, Hazel Carby and others continued this discussion. In particular Cheryl Wall's *Changing Our*

Own Words[88] presented the work of a number of Black feminist scholars who were examining a variety of women writers and related theoretical questions. Michele Wallace's *Invisibility Blues. From Pop To Theory*[89] contains a variety of explorations of Black women in the United States, including film representations. In African feminist work, 'Molara Ogundipe-Leslie's *African Women and Critical Transformations*[90] covers necessary ground as does work by Micere Mugo, Penina Muhando, Ama Ata Aidoo[91] and a variety of African feminist scholars on issues of gender who have offered significant contributions on the conditions of African women.

The contribution of this work is that it continues these discussions of Black women writing and Black feminist theory by broadening the terms of the debate. Because Black women consistently have been perceived as synonymous with US African-Americans, a major limitation in contemporary Black feminist scholarship is that the narrow construction of Black women's writing locates much of the discussion within the terms of what constitutes American (specifically US) literature. Work done by Black women from other parts of the world continues to be marginalized, although we know that many of the writers read and refer to each other across geographical boundaries. For me, therefore, the cross-cultural or comparative approach to Black women writers is an important way of advancing our understandings of Black women's writing. Without it, we remain locked into the captured definition of the term "Black" or "American" or "minority" as it is in the dominant discourse.

In this context, the work of Black women writing in Britain has to be significantly addressed. For here is a whole dynamic of Black women's writing which matches in intensity the output of Black women writing in the United States yet is not considered part of the ongoing discussions of this field unless a critic herself, as did Hazel Carby[92] or Rhonda Cobham, migrates from Europe to the US. A great deal of this writing appears in collections or anthologies, the worldwide distribution of which cannot match that for US books. Writings by writers like Merle Collins, Joan Riley, Beryl Gilroy, Grace Nichols get little exposure in the US. The passion behind much of the work of Black British women writers is creative rather than "high academic." In fact, this in my view is a strength. The collection *Watchers and Seekers. Creative Writing by Black Women in Britain*, edited by Cobham and Collins,[93] contains poetry and prose contributions by a variety of women from a range of ethnic communities, further challenging the location of "Black" as a descriptor wholly located in the African experience. Another collection, *Charting the Journey. Writings by Black and Third World Women*[94] more deliberately expresses the complexity of Black women's experiences in England – using short essays, analyses, reflections and poems and interviews by women of diverse regions, races, sexualities, ages and so on. The editors' brief introductions to each section are conceptually sharp pieces, locating these works within the context of home and exile.[95] Similarly, in Canada there is a growing body of work by Black women, such as Claire Harris, Dionne Brand and Marlene Nourbese Philip and the creative and publishing efforts of Makeda Silvera and Sister Vision Press, which, for example, published an expansive collection, *Piece of My Heart. A Lesbian of Color Anthology*[96] with representative work by women from a variety of communities.

In Brazil, there is a developing body of Black women writing in collections and producing single-authored texts. Some of it arises out of Quilhomboje in São Paulo, a creative collective of men and women, but some from a variety of women's/writings groups in Rio de Janeiro, individual writer/critics like Leda Martins in Belo Horizonte, women like Fatima Fontes in Salvador da Bahia, Miriam Alves and Esmeralda Ribeiro and others in São Paulo.[97]

The various Caribbean Women Writers conferences also testify to the wide range of Black women writing/or who have written from a variety of places, throughout the Caribbean and across language barriers. We are therefore in the middle of a creative explosion by Black women which will go unrecognized unless we mark its diversity, its expansiveness, its challenges to the boundaries of the acceptable.

In this work, therefore, I will not pretend to claim definitiveness or any expansive coverage which matches the breadth of the output. Instead, I offer an approach to more expansive critical work. It will incorporate as wide a range of writing communities as is accessible and possible within this framework, but it will also explore specific texts of individual writers in close analysis. It already accepts that there are several areas where extensive coverage will have to be deferred because of the practical realities of "incompleteness." For example, to explore the range of women writing in South Africa, Australia or Brazil and South America is an enterprise that one is not able to complete from outside or singly. I therefore begin by admitting a tentativeness in relation to Black women's writing asserting the existence of specificity, location, intertextuality and a continuing process of recognition. I offer instead a series of readings of different types in order to problematize the assumptive categories, but always resisting closure.

One of the primary issues that I propose to address in this study, therefore, is the question of theory. How do we theorize, who are the theorists and what is theory? Is theory a hegemonic discourse which imposes a new hierarchy? Is it important to pursue the specificity of Black female identity theoretically? What happens to the readership when the language of theory is deployed? Barbara Christian offered a self-reflexive approach to theorizing as practice in her *Black Feminist Criticism*[98] which included a reading of Buchi Emecheta. bell hooks[99] is making substantial contributions to theory as she criticizes by her process the very nature of theory.

But what about the discussions that surround feminism and deconstruction or feminism and postmodernism? Are they competing, allies, the "master's tools" as some would have it? In Chapter 2, "Negotiating Theories or 'Going a Piece of the Way with Them,'" I propose a model for engaging with a variety of theories and theoretical positions. In this context I find the critical responses of the writers themselves very helpful in pursuing some of the theoretical terms of the discussion. So, for Black women's writing, I believe it is premature and often useless to articulate the writer/theorist split so common in European discourses, for many of the writers do both simultaneously or sequentially. If we define theory as "frames of intelligibility,"[100] by which we understand the world, and not as a reified discourse used to locate, identify and explain everything else, then we have to pursue critically how we theorize, as Barbara Christian says in her important intervention, "The Race for Theory."[101] Theory, in my view, ought not to be an impediment to movement but should be an enabling set of discourses.

The avoidance of the revolutionary possibilities of Black feminist scholarship is an ongoing issue. This can be located, on the one hand, in the inability of Black women critical thinkers to reach a mass audience, and, on the other, in a kind of strategic deafness on the part of many: the media, the academy, Black communities. A number of women have been alarmed, listening to responses of a large number of women of color in the wake of recent public accusations by Black women of abuse by Black men, by the limited knowledge of the history and position of Black women in society. The practical application of Black feminist research has therefore to become as important as its writing. The purpose of scholarly activity ought to be clarified even as the work is being done.

Scholarship and theoretical writing by Black women, because they exist in an academic context, have become distant and removed from the day-to-day lives of most people.[102] But it is not only the fact of the critic distantly removed from the people which is the issue, but the ways in which Black women as writers, academics, teachers, who live lives of multiple oppression, still end up paradoxically unintelligible to those who are unschooled in critical discourses and also to those who are. For the "high theorists," the popular media and the Black male literary establishment still turn a deaf ear to Black feminist critics *vis-à-vis* the politics of citation and other forms of serious engagement with the issues raised. For this reason, the kind of interventions that have been made by women writers and theorists seem to have no impact or little recognition beyond the academy in terms of affecting conceptually how people see things. Questions of audience, about being enmeshed in a certain way of seeing and saying things are relevant for me in this study. Black feminist critics have to make a concerted effort, it seems to me, to do community work whenever/wherever possible.

The theoretical contribution of this book, *Black Women, Writing and Identity*, is the idea of "migratory subjectivity." *Migrations of the subject* promotes a way of assuming the subject's agency. I assert, therefore, that the subject is not just constituted, but in being constituted has multiple identities that do not always make for harmony. The subject here is Black women as it is Black women's writing in their many meanings. Migrations of the subject refers to the many locations of Black women's writing, but also to the Black female subject refusing to be subjugated. Black female subjectivity then can be conceived not primarily in terms of domination, subordination or "subalternization," but in terms of slipperiness, elsewhereness. Migratory subjects suggests that Black women/'s writing cannot be located and framed in terms of one specific place, but exist/s in myriad places and times, constantly eluding the terms of the discussion. It is not so much formulated as a "nomadic subject,"[103] although it shares an affinity, but as a migratory subject moving to specific places and for definite reasons. In the same way as diaspora assumes expansiveness and elsewhereness, migrations of the Black female subject pursue the path of movement outside the terms of dominant discourses. Peter Hitchcock in *Dialogics of the Oppressed*[104] suggests the need to "reassert the sign as a site of struggle, . . . over semantic and social authority. The multiple voicings implied in dialogics does not make for harmony, according to Bakhtin, but for dissonance" (p. 5). We know that questions of subjectivity have moved from the stable, coherent (Euro-Cartesian) to the decentered/postmodernist, to the subject with agency. Paul Smith in *Discerning the Subject*[105] had even argued that

> the current conceptions of the "subject" have tended to produce a purely *theoretical* "subject," removed almost entirely from the political and ethical realities in which human agents actually live and that a different concept of the "subject" must be discerned or discovered.
>
> (p. xxix)

He would even abandon the formulation "subject" for "agent."

A number of feminist scholars have also critiqued the tendency not to see the subject with agency.[106] Kristeva identifies a "subject" with the capability of "traversal," a "subject in process."[107] Hekman suggests that "feminists should be looking for ways to talk about the self and resistance to domination without reference to the constituting subject" (p. 61).

Employing a variety of meanings of subjectivity, I want to pursue the understanding of the resisting subject and apply it in different ways to the diasporic elsewheres of a radical Black *diasporic* subjectivity.[108] As "elsewhere denotes movement,"[109] Black female subjectivity asserts agency as it crosses the borders, journeys, migrates and so re-claims as it re-asserts.

2

NEGOTIATING THEORIES OR "GOING A PIECE OF THE WAY WITH THEM"

I usually spoke to them in passing. I'd wave at them and when they returned my salute, I would say something like this: "Howdy-do-well-I-thank-you-where-you-goin'?" Usually automobile or the horse paused at this, and after a queer exchange of compliments, I would probably "go a piece of the way" with them, as we say in farthest Florida. If one of my family happened to come to the front in time to see me, of course *negotiations* would be rudely broken off. . . .

(Zora Neale Hurston)[1]

the act of theory is the process of articulation, and the event of theory becomes the *negotiation* of contradictory and antagonistic instances.

(Homi K. Bhabha)[2]

The future of our earth may depend upon the ability of all women to identify and develop new definitions of power and new patterns of relating across difference. The old definitions have not served us, nor the earth that supports us. The old patterns, no matter how cleverly arranged to imitate progress, still condemn us to cosmetically altered repetitions of the same old exchanges, the same old guilt, hatred, recrimination, lamentation, and suspicion.

(Audre Lorde)[3]

NEGOTIATING THEORIES

A few years ago a number of young, brave, Black feminist scholars presented papers at a major conference on African literature, at a major Black institution. We were offering readings, from our angles of seeing, of some texts by some well-known African writers. A highly critical Black male scholar in the audience demanded to know what our theoretical framework was and further commented that what was sorely lacking in our work was just that, a theoretical framework in which he could locate what we were doing. Needless to say our responses were defensive, assertive, challenging. More recently, years after Black feminism had found a voice and practice, another Black male scholar, this time a well-known figure in African-American literary criticism, asserted at a symposium at Oxford University on Africanist Discourse, that Black women do not do theory and that indeed he could point to only three Black women scholars who were doing anything close to theory.[4]

The other side of these charges has witnessed the meticulous assembling of scholarly work on Black women which may or may not be defined, by some, as theoretical, depending on how theory is defined. Nonetheless, charges of this sort strike right at the center of what is credible scholarly work in academic contexts today. Demands for theoretical declaration work as positioning, locating or containing strategies in line with the ordering and categorizing that is endemic in academic communities.

Theory, as it is reified in the academy, still turns on Western phallocentric (master) or feminist "gynocentric" (mistress-master) philosophy. Catherine Lutz, in exploring the nature of theory, asserts that "theory" can be said to be writing which identifies itself as "theory." She continues that theory signals itself in certain ways – first, through self-labelling, second, abstract language, identified with levels of difficulty, third, styles and modes of citation of others' work, i.e., theorists cite other theorists and, fourth, the text's positioning of itself at, or in relation to, a moment of origin. Lutz goes even further to assert that theory and non-theory exist in relation to each other in ways which emulate the masculine vs the feminine in society. Theory therefore is anxious about its paternity and its patriliny: "Theories spawn patrilineal offspring who belong more to their father theory than their mother data."[5]

"Theory," applied in a hierarchical way, then, has become a legitimate source of aggravation for many feminists, women of color, academics and students. Although there are a number of paths to pursuing the given definitions of theory, I found interesting Paul Bove's introduction to his *In The Wake of Theory*,[6] which spends some time identifying Heidegger's notions of theory as "a particular form of insight, distantiated and 'penetrating'."[7] Still, according to Bove, theory is not just "penetrating circumspection," or necessarily in opposition to *praxis*, but a certain mode of "envisaging."

Many feminists would find the masculinized language of "penetration" as applied to theory a cause for concern and invalidation. Many of us feel that unless we enter the discussion in precisely the terms presented in Euro-American, male-dominated academic contexts, our words will never be taken seriously. Theoretical orthodoxy is often demanded. The language of theory is loaded with references to European male theorists accompanied by a certain ponderousness and linguistic and syntactic convolution. Additionally, there are definable centers (journals, presses, universities, news magazines) for the canonization of theories and theorists. Further, the mode of dissemination has been the "trickle down" approach to knowledge whereby the theorists theorize; another secondarily positioned group of scholar-disciples write books trying to make sense of the theories/theorists; and another positioned group tries to understand and apply these theories and interpret them to their students. At some point, maybe, the ideas reach the population at large through newspapers, journals, media-misunderstandings and then the language gets (mis)applied without its content.

Academic writing is in many ways an insular type of discourse which circulates among the learned or initiated. So questions of audience are central to the issues of writing and theory. In other words, to whom do theorists speak? Or, what does it mean when sufficiently literate friends and colleagues, otherwise intelligent women, can say to you "I like your book but I couldn't read it because I don't understand any of the language you all are using." In some ways, then, I am speaking about the nature of intellectual work and of the purposes to which this work is put.

Still, this is not to articulate an absurd "against theory"[8] position. For, some women of color who are critical of the convoluted language and direction of recent theory unfortunately come across as standing in a similar space as the older New Critics who want to maintain the canon and criticism as they are. Instead, it is my conviction that one is always acting out of some theoretical position/s whether these are named or not. I therefore agree with Barbara Christian's position, in "The Race for Theory,"[9] that we could effect a shift of language from the noun form "theory" to the verb form "theorize." At the same time one must not concede all the theoretical positions of power to men and white women.[10]

The understanding of "theory" as "frames (or modes) of intelligibility" through which we see and interpret the world or as "discursive ways of making sense of structures of values and belief which circulate in any given culture" and not as a reified discourse for the privileged few offers ways of breaking through the binary of "theory or no theory." According to Teresa Ebert, "Theories produce concepts through which the world is made intelligible and specific social relations are validated, thereby benefiting certain groups while oppressing others, whether or not that is the intention of the theory."[11] For this reason, it is necessary to deconstruct all theories to determine their origin, intent and possibilities. With this in mind, we can also assert firmly that gender/race discourses in the academy as initiated by Black women have had substantial impact on recent theorizings of postmodernism and of feminism without being identified. For example, it is possible to assert unequivocally that many current formulations of race/class/gender/sexuality discourses and the whole understanding of the need to complicate unitary subjectivities come out of the critical speech of a number of subordinated groups.[12]

The metatheories like postmodernism and their theoretical positions like subjectivity end up being constituted at the expense of a range of "others" even as they make the claim of representing them. Susan Hekman in "Reconstituting the Subject. Feminism, Modernism and Postmodernism" asserts that,

> Postmodernism articulates a subject that is subjected to multiple discursive formations. But elements of the postmodern critique address the ethical issue that feminism raises: the need to retain agency. They thus posit a subject that is capable of resistance and political action. This conception of the subject is articulated not by retaining a Cartesian concept of agency but by emphasizing that subjects who are subjected to multiple discursive influences create modes of resistance to those discourses out of the elements of the very discourses that shape them.
>
> (p. 51)[13]

The importance of what bell hooks defines as "critical speech" or "dissident speech" becomes real here.[14] If we look, for example, at Audre Lorde's "Age, Race, Class, and Sex. Women Redefining

Difference," all of Lorde's formulations articulate multiple subjectivities and discursive positions and agency. Not only is the notion of any unitary subjectivity eschewed, but there is also an active recognition of power relations and the necessity for agency, resistance, transformation. Lorde asserts:

> Much of Western European history conditions us to see human differences in simplistic opposition to each other: dominant/subordinate, good/bad, up/down, superior/inferior. In a society where the good is defined in terms of profit rather than in terms of human need, there must always be some group of people who, through systematized oppression, can be made to feel surplus, to occupy the place of the dehumanized inferior. Within this society, that group is made up of Black and Third World people, working–class people, older people, and women.[15]

Lorde's position is therefore highly theoretical here, eschewing binarisms, identifying issues of power and dominance, class, race, gender, sexual oppressions and othering. In fact Lorde articulates very clearly what Teresa Ebert would identify as "resistance postmodernism" which "is not a 'logic' but a *critique* of late capitalism, based on a social and historical rather than a textual theory of difference as the site of social conflict and struggle."[16] For Ebert, too, "resistance postmodernism" is an "oppositional political practice: an interventionist and transformative critique of American culture under the sign of late capitalism."[17]

My position, then, is not to abandon or jettison theory or theorizing, but to offer radical interventions into their claims to complete knowledge and, further, to find ways to negotiate the various theoretical "minefields" as we define ourselves. For example, I would want to apply hooks's formulation of "critical speech"[18] to the meaning of theory here and maybe to advance an assertion that "critical speech" may be more of value than the self-conscious erecting of more new, "high" theories since it (critical speech) has more to do with deconstructing a variety of metanarratives. Critical speech in this context becomes a signifying practice which "reads" theory.

In "Toward a Black Gay Aesthetic, Signifying in Contemporary Black Gay Literature," Charles Nero,[19] following Gates,[20] Smitherman[21] and Claudia Mitchell-Kernan,[22] identifies aspects of signifying which include "capping, loud-talking, the dozens, reading, going off, talking smart, sounding, joaning (jonesing), dropping lugs, snapping, woofing, styling out, and calling out of one's name" (p. 230). All these are ways of "reading" other's behaviors and practices. They are therefore often directed at dismantling dominant or pretentious discourses.

For my purposes, then, it is more significant to go in search of the ideas of a variety of subversive theoretical formulations and work toward the redefining of ownership of knowledge in a variety of areas. For when Black women speak in the proper manner of theory, who hears it or accepts its validity? One runs the risk either of appropriation of one's intent by the "theorists" who have legitimacy in the academy or of direct distortion of one's intent.

The question of theory is one which for us may be more useful if we redefine arrangements, renegotiate our locations. In other words, we must negotiate a channel between the "high theoretical" and the "suspicious of all theories." As Trinh Minh-ha rightly puts it:

> theory is suspicious when it loses sight of its own conditional nature, takes no risk in speculation, and circulates as a form of administrative inquisition. Theory oppresses, when it wills or perpetuates existing power relations, when it presents itself as a means to exert authority – the Voice of Knowledge.[23]

Central to this process is the need to scrutinize the scholars, writers, critical thinkers in our communities for "ways of knowing." For theory, in the academy, turns more on complexity of language and formulations of ways of seeing than it does on original thought. In this way, the critique of theoretical orthodoxy and the "Great Master" – the Western anthropologist, the philosopher (Minh-ha) – is effected. Alice Walker's position in her article "What Can the (White) Man . . . . . . Say to the Black Woman"[24] is an important piece of signifying on the authority of the (white) man to speak definitively on anything that the Black woman should accept. Instead, she moves it to praxis: i.e., he should try to redress wrongs and above all sit still for a century or so and LISTEN.

A variety of recent interventions have further clarified for me ways of reworking the theoretical. Stuart Hall offers, in "Signification, Althusser and the Post-Structuralist Debates,"[25] the concept of "articulation" and the notion of an "arbitrary fixing" without which there would be no signification or meaning at all. Yet, it is the notion of *who fixes and how arbitrary* that still allows some pause, especially when for Black women, so distanced from the centers of power, all fixing of meaning takes place without their consent. As well, arbitrariness often attains a kind of permanence and concreteness. Articulation, nonetheless, allows a kind of open-ended and contingent connection or linking which has constantly to be renewed. A particular articulation may also be overthrown as new connections – rearticulations – are forged. But it must be remembered that Hall was re-reading Althusser and Marx. Hall, nevertheless, sees the purpose of theory as helping us "get a bit further down the road."[26]

This leads to my second helpful intervention, that of Edward Said's "Travelling Theory,"[27] which demonstrates, through reading Lukacs, Goldman and Raymond Williams, that a theory/theory itself can move from its originary points to new uses and new positions depending on time and place and so on. Janet Wolff's "On the Road Again. Metaphors of Travel in Cultural Criticism,"[28] suggests, however, that this does not mean there is something inherently mobile in the *nature* of theory, but that both senses of "travelling theory" are in currency in cultural criticism. Wolff, nevertheless, sees the metaphors of travel as male-gendered (p. 232). Still, I would argue, and the rest of this work will show, that once Black women are accounted for, both "travelling" and "theory" can be also identified as Black women's prerogatives.

A third intervention comes from Homi Bhabha, who is identified in the opening epigraphs. Bhabha, in a defense of theory, asserts that this negotiation "opens up hybrid sites and objectives of struggle and destroys those familiar polarities between knowledge and its objects, and between theory and practical-political reason."[29] So, for Bhabha the distinction between the theoretical and the political is an absurd and unnecessary dichotomy:

> Each "position" is always a process of translation and transference of meaning. Each objective is constructed on the trace of that perspective that it puts "under erasure"; each political object is displacing in relation to the other, and displaced in the critical act. Too often these theoretical issues are peremptorily transposed into organizational terms and represented as sectarianism.[30]

It is the process of "translation" and "migration" and "open-endedness" and even nomadism that is operative here. Deleuze, in "Nomad Thought,"[31] shows that philosophical discourse, related to law, institutions and contracts, and which underpins theory, is "born out of the imperial state, and it passes through innumerable metamorphoses" (p. 148), but is part of the culture of making sedentary. Still there is a counter-discourse which is "nomadic." Nomads, he would argue, are not necessarily migrants. Rather they often stay within a certain geographic range, continually evading the "codes of settled people." Grossberg also argues for a "materialist or nomadic model [which] argues that reality is constructed by the 'anonymous' travels of people within the historically articulated social spaces, places, and structures of practice."[32] Reading Radway,[33] he identifies how "nomadic subjects are always empowered and disempowered, shaped and reshaped, by the effectivities of the practices within which their agency is located" (p. 387). Thus, it is not individual agency which he would privilege, but social practices and the ways the subject can remain "outside of the particular practice," but "able to articulate it" (p. 387). Despite this, nomadism is still a mobility, limited geographically nonetheless. However, all journeys do not necessarily entail major physical movement, nor crossings of large geographical spaces. Deleuze would assert that "some voyages take place in situ, are trips in intensity."[34]

I want to assert, while recognizing the validity of their interventions and clarifications, that it is not an accident that it happens to be men who are asserting the right to theory and travel. Although I support their positions, I recognize again that we are nevertheless interpellated in a variety of discourses based on gender, race, declared sexuality and so on. So, for example, Teshome Gabriel, in "Thoughts on Nomadic Aesthetics and the Black Independent Cinema. Traces of a Journey,"[35] offers important ideas on theorizing movement. Still it is a masculinized set of formulations with woman as object, "aesthetics as woman" and so on. His "Poetics of Nomadic Aesthetics" offers a useful series of ideas of modes of interrupting, disrupting linearity, fixity, sedentariness and so on.

The hierarchies which exist are able to locate us as thinkers, authorized speakers, yes, theorists, at various levels based on these same categories which are already installed, and masculinity is one which has historically guaranteed one a hearing.

One can test this "politics of citation" by attempting to produce a professional paper and citing only Black women/women of color critical thinkers. So far there have been few such attempts and these are doomed to non-recognition at the high academic level, the charge of "not doing theory" or the absence of theoretical framework with which I began. It is essentially, then, a question of speech, language and authority. These are some of the areas that I want to disrupt in the rest of this chapter by first of all locating a theoretical position of migratory subjectivity in Zora Neale Hurston's narrative description of cultural, performative practice.

GOING A PIECE OF THE WAY WITH THEM

The subtitle of this chapter, "Going a Piece of the Way with Them," is constructed on the model for relationships with "strangers" which Hurston identifies in "How It Feels to Be Colored Me." In this model of offering courtesies to visitors, which comes out of several African and African-based cultures, the host goes a "piece of the way" with friend or visitor, the distance depending on the relationship.

In using this formulation, then, I want to engage all these theories as visitors. This comes from the recognition that going all the way home with many of these theoretical positions – feminism, postmodernism, nationalism, Afrocentrism, Marxism, etc. – means taking a route cluttered with skeletons, enslavements, new dominations, unresolved tensions and contradictions. Following many of the theories/theorists "all the way home" inevitably places me in the "homes" of people where I, as a Black woman, will have to function either as maid or exotic, silenced courtesan, but definitely not as a theoretical equal. Going all the way home with them means being installed in a distant place from my communities.[36]

I believe that the "visitor theory" approach offers a technique of interaction similar to the intention of "multiple articulations."[37] It becomes a kind of *critical relationality* in which various theoretical positions are interrogated for their specific applicability to Black women's experiences and textualities and negotiated within a particular inquiry with a necessary eclecticism. It is a particular way of reading or writing the Black/female experience which plays on a variety of possible configurations. It is at once a process and a pattern of articulations. This particular negotiation which Hurston identifies is a way of conceptualizing the practical work that many of us do already. It builds on that work and goes beyond the now clichéd "race, class, gender" formula that has made its way into and affected the academy. It moves beyond that formula because those three also turn on some exclusions, silences and camouflages, for example, sexuality, age, ability, national or cultural origin, educational level and the like.

I want to submit that Hurston's articulation of "going a piece of the way with them" is inherently a statement which assumes agency. Journeys, Teshome Gabriel asserts, "acknowledge encounters with others, with known and unknown forces, happy or horrendous . . . the journey is the link[age]."[38] This journeying, then, is not so much an "oppositional consciousness" which can suggest a certain fixity, but a consciousness which turns on "migration," mobility, movement, departure, return, re-departure (Trinh T. Minh-ha) and transformation. Chela Sandoval in "U.S. Third World Feminism. The Theory and Method of Oppositional Consciousness in the Postmodern World,"[39] places "Third World feminism" in the US in a space or "topography or cultural region which delineates the set of critical points around which individuals and groups seeking to transform oppressive powers constitute themselves as resistant or oppositional subjects."[40] At the furthest point of Sandoval's articulation is her notion of "differential consciousness" comprised of "seeming contradictions and difference which serve as tactical interventions in the other mobility; a kind of anarchic activity or ideological guerrilla warfare; an opposition to repressive authorities in a highly technological and disciplined society." For her "differential consciousness implies or requires an emotional commitment to shattering of the unitary self as the skill which allows *a mobile identity to form* takes hold."[41] It is this "mobile identity" which Hurston captures as a non-Western, rural or "Third World" mode of offering courtesies to visitors that allows me to advance the validity of this multiply articulated approach. Hurston's own critical academic work was based on a series of physical migrations and her own migratory subjectivities.

Jamaica Kincaid in *A Small Place*[42] asserts that if Africans had travelled to see the Europeans (as we know they did), they would have said "how interesting" and gone back home and told their people and not sought to conquer. A way of relating to visitors or difference is imbedded in this approach. *Critical relationality* thus means negotiating, articulating and interrogating simultaneously a variety of resistant discourses relationally and depending on context, historical and political circumstances. It is not opportunistic, in the sense of conveniently articulated, but progressively multiply articulated in the face of a variety of dominant discourses.

47

Thus, I differ slightly with Sandoval in her "car clutch metaphor," which asserts that differential consciousness goes into gear tactically. But even gear shifts require a hierarchical sequence which I reject on principle. So rather than "choosing tactical positions," I am asserting an interrogation of a variety of positions and a fluidity of movement which, more like a spider web, asserts itself in multiple ways. I therefore reject the Bhabha notion of "hybridity" for the same reason and share the position of Becquer and Gatti in "Elements of Vogue,"[43] which suggests "syncretism" and "syncretic articulations" as "*antagonistic*, i.e., in relations which are animated by the partial presence of the other within the self, such that the differential identity of each term is at once enabled and prevented from full constitution,"[44] while hybridity, they assert, offers two essentialized poles from which something new grows. "Vogueing," and similar signifying articulations, thus becomes one of those articulatory discourses which "traverse sexualities, genders, races, and classes in performance" in multiple ways.[45]

Antonio Benitez Rojo in "The Repeating Island"[46] has a wonderful analysis of the Caribbean islands, using postmodernist formulations to identify what already is in Caribbean geography – that repetition which lends itself to new analyses:

> This archipelago, like others, can be seen as an island that "repeats" itself. I have drawn attention to the word "repeats" because I want to give it the unsettled meaning with which it appears in post-structuralist discourse, where all repetition brings necessarily a difference and deferral.
>
> (pp. 431–432)

I am saying, too, that the experience of Black women lends itself to the notion of fluidity, multiple identities, repetition which must be multiply articulated. Lata Mani, in her "Multiple Mediations. Feminist Scholarship in the Age of Multinational Reception,"[47] calls, with Chandra Mohanty, for the need to reflect on the process of "moving between different 'configurations of meaning and power' [which] prompts different modes of knowing." The rest of her essay raises a number of questions but never reaches the point of identifying in practice how these processes might be activated.

My position is that "going a piece of the way" with its implied multiple, discursive articulations and movements offers such a model and lines up well with "syncretic articulations," "vogueing," creolizations and other migratory formulations.

PROBLEMATIZING THEORETICAL BLACK NATIONALIST HOMELANDS

The entire construction of "going a piece of the way with them" turns on a concept of home, i.e., going a piece of the way and returning. It nonetheless realizes that "home" (as expressed in a wide range of feminist theoretical and creative works) is one of the principal sites of domination and conflict for women. Resisting specific identities and "theoretical homelands" can lead to a "theoretical homelessness," as shown in the question with which I began: "What is your theoretical framework?" Thus, the sense of "homelessness" which is activated in postmodernist discourses is already simultaneously articulated in Black female experiences of conflict with "home." Home, here, is being used in a way much like Martin and Mohanty,[48] within the context of self, home, community, nation constructions and the need for re-mapping boundaries and renegotiating connections.

But home in this new understanding can be seen as multiple locations. Gloria Anzaldua identifies "borderlands" using the Chicana/US experience to identify how people live in more than one location at the same time.[49] A similar conceptualization appears in Flores and Yudice's "Living Borders."[50] bell hooks contributes another helpful way of seeing constructions of home:

> the very meaning of "home" changes with the experience of decolonization, of radicalization. At times home is nowhere. At times one knows only extreme estrangement and alienation. Then home is no longer just one place. It is locations. Home is that place which enables and promotes varied and everchanging perspectives, a place where one discovers new ways of seeing reality, frontiers of difference. One confronts and accepts dispersal, fragmentation as part of the construction of a new world order that reveals more fully where we are, who we can become, an order that does not demand forgetting.[51]

Any articulation of a critique of home for Black women has to begin with an examination of the totalizing nature of nationalist (Africa-diaspora) discourse. Pan-Africanism, Black/African nationalism and Afrocentricity are "totalizing discourses" which can tolerate no different articulation and operate from a singularly monolithic construction of an African theoretical homeland which asks for the submergence or silencing of gender, sexuality or any other ideological stance or identity position which is not subsumed under Black/African nationalism. An engagement with nationalism for Black feminist critics is one which has to interrogate a number of theorists of nationalism to locate specific positions on gender and determine how far we can "go down the road with them." Thus, "Afrocentric feminism" sounds like a contradiction in terms, for if it is "Afro-centered" then the feminine/feminism is already an appendage, an excess, easily expelled or contained within.

According to 'Molara Ogundipe-Leslie,[52] if one is a woman one often has to run in the other direction when some African men start talking about culture and, I would add, by extension, of "Afrocentric theoretical homelands." Many of these "homelands" become constructed spaces as "under apartheid" – as reserved spaces – or in North America – reservations. Cynthia Enloe, in *Bananas, Beaches & Bases. Making Sense of International Politics,*[53] asserts correctly that "nationalism typically has sprung from masculinized memory, masculinized humiliation and masculinized hope."[54] The link between nationalism and masculinity is, I believe, also made in *Motherlands* by Elleke Boehmer in her opening section, "Stories of Women and Mothers. Gender and Nationalism in the Early Fiction of Flora Nwapa."[55]

In the tradition of "critical speech" (bell hooks) or "specifying" (Valerie Smith) or "signifying" (Henry Louis Gates Jr), *critical relationality* assumes a critical practice which carries a certain iconoclasm as one "reads" named (father) figures like Fanon, Garvey, Sekou Toure, Kwame Toure, C.L.R. James, W.E.B. Dubois, Malcolm X, Mandela, Nkrumah, Cabral, Fidel Castro and others on gender. Some of this analysis has been done, or is in process; some of these analyses will be very easy as the responses have been so explicitly misogynist; some lesser known African intellectuals will look better than the popular ones once gender is factored. Black feminist critique has already challenged the aspects of nationalism with which we had worked without question.

In other words, how can a Black feminist activate a race-based, Afrocentric discourse which already defines itself in a static, essentialized, nativized, flawed, historical context? At this level, the negotiating approach is as well a rejection of a philosophical fundamentalism. A rejection of fundamentalist Black/African nationalism, as in the attack on the father, often assures a "theoretical homelessness" unless one reactivates a more transcultural conception of "home."

While one, of necessity, has to identify with Africa as the imaginary/historical basis of identity or self-assertion, the unproblematic, sacred homeland definition on which nationalist discourses turn is oppressive. The transportation of African peoples to the New World unified Africans across their ethnic differences and cut them off from their past, creating what Benedict Anderson calls an "imagined community." But what is asked of women in some of these nationalist discourses is that they accept their own oppressions as a given (using some examples from the US), accept commodification (2 Live Crew), abuse (Shaharazad Ali), death (Suti in India), silencing (Anita Hill), rape (Desiree Washington), to allow race-based discourses, i.e., Black/male discourses, to exist.

The re-emergence of nationalist discourses will be an area of ongoing engagement at specific historical junctures. Nevertheless, I still believe that given the interventions of Black feminist discourses, they can never pretend to be the same. The role of women in nationalist discourses is an important issue, for historically women have expressed nationalist zeal and patriotism,[56] although, often, they have been dispossessed in the documenting of nationalist struggles and/or in the shaping and reconstruction of new societies.

RE-READING POSTMODERNISM AND FEMINISM

Postmodernism is an area of theoretical engagement which, although relatively new, has to be subject to the same scrutiny as any of the theoretical positions it would delegitimize. In the construction of "going a piece of the way with them," it seems possible to raise some of the questions postmodernism raises and at the same time challenge any totalizing gestures on the part of this theoretical approach. Postmodernism offers a disruption of metanarratives of all sorts and it is primarily at that level that one can see how that deconstruction of race or gender discourses which assume totality, can be activated by Black feminist critics. But what about essentialism and the question of "race" under erasure and "gender" under erasure? We can ask, together with Toni Morrison in "Unspeakable Things Unspoken,"[57] why it seems strange that the people who lived by asserting that "race" was everything (or "gender" was everything) are now, when it seems people are activating race and gender for empowerment, saying that we should forget about race. Morrison was nevertheless speaking in the broad categories of race and gender that are easily essentialized. So, is Black identification an ideological position, a political stance or a rhetorical gesture?

Similarly, Michèle Barrett and Anne Phillips in their introduction to *Destabilizing Theory. Contemporary Feminist Debates* assert that "Feminists have become deeply suspicious of theoretical discourses that claim neutrality while speaking from a masculinist perspective, and have at times despaired of the possibility of 'gender-neutral' thought."[58] A second aspect of the work would be the self-critique of feminist theories and assumptions themselves. Many point to Susan Bordo's[59] work on the assumptions of "Western intellectual tradition" which underpins all philosophical/ theoretical projects that come out of the West. Similarly Nancy Miller's "Changing the Subject. Authorship, Writing and the Reader,"[60] argues that "the postmodernist decision that the Author is dead, and subjective agency along with him, does not necessarily work for women and prematurely forecloses the question of identity for them."[61] The discussions generated by Linda Alcoff's "Cultural Feminism Versus Post-Structuralism. The Identity Question in Feminist Theory,"[62] point well to the ways in which feminism has not had an easy set of coincidences with postmodernism. Teresa Ebert's "Ludic Feminism, the Body, Performance and Labor. Bringing *Materialism* Back Into Feminist Cultural Studies,"[63] offers a critique of certain forms of feminism and a way of allying it with her formulation of "resistance postmodernism" identified earlier.

For Black feminist criticism, though, bourgeois, Western feminism which has held the dominant position in definitions to date is also an inheritor of that same Western intellectual tradition, like postmodernism, even as it critiques it. It is a position which Gayatri Spivak, Trinh Minh-ha, bell hooks, Chandra Mohanty and a wide range of other non-Western/Black feminists have argued well. One has, therefore, to examine the location in history of specific discourses and not see them as consistently dominant, and thus begin examinations of their occurrences in history, their alliance with dominant politics and so on. An anti-occurrence position, as identified by Ernesto Laclau and Chantal Mouffe,[64] leaves room for a host of alliances. Leaving "home," Mohanty and Martin would assert, activates the dialectical journey back and forth.[65] Still back and forth suggests only two axes or poles of interaction. Trinh Minh-ha's concept of *re-departure*[66] may allow a bit more opening as it suggests, "Identity is a way of re-departing. Rather, the return to a denied heritage allows one to start again with different re-departures, different pauses, different arrivals" (p. 328). I do not necessarily agree that in all cases re-departure is allied with "the pain and frustration of having to live a difference that has no name and too many names already."[67] It is for a number of migrants identified with the conjunction of both joy and pain of nostalgia, longing and desire as in *saudade* in Brazilian cultural contexts.

Stuart Hall, in "The Local and the Global,"[68] asserts that various discursive positions have validity as arguments within specific contexts when they have to be activated. There is also a certain migrancy or discursivity between the local and the global in postmodern contexts. Chandra Mohanty sees location as "temporality of struggle."[69] For example, talking with an entrenched "old/new" critic, traditionalist, who wants to maintain the canon as it is, it is impossible not to activate some postmodernist positions. Or listening to an attack on a female colleague for her assertions into male space, can activate a feminist position. A nationalist, anti-imperialist position has to be articulated when Black students are under attack. In other words, each position is deployed when each necessitates its own specific critique and one journeys accordingly or activates them simultaneously, braid-like as I have suggested elsewhere.[70] Similar interrogations of Marxism[71] and queer identity[72] are themselves interrogated by the critique of gay-people of color who challenge the dominance of monolithic gay/queer nation theories.

Postmodernism and feminism, with their destabilization of metanarratives, offer important avenues for the critique of establishment positions. More innovative approaches to philosophy and philosophizing, reading and cultural and literary criticism by women of color offer that nationalism, feminism, poststructuralism and postmodernism, queer theory and other discourses which open up the space for articulations also, when looked at from other angles, become totalizing discourses and thus subject to critical interrogation, "reading" or dissident speech.

The type of political critique of a variety of theoretical positions that I envisage and appreciate, activates my own notions of theoretical negotiations and *critical relationality*. Benitez Rojo, speaking of repetition and polyrhythms in the Caribbean cultural space, says that European rhythms try to command a center, but the "rhythms of the People of the Sea . . . float toward the pleasurable condition of 'totality' which finally is nowhere" (p. 450). Thus, even the mixtures that are produced by these rhythms cannot be fixed, as to do so would assume a certain "positivist logocentric argument" concerning identity. At each moment when unity seems to be arrived at, it "explodes and scatters" (p. 451) toward beginning again.

It is this kind of space that some resistance/postmodernist discourses allow us for recreation of meaning and pushing forward new forms of knowledge. Elsa Barkley Brown articulates similarly in her "Polyrhythms and Improvisation. Lessons for Women's History"[73] when she talks about listening to multiple conversations/multiple rhythms being played simultaneously, or the variegated patterns of quilting, as a primary way of seeing a world that is fundamentally different from European bourgeois, male formulations which demand linearity. "Going a piece of the way with them" is a pretext which engages the intent of what are now postmodernist discourses for their sense of rupture and destabilization, but accepts the need to read ways in which these disruptions already exist in non-Western/woman-centered cultures.

CRITICAL RELATIONALITY: COMPLICATING WOMEN OF COLOR FEMINIST CRITICAL POSITIONS

I want to end this chapter by affirming Audre Lorde as an important example of one who challenges that split between writer and theorist, between theory and practice, between the borders of different theoretical positions.[74] Moreover, her formulation of herself as "sister outsider,"[75] emulating in her self-naming the language used in Caribbean islands to refer to those who occupy the immigrant slot, names herself as crossing boundaries yet remaining outside a number of them, by choice and ideological positioning. Her words with which I began this chapter assert all the critiques of binary thinking that, for example, Kobena Mercer identifies in his "Black Art and the Burden of Representation."[76] Similarly, Ama Ata Aidoo, whose work I will discuss in the following chapter, effected an important discourse on marginality and the construction of African female subjectivity in her play *Anowa* (1970) before the critics had terms to write about these.

A number of critical thinkers/cultural workers are creative writers, and vice versa, who consistently disrupt the separations inherent in these enforced constructions of being one or the other. The writer/ theorist split is obviously a recent disciplinary move meant to keep the functions separate. It is my view that it may be more important to interrogate the ideological positions of the writer/theorist than to activate the split. At one level, it does offer a way around the "death of the author" syndrome of some post-structuralist positions. But one has to simultaneously reject approaches in which the author's interpretation becomes the final and only interpretation of the text.

At this point, though, it is necessary to trace a variety of women of color feminist critical positions. Black feminism is sometimes reduced to one generalized category which hides all kinds of differences and subsumes all sorts of submerged identities. Instead, I would offer recognition to a number of intersecting circles, with a range of critics, theorists and writers all articulating different positions from their particular locations in and out of the academy. All of these theorists articulate the need for a transformative process which takes into consideration multiple spheres of interest. They offer, to Black/feminist/critics/theorists/activists, possibilities of intersecting and reading a variety of cultural texts. In this approach, the politics of transformation, without the enforcement of one totalized way of seeing or being, is struggled with. At this point, then, we have to admit that many scholars in the academy participate in the devaluing of Black women who are writers and theorists by not recognizing them or engaging their ideas.

My contention is that postmodernist positions or feminist positions are always already articulated by Black women because we experience, ahead of the general population, many of the multiple struggles that subsequently become popularly expressed (for example, drugs in communities, teen pregnancies, struggle for control of one's body, one's labor, etc.). Black feminist criticisms, then, perhaps more than many of the other feminisms, can be a praxis where the theoretical positions and the criticism interact with the lived experience.

The clusters or circles of non-Western (Third World) feminist positions can include, Black British feminisms, native American feminisms, Latin American feminisms, Chicana feminisms, Brazilian feminisms, Asian feminisms, African feminisms, African-American feminisms, US Third World feminisms, Caribbean feminisms, Black/Australian feminisms and so on. One can therefore see a pattern in which each of the circles intersect, collide, bump against each other, relate, re-energize, separate and reorder themselves. Each feminist articulation is intersected by geography, sexuality, class, cultural identity, economics, history, social factors, race, ethnicity, age, ability, language. Thus, one can also speak specifically of, for example, an Asian feminism or a US Latina lesbian feminism in more particular terms as well as a general discussion of Black feminisms or women of color.[77] The need for complicating black feminisms assures an interruption of monolithic assumptions of any discourse, such as specific definition, of what feminism is or what Black feminism, or Third World feminism, itself can be. The word "defining" originally meant "setting up of boundaries or enclosures."[78] An anti-definitional stance moves us out of minority status into possibilities of alliances which recognize specificities and differences.

This kind of critical relationality asserts the specificity of the other, but works together and from each other in a generalized purpose of resistance to domination. Critical relationality, then, moves beyond singularity or sameness to varied interactions, transgressions and articulations. Critical relationality becomes a way in which other theoretical positions interact relationally in one's critical consciousness. Critical relationality moves beyond a singular, monochromatic approach to any work to a complexly-integrated and relational theoretics; it allows the situation of a text in its own context, but provides an ability to understand and relate it to a range of other dimensions of thought. Critical relationality is then inherently migratory.

In order to read Black women's writing in a cross-cultural or transnational perspective, the critical consciousness has to demonstrate this expansiveness and relationality. Critical relationality is not interruptive or a series of interruptions (as in Marxism/feminism or race/class or gender/ethnicity formulations, nor does it embrace the hierarchy embedded in subalternization. Rather, it argues for the synchronic, multiply articulated discourses, which operate braid-like or web-like as a series of strands are woven.

The ways in which other women of color address issues of identity and writing become of major importance in critical relationality. Scholars like Trinh T. Minh-ha, in *Woman Native Other* and *When the Moon Waxes Red*[79] and her more recent collections of essays, are important for their unpacking of the issues of theory, spectatorship, location. The work of Gayatri Spivak[80] has been helpful because it addresses the issues of gender, class, nationality, identity and "worlding" in hegemonic Western theory. Spivak's subjecting of Indian women's texts to critical and theoretical examination broke a number of barriers to the recognition of women's writing from the "other worlds." Gloria Anzaldua's *Borderlands/La Frontera* and her collection *Making Face, Making Soul/Haciendo Caras*[81] have been important contributions which have aided the explorations that some of us undertake. In particular, the identification of border cultures of race, nationality, sexuality and how boundaries are set up between peoples has allowed me to conceptualize a range of borderlands in a variety of practical realities. Similarly, Paula Gunn Allen's *The Sacred Hoop. Recovering the Feminine in American Indian Traditions*[82] offers an important insight into ancient traditions of womanhood beyond the white female understandings. *Opening the Gates: A Century of Arab Feminist Writing,*[83] which brings together a variety of essays on women's identity by Arab women, has also aided my understanding of the long history of feminist struggle which predates the Western articulations of women's rights. Ifi Amadiume's *Male Daughters. Female Husbands*[84] and work now being done by other African women provide cultural groundings and pretexts and analyses for questions being debated in the West that have to do with accepted definitions of gender. In other words, the search has to be continued for ways of seeing our worlds beyond the given. Two collections, Chandra Talpade Mohanty, Lourdes Torres and Anne Russo, *Third World Women and the Politics of Feminism*[85] and Susheila Nasta's *Motherlands. Black Women's Writing from Africa, the Caribbean and South Asia,*[86] add new options for the kind of critical relationality which I identify.

An intersection may be encountered as a site of conflict, confusion, anger or be seen as a nexus of engagement, growth of specific identity and creativity. This therefore eschews questions of how to identify specifically women's issues within any of the other identity discourses. I propose to explore throughout this text the ways in which we can negotiate a variety of identities, theoretical positions and textualities without falling prey to schisms and dualistic or binary thinking that dismisses one dynamic to privilege another. So, what is the theoretical framework or are we doing theory? I close with an appropriate poem by Joyoti Grech[87] as a way of eschewing closure, maintaining provisionality and ambiguity:

In Answer to Some Questions

In answer to some questions that miss the point
or
yes but where are you from?

What I don't have
is a land
is a lover
is a language
to say, is mine

What I don't have
are ropes
of romance
of nationalism
of words to tie me down/in smug belonging
to stop me knowing
what more there is

What I don't have
is pencil lines
drawn around my/self
by pale people
who know nothing/of my terrain

What I don't have
are someone else's borderlines

I rub them out with my desire
                    with action
and a need to know

I am never satisfied

I flood their borders
with the sea of my sisters names
and my brothers
whose lives keep their blood
red like mine.

3

DECONSTRUCTING AFRICAN FEMALE SUBJECTIVITIES

Anowa's borderlands

The politics of domination, migration, subjectivity and agency are multiply articulated in Ama Ata Aidoo's play *Anowa*. It is a text which has to be foregrounded in any theoretical examination of Black women's writing for it offers a way of "creative theorizing" which I am arguing is a central aspect of some Black women's writing. *Anowa* refigures the New World/Old World signs of rupture, schism, opening and othering as it simultaneously embodies the critique of constructions of the woman in society. It also prefigures issues of Black female subjectivity and identity that would be located in subsequent/current texts by Black women writers. The material of the play itself traverses boundaries that have to do with orality, writing and performance, gender, marginality and the social construction of identity, the patriarchal assumptions that are generally allied with capitalist exploitation.

In an earlier work, I addressed issues of marginality, minoring and effacement,[1] showing how the "(op)positional status of the African woman writer in relation to literary canonicity" reveals itself as a *multiple marginality, minoring* and *effacement* against which she writes anyway. The play, *Anowa*, therefore offers an important approach to the "politics of exclusion," both within the text of the play and in its reception. Published in 1970, by the Ghanaian playwright, the work has received little critical attention and as a result occupies a marginal position in African literary studies[2] and feminist criticism.[3] Aidoo herself has said that "[w]hen a critic refuses to talk about your work, that is violence; he is willing you to die as a creative person."[4] It is this same "politics of exclusion" which revels in the constructed binaries of masculinity/

59

femininity, sanity/insanity, home/exile, center/margin, witch/ priestess which this chapter attempts to disrupt.

The intersections of coloniality, male dominance, class preju- dices, economic exploitation, power and gender dynamics which are explored in this play, perhaps placed it ahead of its time. In a way, then, this text, like many other works by women such as Zora Neale Hurston's *Their Eyes Were Watching God* (1937),[5] seemed to have to await the theoretical discourses on subjectivity and of feminist critical practice which would allow it to be read seriously. I want to read *Anowa*, therefore, also as a kind of theorizing within the creative text. As I assert in Chapter 2, it is the nature of the engagement with multiple subjectivities that places some works, like this one, solidly in contemporary theoretical explorations of colonial discourses and female subjectivity.

The play *Anowa* is constructed in three movements: Phase One takes place at the village, Yebi, in the 1870s, locating Anowa's resistance to societal prescriptions of what is appropriately female as expressed by her parents and by "The-Mouth-That-Would-Eat- Salt-and-Pepper." It ends with her choosing her own mate and leaving the village. Phase Two takes place on the Highway where Anowa and Kofi Ako her husband are the primary actors, leading nomadic lives. She is working as a partner in the business they are building; he is planning to install her in the position of "wife." They debate here his route to financial success through expropriat- ing other people's labor and dealing in "skins." Phase Three is located in "The Big House at Oguaa" where Kofi Ako is now installed as chief and successful businessman. Anowa, who has now become a displaced figure, resists all prescriptions concerning modes of behavior befitting her husband's status and does not partake in his riches. She therefore comes across to those around her as a mad woman. The play ends with Anowa discovering that Kofi has lost his "manhood" and with the self-immolation of Kofi Ako and Anowa being recorded by the community's voice. Framing the text and serving as commentator on events is "The-Mouth-That-Would-Eat-Salt-and-Pepper," an old man and woman, who function as representative spokespeople of the com- munity. They also function as intermediary readers of the text of Anowa's life,[6] standing between the readers/viewers reading the play and Anowa and allowing us to do a double reading the text and of their responses to the text of Anowa's life.

The significance of the play as a rewriting of one of the oral narratives of the girl who would choose her own husband is that the writer, the play, the readers are able to traverse the boundaries of orality, writing and performance. In describing the play, Aidoo says,

> [i]t's more or less my own rendering of a kind of . . . legend, because, according to my mother, who told me the story, it is supposed to have happened. The ending is my own and the interpretation I give to the events that happen is mine. A girl married a man her people did not approve of; she helped him become fantastically rich, and then he turns round to sort of drive her away. The original story I heard, which in a way was in the form of a song, didn't say why he did this, and I myself provide an answer to this, a clue, you know, a kind of pseudo-Freudian answer. . . . [7]

The play therefore performs, multiply, a range of questions around orality and writing, reading, storytelling, spectatorship, agency, subjectivity and location. I propose to read the text within the context of four major questions: first, the issue of marginality and authority, second, the constructions of femininity and masculinity, third, the embodiment of the African woman and African female subjectivity in the trope of "dark continent," and finally, the questions of witchery and madness.

Textual constructions of territoriality and exile are central to this reading of the play. "Home" and interior spaces are problematized. Home is a place of disorientation and social conformity. It is not a comfortable or safe space for Anowa. Anowa is freest in the deliberate center of the play which is located paradoxically in a borderland, frontiered space, a highway. She is first constricted in her village where gender politics enforce female subordination. She is further enclosed in the "Big House" which her husband acquires. This "Big House" becomes an external reference for the entrenchment of colonial power and male dominance. It is also the site of final resistance for Anowa. Her exit from the play can be read as a tragedy of historical closure for women.[8] But also, read discursively, it represents a kind of re-oralization, a re-entering of Anowa into the narratives surrounding her. In the final commentary of the play, the old woman says: "This is the type of happening out of which we get stories and legends" (p. 63). In response, the old man says:

They used to say around here that Anowa behaved as though she were a heroine in a story. Some of us wish she had been happier and that her life had not had so much of the familiar human scent in it. She was true to herself. She refused to come back here to Yebi to our gossiping and our judgments. . . . If there is life after death, Anowa's spirit will certainly have something to say about that.

(p. 64)

More recent readings of Anowa see her as a "figure of transformative poetics and politics,"[9] a figure of feminist possibility. One can therefore read Anowa intertextually with a variety of other texts. For example, Sekyi-Otu[10] sees an intertextuality between Anowa and "Anoa" of Ayi Kwei Armah's work in which Anoa, the historic Akan reference, becomes the spirit of woman as healer/oracle.

Anowa who dies in the tragic revolt against enslavement is reborn in *Two Thousand Seasons* as Anoa, the archetypal visionary of Africa's and humanity's revolutionary homecoming. For Anowa is not a name, figurative or literal, of a known and knowable place, a fixed address for the isolate residency and exclusive pleasure of women's power. Anowa is possibility. . . .

(p. 73 ms)

Reading *Anowa* intertextually as well within the oral tradition allows us to read "beyond the ending." Anowa's last words as speaking subject, in deliberate self-construction, are "it matters not what the wise ones say,/For/Now, I am wiser than they" (p. 62). Since Anowa is based on a mytho–legendary figure of the same name, in the Akan oral literary corpus, Aidoo's rewriting of Anowa performs the act of reclaiming. Aidoo, in the stage directions, also allows for a certain open–endedness in the play, permitting alternative and varied endings.

Aidoo therefore produces a "version" of Anowa which offers many of the complexities of desire and the young girl/woman. Her protagonist breaks from traditional expectations as does say *Foriwa* by Efua Sutherland, a play by another Ghanaian woman writer. Yet we see Foriwa only at the point just before her marriage and not beyond it as in *Anowa*. In other words, each targets different points in the woman's life cycle. Foriwa also had a supportive "queen mother" and existed in a different class position to Aidoo's Anowa, with a different mother-daughter dynamic. Read inter-textually and against the oral narrative of the girl who would choose her husband, both texts become popular rewritings and re-oralizations of the oral narrative.[11] Anowa says in the end that she has "nowhere to go" (p. 57). She is homeless.[12] Still, she functions as a figure of resistance to specific societal prescriptions and patriarchal assumptions about woman's place. Her homeless-ness can be read discursively as movement outside of all society's limiting structures.

BORDERLANDS AND MARGINALITY

In order to unpack some of the complex issues of *Anowa* as an analysis of the social construction of the colonized African female subject, I begin with an examination of issues of marginality as they are represented textually. I am proposing, therefore, a series of reading strategies for *Anowa*, within the context of (post-) representational ideology critique, i.e., a critique of the ways meaning and identity are installed.[13] "Resistance postmodernism," Ebert insists, is a mode of reading which directly confronts how meaning is arrived at and/or the modes of sense-making in a given text. This is not, then, so much a question of language as in certain brands of postmodernist discourse, but a challenge to the ways in which domination installs power relations between groups and seeks to maintain this domination through a control of the sense-making devices.

I propose also to read *Anowa* through Gloria Anzaldua's theory of "borderlands" which expresses the multiple discursive and political positions that subjects occupy or resist in a variety of given situations.

At the level of spatial structure, the play foregrounds the ways in which marginality is woven into the fabric of dominant/subordinate male/female relations. The centered action is on a highway where Anowa is freest. Paradoxically, this free space is contained by the constructions on either end – the village, the house – the sites of gendered subordination. The highway, then, becomes the locus of potential negotiated gender and class relations for Anowa. On the highway, she and Kofi Ako confront simul-taneously the social construction of gender and the nature of exploitation. On the highway, there is mobility and the chance of constructing new relations. But it is also on the highway that Kofi Ako, alone with Anowa, moves to assert the dominance that he did not have in his village, to enforce a specific male-dominated version of their relationship and the specifics of exploitative economics.

Importantly, it is when Anowa challenges his capitalist project and its implications that he activates patriarchal rules. Up until that time he had talked about them being the new man and woman, about their working together, about her being more a sister than a wife. And it is also significant that his projected mode of acquiring wealth involves the acquisition of slaves. Dominance is therefore installed through the subordination of other human bodies (male and female) and the expropriation of their labor and, therefore, of their *selves*.

> Kofi Ako: What do you want to say? I am not buying these men to come and carry me. They are coming to help us in our work.
>
> Anowa: We do not need them.
>
> Kofi Ako: If you don't, I do. Besides you are only talking like a woman.
>
> Anowa: And please, how does a woman talk? I had as much a mouth in the idea of beginning this trade as you had. And as much head!
>
> Kofi Ako: . . . Anowa who told you that buying men is wrong? You know what? I like you the way you are *different*. But Anowa sometimes you are *too different* [Anowa walks away from him] I know I could not have started without you, but after all, we all know you are *a* woman and I am *the* man [my emphases].[14]

The specificity involved in the use of language for dominance is clear in Kofi Ako's use of the definite article "the" in front of man, for example, as opposed to Anowa being preceded by an indefinite "a" woman. She becomes any woman, he the identified male. Further, her critique of his attempts at involvement in slave trade is constructed as "woman talk" and contained within the context of societal prescriptions concerning women's speech. As well, in a move which "others" Anowa, Kofi Ako aligns her "difference" with negativity.

Anowa resists his attempts to locate her and specifically constructs herself as a "wayfarer," thus positioning herself on the same plane as the captives: "What is the difference between any of your men and me? Except that they are men and I'm a woman? None of us belongs."[15] She therefore activates in a pre-colonial context what would now be called postmodernist notions of displacement, deterritorialization or homelessness. She says: "to call someone a wayfarer is a painless way of saying he does not belong. That he has no home, no family, no village, no stool of his own; has no feast days, no holidays, no state, no territory."[16] In the end, when Kofi Ako asks her to leave and she continues to restate that she has nowhere to go, Anowa seems to have reached the end of alternatives within the context of that society and that historical period.[17]

The play, therefore, rehearses the split between home and not-at-home. For women, home and/or village, as we have already discussed, are often sites of compulsory domesticity and the enforcement of specific gendered relations. Much of this is seen in the exchange between Badua, her mother, and Anowa, between her parents, Badua and Osam, and between Anowa and the community, in the beginning and at the play's conclusion. But there are different versions of homelessness activated at each point of the play. A sense of hope for new relationships at the beginning gives her initial homelessness a sense of possibility. The hopelessness at the end activates this difference, making Anowa technically a refugee. According to Chandra Talpade Mohanty and Biddy Martin, "not being home" is a matter of realizing that home was an illusion of coherence and safety based on the exclusion of specific histories of oppression and resistance, the repression of differences even within oneself.[18]

This construction of home as problematic space calls into question the notion of stable, continuous identities. For home is often situated as the site of calm, security and comfort. It is this critique of these stable notions of home that recurs in Black women's writing and which Aidoo captures well here. Badua in her response to Osam upon reflecting on Anowa's departure says: "I haven't heard the like of this before. A human being and a woman too, preferring to remain a stranger in other people's lands" (p. 31). Anowa had earlier said in response to Kofi Ako's suggestion that she stay at home: "I like being on the roads. . . . There are worse things in villages and towns" (p. 28).

Anowa chooses exile over "home" in its dual senses. She refuses to accept the given terms of "home" as equated with female domesticity. And in the final phase of the play, the problematic of home is maximized. The "Big House" which her husband acquires much to her dismay is a site for the further layering of the problematics of "home." "Home" is reduced to constricting walls with icons of empire and masculinity superimposed. We should also note the earlier link the play makes to European big houses in Anowa's dream of slavery. The semiotics of the "Big House" is a common staple of African and Caribbean anti-colonial literature. In a similar way, Hurston in *Their Eyes Were Watching God* makes much of the link between Joe Starks and the "Big House," the sign of the colonized male's entitlement and concomitant female disempowerment. The "Big House," as acquired by the Black male, then becomes in literature by Black women a trope for Black/African nation(alism) and the parallel locus of final destruction of any positive relationship between Black men and women as Black manhood aligns itself with male dominance. In the "Big House," a more constricting space than her village, Anowa lives as a ghost of her former self unable to come to physical terms with it as home even in a conflicted way.

While discourses of marginality in many ways accept a static center-periphery arrangement with some dialectic movement, "borderlands," as posed by Gloria Anzaldua, allow a sense of myriad possibilities and conflicted spaces that are expressed in the text. Anowa defies marginality in terms of her many relationships and exists instead in borderland spaces. Borderlands for Anzaldua are physically present wherever two or more cultures edge each other, where people of different races, sexualities, classes, genders occupy same territory. One can also think of borderlands as places where multiple identities collide and/or renegotiate space. Some would argue that the postmodern condition is that sense of "living on borders and margins, keeping intact one's shifting and multiple identities" and integrity. But "borderlands," Anzaldua holds, are set up to define the places that are safe and unsafe, to distinguish "us" from "them." Nevertheless they are unnatural boundaries, the sites of constant transition. Similarly, Donna Haraway in her chapter, "Situated Knowledges," suggests that

> boundaries are drawn by mapping practices; "objects" do not pre-exist as such. Objects are boundary projects. But boundaries shift from within; boundaries are very tricky. What boundaries provisionally contain remains generative, productive of meanings and bodies. Siting (sighting) boundaries is a risky practice.[19]

Anowa's preferred space is that shifting site of transition and movement. *Anowa*'s borderlands are the intersections of gender and class, colonial and neo-colonial relationships, masculinity and femininity, freedom and constraint. Anowa attempts a "re-mapping of boundaries" and a renegotiating of connections. We can read Anowa's own internal contradictions as borderlands as well: her responses to polygamy, childlessness, heterosexual family relations, the societal definition of her independent spirit as witchery. The borderline (case) in psychoanalysis is the space of the transgressive or undefinable, the uncertain, the contradictory, a kind of catch-all reference for those people unable to deal with their worlds and social norms as they exist. Anowa seems in the end to exist in such a space. A girl like Anowa is suspended in time and history, over-determined by place/space constraints. Anowa's initial resistance to this looming possibility of suspension is what moves this play. Badua tells Anowa as she departs after challenging her mother's prescriptions: "I am waiting for you to come back with your rags and nakedness."[20] Badua almost seems to be wishing Anowa's return to the womb, to that symbolic nakedness: the self stripped of all that is not biologically defined. Anowa's response is: "I shall walk so well that I will not find my feet back here again."[21] In the end she says to Kofi Ako, "I swore to Mother I was not returning. Not ever."[22]

Where does a woman go after leaving "home"? This is one of the text's central questions. Anowa says she has nowhere to go. And central to this nowhere to go is the inability of the mother line to activate itself in a way that would facilitate openness. Another possible opening response, in my view, would be to allow Anowa the space to become a perpetual wayfarer or Sojourner, which seems much more in character with the Anowa of the beginning but which Anowa doesn't choose in the end.[23] The common approach is to stay and accept subordination. A more interesting option is to locate oneself in the struggle for social transformation.

WHAT IS A WOMAN? WHAT IS A MAN? SOCIAL CONSTRUCTIONS OF MASCULINITY AND FEMININITY

In the prologue we are told by "The-Mouth-That-Would-Eat-Salt-and-Pepper" that Anowa is not a girl to meet everyday (p. 7). Throughout the text of *Anowa*, Aidoo offers a number of explorations of what it is to be a woman in her particular culture, nation and in the world. Aidoo has also explored this issue in "To Be a Woman," in which she says, "the position of a woman in Ghana is no less ridiculous than anywhere else. The few details that differ are interesting only in terms of local color and family needs."[24] What is a woman in any given society? Aidoo seems to say that being a woman is a position often defined in relation to serving the male. Woman, then, comes to occupy the position in society against which male identity is installed. Anowa expresses a related position, ironically and rhetorically:

> Someone should have taught me how to grow up to be a woman. I hear in other lands a woman is nothing. And they let her know this from the day of her birth. But here, O my spirit mother, they let a girl grow up as she pleases until she is married. And then, she is like any woman anywhere: in order for her man to be a man, she must not think, she must not talk. . . .[25]

That she is addressing her discussion to the photograph of Queen Victoria should not be lost in terms of its irony and its address to the Western, ruling-class woman. 'Molara Ogundipe-Leslie asserts, in "Not Spinning on the Axis of Maleness," that the "woman as daughter or sister has greater status and more rights in her own lineage. Married she becomes a possession, voiceless and often rightless in her husband's family, except for what accrues to her through her children."[26] While Ogundipe-Leslie was referring specifically to Nigeria here, the relative sense of "rights" discourse which is activated and which Anowa expresses has resonance. Spivak, probably more than most other feminist theorists, has addressed how women begin to be constructed as the object of super-exploitation within capitalist economies.[27] It is necessary to read the exploitation of Anowa's labor and ideas on which Kofi Ako advances as producing her "alienated labor" position at this point. And Anowa's status as a woman in marriage is directly implicated.

On the directly social plane, Anowa's alienation is generated by the inability of some forward women to accept societal prescriptions. This had been raised preliminarily by Juliet Okonkwo in "The Talented Woman in African Literature."[28] Anowa is defined as exceptional in her particular society, so by extension there is no space for her except outside the given normative paradigms. Kofi

Ako, at one point, asks Anowa: "Why are you like this, Anowa? Why? Can't you be like other normal women? Other normal people?" Her response is disruptive, carnivalized laughter[29] and her comment: "I still don't know what you mean by normal. Is it abnormal to want to continue working?"[30] The assumption is that Anowa is not meeting the particular norms of her society in terms of female behavior and socio-economic class. If we follow Steady[31] on this point, though, the desire to construct African women "in the home" carries with it the African male's accession to Western/class-based expectations about the position of the woman. One acceptable societal option for the forward woman or the woman unable to live within the confines of patriarchal dictates, is to become a priestess: "Osam: . . . apprentice her to a priestess to quieten her down" (p. 11). Her mother, however, rejects this approach and instead articulates the classic mother's "wish," expressed in the text in the poetic lines:

> I want my child
> To be a human woman
> Marry a man
> Tend a farm
> And be happy to see her
> Peppers and onions grow.
> A woman like her
> Should bear children
> Many children,
> So she can afford to have
> One or two die.
> Should she not take
> Her place at meetings
> Among the men and women of the clan?
> And sit on my chair when
> I am gone? And a captainship in the army
> Should not be beyond her
> When the time is ripe.[32]

Much of the definition of woman is verbalized primarily by the mother and by Kofi Ako, and secondarily by the community and the father. The mother and husband seem entrusted and empowered by society to translate the rules of patriarchy. Badua's definition of what is acceptable for her daughter seems to be positioned in the order of preference – marriage, domestic production, child-bearing, communal involvement, inheriting of the mother's place in society, patience in accepting the rewards of seniority, material wealth and perhaps, eventually, leadership in the defense of the community. Paradoxically, the mother's wishes for her daughter's material success are what the daughter can acquire in the end.[33] But, we learn from the Old Man that "Anowa is not a girl to meet every day" (p. 7), from Osam, her father, that Anowa is not every woman (p. 33) and from Kofi Ako that she "ought to have been born a man" (p. 24); and further that she was not behaving like his vision of a good wife. The spokespeople for the community offer judgment within their own constructions of the woman: i.e., what is a woman? what is a good woman? She is first of all a good wife, most seem to say. The community also struggles for other terms to describe Anowa's behavior and, finding no other, censures her.

Anowa is thus read against normative femininity. The difference she embodies is misrecognized as she struggles to be recognized. The issues of enforced heterosexual constructions are therefore central to the text's unfolding. For Anowa does not live the acceptable patterns of female behavior, and this places her outside the traditional symbolics of gender in her group. Teresa Ebert offers a useful summary of the ways that woman's social subjectivity is produced in patriarchal contexts which I find helpful in reading the text of Anowa's life. The Ebert analysis actually retraces, in the language of the postmodernist critic, much of the ground Aidoo had covered in her statement on the social construction of the African woman in "To Be a Woman." Ebert suggests that concerning "woman",

> We can read her as a social subjectivity produced by the economic, political and ideological practices organizing the economy of signification around the dominance of the phallic signifier. Woman is produced in social signification as the other on which the very existence of man and the asymmetrical relations of exploitation, power, and privilege in patriarchy depend. Woman, then, would not be in and of herself an oppositional presence to man and patriarchy, but would be revealed as simultaneously in a position of oppression in patriarchal capitalism and as one of the crucial supports of that system.[34]

Aidoo, therefore, positions Anowa as a figure who disrupts the very foundations on which patriarchal dominance depends. The issue of the definition of woman in society has plagued feminist theorists for a long time. Kristeva had asserted that "Woman Can Never Be Defined": "In 'woman' I see something that cannot be represented, something that is not said, something above and beyond nomenclatures and ideologies."[35] Further, in order to identify woman "this process involves going through what is repressed in discourse in reproductive and productive relationships. Call it 'woman' or the 'oppressed social class': it's the same struggle and you never have one without the other" (p. 141). Feminist theorists are beginning to concur that the category "woman" is a social not natural/biological construct. Women's bodies become the locus for a certain social definition of gender with specific economic import to this social construction.[36] The working class, African peoples and Black women have historically been socially constructed and defined as inferior for economic gain.

Aidoo importantly had creatively located the multiple subject positions of women in this play, staged in the 1960s. She had similarly linked economics to gender in a materialist-feminist approach that offers an African pretext to this on-going discussion. Lloyd Brown, for example, shows that it is Anowa's "moral energy which enables her to perceive the woman's situation as the symbol of African history – a history of slavery, colonialism and repressive power. . . ."[37] For example, much of Kofi Ako's struggle with Anowa is to get her to live comfortably in "the domestic mode of production" and further to layer class over gender, by exploiting the labor of others, in order to situate her firmly in the house. There is then a deliberate linking of dominance to masculinity and phallic power and/or the equation of phallic power with economic success, as whiteness is often coupled with dominance. The community is therefore heavily implicated. Kofi Ako in his village context is described as a weak man, "a watery cassava man." But, Kofi Ako, even as procurer of slaves, is termed a "successful one of us." Kofi Ako's need to assert his masculinity, and thus achieve full acceptance in his community, hinges both on oppressing others as in slave labor (or the expropriation of others' labor) and on subordinating the female.

The idea of the existence of a male economy (capitalist, patriarchal) that circulates differently, has been offered by a number of feminist critics.[38] It is the context in which the repression of women and non-Western peoples has been perpetuated repeatedly. Kofi Ako's participation in the trade of skins signifies his accession to this oppressive economic mode, thus making the link to European imperialism. "Skins" become a reference to the fictive covering of "bodies," the practically located human existence which can be exploited for a variety of reasons. Thus, there is a practical movement from "skin" to "body," from the exploitation of animals to the exploitation of humans. Anowa constantly asserts her opposition to this path. She rejects the need to exploit human labor and thereby become a person who does not work manually anymore. She expresses, as Brown says, an "aversion to exploitive patterns of power . . . ranging from her spirited opposition to slavery and her continuous determination to remain independent."[39]

The play therefore offers an interesting reading of a certain homosociality in the construction of masculinity. Kofi Ako, a man scoffed at in his village because he does not conform to the standard of what is a man, feels compelled to invoke male power over Anowa and the bonded men in conventional phallic terms in order to camouflage his own inability to meet, initially, community significations of masculinity. In Lacanian terms, he asserts a response to the fear of castration as well as a refusal to accept masculinity in non-traditional ways or redefine masculinity to meet his needs. Thus, his deployment of the phallus is as an empty/loaded signifier of male power. A number of male scholars, such as Ian Craib in "Masculinity and Male Dominance,"[40] are beginning to offer interesting readings of this social construct in the task of uncoupling masculinity from dominance.

Hélène Cixous has also asserted, although in broad generalization, that male homosexuality can be seen as essentially different from female homosexuality in its possible alliance with male power and a certain male exclusivity. In other words, the tendency is often to equate gay and lesbian identity, but these are not symmetrical. For Kofi Ako can become, in spite of his questionable "masculinity" by the society's standards, a man of significance, while Anowa is not allowed to occupy the sexually transgressive position (read as "lesbian" in the West), i.e., constructed outside heterosexuality and wifehood.

The play's resolution is the moment Anowa recognizes this link, i.e., that Kofi's assertion of masculinity through the deployment of the phallus as expressed in economic power and social dominance is tied to his need to defend his "manhood" in societal terms. Kofi, like Jody in *Their Eyes Were Watching God*, is unable to begin afresh and on new terms once this challenge is made. Anowa in the resolution of the play says:

> Anowa: . . . And for years now, I have not seen your bed. And Kofi (getting hysterical) now that I think back on it, you have never been interested in any other woman. . . .
>
> Kofi Ako: What are you saying Anowa?
>
> Anowa: Kofi, are you dead? [Pause] Kofi is your manhood gone? I mean you are like a woman. [Pause] Kofi, there is not hope any more is there? [Pause] Kofi . . . tell me, is that why I must leave you? That you have exhausted your masculinity acquiring slaves and wealth?
>
> (p. 61)

The text's silences and pauses speak eloquently to the hidden subtext of Kofi's life. Kofi's question seems to beg recognition of his submerged sexual identity as it fears that same recognition. Neither Anowa nor Kofi Ako seem to have the language to express this reality.

The traditional alliance of masculinity with blackness is I believe an important issue here because of the ongoing denial in African/ Black nationalist circles of homosexuality in African and black communities. In other words, the need to construct a black manhood spills over into an African homeland where homosexuality, the nationalist narrative says, did not exist until the Europeans or Arabs came. But there is growing information about the silenced issues around sexualities in African contexts. A number of black gay men are resisting the nationalist construction of masculinity, for example, Essex Hemphill and Kobena Mercer in "True Confessions. A Discourse on Images of Black Male Sexuality" in the collection *Brother to Brother. New Writings by Black Gay Men*.[41] The link is significant here because this is, in effect, Kofi Ako's story. With no alternative paradigms allowed, he chooses the path of oppressing Anowa to prove his manhood in conventional terms, and when that fails self-destruction is his preferred option. According to the nationalist narrative, the historical location of the play is significant because it is set at the time when African men were being enslaved and therefore "demasculinized." But, according to Mercer and Julien, "Racism defined African peoples as having only bodies and no minds: Black men and women were seen as muscle machines and thus the superexploitation of slavery could be justified" (p. 171). Just as (white) femininity is constructed, so is (Black) masculinity, and those who reject the given societal norms become locked or displaced in these constructions. Julien and Mercer also link this to patriarchal power and control which needs normative "masculinity" in order to ensure "femininity."

Recent work on theorizing gender locates both masculinity and femininity as certain performances of gender. It is appropriate to identify Judith Butler who, in *Gender Trouble*,[42] advances this discussion when she argues that "gender ontologies always operate within established political contexts as normative injunctions, determining what qualifies as intelligible sex, invoking and consolidating the reproductive constraints on sexuality, setting the prescriptive requirements whereby sexed or gendered bodies come into cultural intelligibility."[43] This performance of gender is what Anowa recognizes and what marks her ability to transgress the class boundaries by *not dressing and playing the part*. She therefore cannot behave like "every normal woman" and accept the given boundaries of maleness or femaleness. She consistently remains outside them.

WITCHERY AND MADNESS AND ANOWA'S DESERTION OF SELF-EMPOWERMENT

Anowa's failure to transform her position in society seems to have been because what she feared most was the source of her own power: the societal stigma of being called a witch or the transgressive position of actually "becoming a witch." According to Gauthier in "Why Witches?,"[44] witches are the most deliberate violators of societal tradition: "If the figure of the witch appears wicked, it is because she poses a real danger to phallocratic society."[45] It is how society defines those women who break conventions, as in "conjure women" in Afro-American cultures, that is important. The "witch," then, is often a political revolt by women against "category maintenance." The witch is not a priestess in the sense of a servant to a god or goddess, although she may be, but a source of transgressive female power. It is interesting that in *Anowa* both mother and daughter are repeatedly called "witches." In fact, the "witch" identification has multiple meanings and references in the play.[46]

In attempting to understand this issue, I surveyed a wide variety of sources on witchcraft from a wide variety of African peoples.[47]

While there were variations from place to place, with the witch distanced in some communities, and welcomed or at least accepted in others, there were some constants. On a basic level, having the power[48] of the witch is referenced as possessing the gift, skill or knowledge of extra vision, "the third eye" or "four eyes" in some descriptions. The knowledgeable witch also has power of trans-formation, transmigration, transmogrification, transfiguration, transmutation. She has the power to heal or to hurt. She often resides in the area of the unexplainable, mysterious. She owns the power of possession. She has power, some would assert, over life and death. According to Naana Banyiwa Horne, she stands be-tween the community and what it is unable to attain, as does Anowa.[49]

It is also important to note that Badua's role in identifying Anowa as witch but also forbidding her to become a priestess is contradictory and pivotal. The mother is adamant that she is not going to turn her daughter into a priestess because they become "too much like the god they interpret" (p. 12). What follows is, in the author's stage directions, a cataloging of, for her, the despised qualities of the priestess in a voice that grows "hysterical and terror-stricken" (p. 12). She is opposed to "possessed women" on the dancing ground (p. 32). Still, from all my research it seems the witch/priestess split is a Western invention of an opposition. A great deal of the misunderstanding lies in language and the prob-lematic application of Western meanings of the word "witch" to African contexts. A priestess, therefore, may possess the knowl-edge which can be identified as "witchcraft," an already loaded term. According to Naana Banyiwa Horne, Badua's opposition to her daughter becoming a priestess also has to do with her wanting a successful daughter in the current, material-based terms the society was developing. For the priestess would have power, but not that generated by material wealth.

It is important that there are multiple meanings and definitions of a witch in the text of *Anowa* itself. One comes in Anowa's early, visionary understanding of the nature of slavery and the African diaspora.[50] Cast as a dream and a discussion with her grandmother, it later allows the community to approach her with the awe felt for a "seer" and leads to the grandmother identifying her as a "witch," which means, in this context, as a "wisechild," and to subsequent talk of apprenticing her to a priestess (p. 47). In a way, the witch/priestess split collapses exactly in the grandmother's

understanding of Anowa. The fact that the grandmother had travelled previously and returned with visions of other lands is also
significant. For it invokes a matrilineal critique of male dominance
and European conquest which Badua seemed to have missed. In an
extended monologue, Anowa locates her abhorrence for Kofi
Ako's trading in slaves in a series of questions she had posed to her
grandmother:

> Anowa: . . . What is a slave, Nana?
> Shut up! It is not good that a child should ask big questions.
> A slave is one who is bought and sold.
> Where did the white men get the slaves? I asked.
> You frighten me, child.
> You must be a witch, child. . . .
>
> I was very ill and did not recover for weeks. When I told my
> dream, the women of the house were very frightened. They
> cried and cried and told me not to mention the dream again.
> For some time there was talk of apprenticing me to a priest-
> ess. I don't know what came of it. But since then, any time
> there is mention of a slave I see a woman who is me. . . .
>
> (pp. 45–47)

This is an important section of the text because Aidoo performs the
multiple moves of identifying the metaphorical big house, the nature
of oppression, imperialism and slavery, the location of the visionary
woman in society. Also, she conflates Anowa with slavery and with
"Mother Africa." It is a kind of reclaiming of the maternal as a site of
dispossession and rupture, but also of new births. Anowa's resistance to Kofi Ako, who, as the stage directions say, is dressed and
decorated in the trappings of conquest and surrounded by all the
material evidence of his trading success, is located historically and in
terms of class hierarchies. Anowa, by contrast, is described as
wearing old clothes and is barefooted (p. 44).

The contradictory meanings of witchery are identified in the link
between witchery and insanity in the dream of Africa and the
diaspora in her childhood and also in the community's perceptions
of Anowa's revolt. In calling Anowa a witch or madwoman in the
end, she is allied with everything evil, but also everything transgressive, because she refuses to participate in Kofi Ako's wealth
(p. 40). Still, Anowa had herself called her mother a "witch" –
"Please, Mother, remove your witch's mouth from our marriage"

(p. 18) – and in this context is invoking the power of the mother, allied with creation and mystery. This is related to the way the concept *gelede* among the Yoruba identifies an equation of the mother with power which is translated in European discourse as "witchery."[51]

In Western women's discussions of this point, Cixous in "The Laugh of the Medusa" and Clement in her analysis of female hysteria in *The Newly Born Woman*[52] assert that the witch and the medusa are two constructions of women who respond overtly to patriarchal dominance. And feminist discussions of women and madness identify the trope of the madwoman as resisting figure, as do Gilbert and Gubar in *The Madwoman in the Attic*.[53] A distinct slippage between the categories seems to occur in formulations of the resisting woman. But Bessie Head's *A Question of Power* similarly asserts the link between power and dominance and "madness" in the context of the oppressiveness of South African state power. Thus, Foucault's *Madness and Civilization* is clarifying. Maryse Conde's *I Tituba* also makes a contribution to this discussion by associating "witchery" with the transgressive knowledges of women resisting dominance.[54] Here, the power which comes in the knowledge of traditional modes of healing and "conjuring" is passed down through women but is submerged, in Tituba's case, by both her desire for masculine/sexual affection and Western/Christian prescriptives.

All deviants occupy challenging positions in cultures. However, the madness does not change the structures, it makes them and it more comfortable. The hysteric interrupts phallic mastery but does not change it. This is easily applied to Anowa and her relationship to her society which marks her as deviant. She will not wear the skins – the dresses the appearances of which identify women in terms of their social status and wife position in that society. In *Vested Interests*,[55] Marjorie Garber shows that clothing is politicized historically, particularly as the marker and transgression of gender. For Anowa, there is no cultural code to render her behavior intelligible, so her dressing down in terms of class, at least, provides a textual statement which can be read discursively as resistance.

Anowa's position poses an open question for us to deal with: who has an alternative way to the modes in which women are located? That alternative way, it can be argued, resides in the rejected role of priestess[56] or "mother-healer" as I call it elsewhere,[57] a role which gives African women a great deal of power in their societies. In other words, in Western culture the witch position carries women's transgressive power, but is consistently allied with evil or identified as consorting with the devil, a very specific Christian definition of the limits of female power.[58] For this reason, feminists like Barbara Ehrenreich and Deirdre English realign witching with healing in a text entitled, *Witches, Midwives, and Nurses. A History of Women Healers*,[59] which begins by saying that from earliest times these healers were called "wise women" by the people, "witches" by the authorities (p. 3).

I would propose, therefore, that we go beyond the witch/priestess binary to understand how women who transgress male power get configured. New studies of gender, divination and power in African (also Afro-Brazilian, Afro-Caribbean) contexts, are revealing the complexity of the functions of African women who occupy the priestess position in their societies.[60] Yet, in my view, the ritual power that women get in the "mother-healer" position, nevertheless, does not translate into social and political power by which international communities operate. Thus Anowa, a dislocated figure, who has rejected all the possibilities for containment or power within her society, sees beyond them, but nevertheless becomes in the process "wiser than they." Thus she is propelled into the future/our present/the space of the postmodern.

WOMAN AS DARK CONTINENT

In Anowa's dream, the definition of woman as dark continent, popular in recent French feminist constructs, was already very definitely and explicitly made. The link between women and slavery – "the traffic in women" and the "traffic in slaves" – is contained in the dream and carried throughout the text. Anowa reveals an acute awareness of past and present which fires her. The metaphoric convergence of the dark continent as Africa and the African woman is critical to the construction of African female subjectivity: "I dreamt that I was a big, big woman. And from my insides were huge holes out of which poured men, women and children" (p. 46). Ama Ata Aidoo has a more recent discussion of the disempowerment of the African woman by the cumulative effects of African patriarchal definitions, Western enforced systems and so on.[61] Black women, therefore, following Aidoo, become the embodiment of converging identities, hierarchies, politics and so on.

The convergence of woman as the dark continent to be penetrated and pacified, the notion of conquering her and leaving her borders, the site of obligatory civility meant to be invaded and colonized as expressed by Cixous had been previously articulated in *Anowa*. Hence in the play, there is the conflation of the Black woman with the ultimate "dark continent" which is similarly made between Mother and Africa in nationalist discourses (the unknown, resourceful, bountiful mother). But, mother in feminist discourses also exists as a figure of expropriated labor: her productive and reproductive capacities exploited as in *Beloved*, which I will discuss in a succeeding chapter. Hence, the deliberate construction of Anowa's childlessness has particular meaning – the specific eschewal of the biological/institutional motherhood. *Anowa* in these terms proves Barbara Christian's contention in "The Race for Theory," that theory as it is reified in the academy moves too quickly over the fact that Black people have theorized in their fiction, their folk-tales, their creative acts.

Hortense Spillers, in "Mama's Baby, Papa's Maybe,"[62] identifies bodies and flesh as the site of lacerations, woundings, scars, markings and captivity. Kofi's trading in animal skins and his later trading in human bodies shows how the bodies and their signifying "skins" get marked for/by oppression. Anowa then becomes an effective link to African-American and Afro-Caribbean rewritings of the construction of patriarchy and capitalism on the bodies of Black women. *Anowa* is thus a text which I am foregrounding in my theoretical understandings of Black women's writing. Reading strategies which make room for the cross-cultural allow ways of cross-readings which challenge specific ideologies of placement and location. They identify how the politics of race, gender, class, sexuality intersect and interrelate as they allow meaning to be formed and installed.

4

FROM "POST-COLONIALITY" TO UPRISING TEXTUALITIES

Black women writing the critique of Empire[1]

Signifying post-colonial narrative

After the quarrels and the departures and the signing of formal separation papers, the wife puts up flags of independence, cleans out his presence from her space and defines a new identity. Not long after that, the husband who had moved miles away, moves back into the general neighborhood and seeks indirectly to reassert his removed presence in a series of scenarios that have to do with money, the children and so on. The woman has a "choice" to relate to him in order to ensure some continuity in their general well-being. But there are other possibilities.

ON POSTING AND POSTPONING: POST-COLONIALITY OR THE RE-MALE-ING OF CURRENT DISCOURSES

A question often asked by those sensitive to gender, race and postmodernist discourses is: where are the women in the theorizing of post-coloniality? Although there are growing numbers of titular identifications of post-colonial feminist discussions, it seems so far that the discourse of post-coloniality is not, at this point in history, overly populated by "post-colonial women." Trinh Minh-ha's *Woman Native Other* which is subtitled *Writing Postcoloniality and Feminism*[2] does not deal in any substantive way with theorizing post-coloniality. That she is participating in the post-colonial project has to be inferred. Examining Dangarembga's *Nervous Conditions*, Sally McWilliams offers the useful definition that "post-colonialist theories are trying to unweave the complex structures put in place by colonialist rule . . . revealing the complex inter-actions of colonizer and colonized . . . to discuss how subjects are constituted now that the colonial powers no longer have overt, political control."[3] Yet in order to agree with her position it would be necessary to accept that any articulation of non-Western cultural particularities or gender specificities is by extension within the "post-colonial" subject. This, of course, I disagree with substan-tially for, in effect, it assigns to post-coloniality the same totalizing posture as any other master discourse.[4]

While there may be some basis to an articulation that "a reshap-ing of cultural codes and structures is a reversal of the process of colonization,"[5] the assumption is that the formerly colonized have no basis of identity outside of the colonizers' definitions. Also, in my view, reshaping is not symmetrical with decolonization pro-cesses. Paradoxically, Minh-ha's deliberations throughout *Woman Native Other* escape the kind of singularity and ownership to the narrative of development which post-coloniality implies. In fact, the entire approach of her work is to repudiate that kind of dichoto-mous construction. Thus any attempt to impose a master structure to any set of articulations comes out of a particular academic need to codify, manage and categorize.

My positions are that post-coloniality represents a misnaming of current realities, it is too premature a formulation, it is too totaliz-ing, it erroneously contains decolonizing discourses, it re-males and recenters resistant discourses by women and attempts to submerge a host of uprising textualities, it has to be historicized and placed in the context of a variety of historical resistances to colonialism, it reveals the malaise of some Western intellectuals caught behind the posts and unable to move to new and/or more promising re-/articulations.

The definition of post-coloniality, it seems to me, took place in the face of the growing theoretical consecrations of postmoder-nism, but also because of the space created by postmodernism and its disruption of metanarratives. A number of scholars had felt a need to articulate transformational discourses: the presence of the literatures of decolonization, resistance and self-articulation of non-Western peoples. There was a growing sense in which these "minority discourses" were beginning some self-articulation. Particularly important were the ways in which Deleuze and Guattari, Kubayanda, Christian and others had begun to address the meaning of "minority literatures."[6] That space of self-articulation suddenly became filled with the macro-discourse of post-coloniality.

Post-coloniality, in this context, has become the center announcing its own political agenda without reference to indigenous self-articulations. For post-coloniality is a theoretical production of the Western academy (even though by some non-Western scholars) within which writers and teacher-critics are asked to locate their work. Ashcroft, Griffiths and Tiffin, who are credited with providing one of the first widely disseminated major formulations of post-coloniality in *The Empire Writes Back. Theory and Practice in Post-Colonial Literatures*, defined the term "post-colonial"

> to cover all the culture affected by the imperial process from the moment of colonization to the present day. This is because there is a continuity of preoccupations throughout the historical process initiated by European imperial aggression. We also suggest that it is most appropriate as the term for the new cross-cultural criticism which has emerged in recent years and for the discourse through which this is constituted.[7]

The result, however, was a broad-based totalizing of wide geographical areas from the Caribbean to Australia and the US under this umbrella. Even more troubling was the attempt to include all the recent cross-cultural criticism under the general rubric of the post-colonial. The intent may have been a timely gesture of articulating a counter-discourse, but the effect has been a highly problematic subsuming of non-Western cultures, reducing these cultures while further hegemonizing the West. Further, like most theories and/or discourses that come out of the Western tradition (including counter-discourses like Afrocentricity, feminism, postmodernism, queer theory and so on) post-coloniality arrogantly makes such a broad historical and conceptual sweep that it attempts to contain all of these cultures, movements and peoples in some giant conglomerate-like, monolithic sprawl. Thus, any indigenous, vernacular movements past and present must be placed under the sign of the post-colonial.

In this context, Ama Ata Aidoo makes an important distinction in her critique of the term post-colonial by suggesting that it "may be relevant to the United States after its war of independence, and to a certain extent, to the erstwhile imperial dominions of Canada, Australia and New Zealand," but "applied to Africa, India, and some other parts of the world, 'postcolonial' is not only a fiction, but a most pernicious fiction, a cover-up of a dangerous period in our people's lives."[8]

Lata Mani and Ruth Frankenberg in their "Crosscurrents" conversation try to examine the post-colonial in relation to what they define as post-Civil Rights in the United States. In this way they are able to make some important distinctions in terms of what has passed and what is still with us and thus conclude "that white, Western 'postcolonial' subjects are still interpellated by classical colonialism itself" and that "location is in many respects key in determining the importance of the 'postcolonial' as an axis staging cross-racial encounters" and "not all places in this transnational circuit are, however, similarly 'postcolonial.'"[9]

The concept of post-coloniality, in my view, almost mandates that one ignores or rationalizes the numerous colonizing operations still taking place. The numerous peoples that are still existing in a colonial relationship or struggling with an actively present colonizer, as is Curaçao and the Netherlands Antilles, Puerto Rico, Virgin Islands, Guadeloupe, Northern Ireland, Palestine, have to automatically participate in the post-colonial moment whether their experience warrants it or not, or remain somehow outside of the bounds of the discussion or be explained away. Further, people within certain nations who have been colonized within the former/colonies (Native Americans, African-Americans, South Africans, Palestinians, Aboriginal Australians), become contained again within the post-colonial or are erased from current discussion.[10]

It is still necessary, then, to make room for the assertion of the ways in which countries and peoples have become effectively recolonized to various political, commercial and military operations and interests. The frightening reality is that we are not beyond Western colonialism, that Western colonialism is not the only colonialism around. In the assumption of post-coloniality, we are automatically interpellated in ideologies of posting or post-poning. Quite clearly, Western bourgeois culture feels it has reached, rather arrogantly, a certain alreadyness. So, any current formulations wanting to be identified as theoretically current have to construct themselves within the context of this alreadyness or afterness, or even done-by-Europeanness.

It is a given that master discourses, like colonialism, apartheid and Soviet Communism have been/have to be radically ruptured. Yet, although a condition is *named* as having been moved beyond (as in post-apartheid) it does not ensure that the particular oppressive system has really been vanquished. Have we really left them behind or has the oppression not simply evolved with time? In fact, the ideology of most "postings" conveys that the older systems, as well as their after-effects, are carried over into the present or future. Bereft of their singular and prominent identifications which fuel the opposition or energy of resistance, they become empty positionalities which obscure oppression (i.e., post-feminism means one no longer has to struggle against patriarchy).

Implicit in the ideology of "posting" is the argument, on the part of some disillusioned Western intelligentsia and their cohorts in the "Third World," that the West has already invented everything, done everything, experienced everything or thought of everything worthwhile, and therefore all we need do is sound the last post as the world collapses.[11] Ian Adam and Helen Tiffin, *Past the Last POST: Theorizing Post-Colonialism and Post-Modernism*, is an example in point. Even as its title signals a going past (an after-life/after-death), it reinscribes, as do most post-colonial discourses, the colonial period under pretentiously new terminologies.[12] Similarly, "Post-Post-Modernism? Theorizing Social Complexity" by Sylvia Walby[13] carries a sense of doubled afterness even as it questions the trajectory of a central theoretical mode.

In an early intervention now published as "The Nature of Things. Arrested Decolonization and Critical Theory,"[14] Biodun Jeyifo argued that we had too easily elided discourses of decolonization. He also made the point that "every single theoretical school or approach is only one layer, one tier in the exclusively and prescriptively *Western* monument of High Theory" which is in turn "an aspect of the intellectual division of labor of the metropolitan centers of the world system of late capitalism."[15] Benita Parry in "Problems in Current Theories of Colonial Discourse" critiqued the work of Homi Bhabha, Abdul Jan Mohammed and Gayatri Spivak, on the basis that "the protocols of their dissimilar methods act to constrain the development of anti-imperialist critique."[16] Parry further argued that:

> The labor of producing a counter-discourse displacing imperialism's dominative system of knowledge rests with those engaged in developing a critique from outside its cultural hegemony, and in furthering a contest begun by anti-colonial movements, theorists of colonial discourse will need to

pursue the connections between imperialism's material aggression and its epistemic violence, and disclose the relationships between its ideological address to the colonial world and the imperialist culture of the metropolitan world.

(p. 55)

The essay which expresses many ideas which I share is Arun Mukherjee's "Whose Post-Colonialism and Whose Post-modernism?"[17] Her early assertion that this is contested terrain, both at the level of ideas and in practical realities, finds a certain responsiveness in my own reading of the issues. Among her contentions are post-coloniality's erasure of "race" as an analytical category, that coloniality and "post-coloniality" are lived histories and not just literary and cultural movements, that the differences between the various communities get elided, that white and non-white post-colonial settler colonies are treated as relatives not as "subjects," the absence of "cultural insiderness or inwardness" on the part of most post-colonial critics, the perpetuation of a center-periphery relationship between the post-colonial and the post-modern for example, its suggestion that the subjectivities of the post-colonial cultures and their occupiers are inextricably linked. Thus, she concludes, this "leaves us only one modality, one discursive position. We are forever forced to interrogate European discourses, of only one particular kind; the ones that degrade and deny our humanity" (p. 6).

The result of the construction of post-coloniality, then, is a replaying of the tendency in the Euro–American/modelled academy to create another sweeping, totalizing and reductive discourse to cover huge and sometimes unrelated discursive fields. For these reasons, it is troubling to find essays which self-consciously mark themselves, as does Zakia Pathak, "A Pedagogy for Postcolonial Feminists,"[18] but which are actually doing something else. Pathak deals principally with feminist teaching practices and textual readings. Clearly in all the formulations of post-colonial there is the automatic attempt to subsume a variety of emergent discourses of "Third World" and "minority" "resistance" and certain "feminisms" or women's discourses.

Post-coloniality itself, as it makes a play for being a master narrative, must be deconstructed and its elision of gender is a principal angle of this critique. First on the agenda is the decentering of the former and current colonial paradigms, and the displacement

85

of the implied focus on, and relationship to, things European even as we talk about ourselves, i.e., its reproduction of the same discourse of dominance it seeks to challenge. We have to at least assert that some people have no desire "to write back to the center."[19] Others still assert that the center is a site of emptiness and lack. And further, texts like Ngugi's *Moving the Centre*[20] seek to challenge the centre's primacy. The earlier formulation of the Centre for Contemporary Cultural Studies, *The Empire Strikes Back*,[21] has the sense of more "resistance" in its intent as it engaged the center on home base on issues of race and racism in the 1970s.

It seems to me, then, that a lot of the language of post-coloniality comes out of a certain period in which its practitioners know intimately the formal colonial period and find it so overwhelming that it remains almost a fixation. Clearly there was a need for anti-colonial struggles and certain positions had to be taken given the historical reality and pervasiveness of colonialism. It is not expressing nostalgia to assert that there is still a need for the (not "ambivalent") standpoint against colonizations. Further, there are other constituencies which cannot/do not accord Europeanity such an important position in the scheme of things and feel the need to articulate the discourse in completely different ways, refusing to formulate it even as an "After Europe."[22]

I would further offer that post-coloniality can only have meaning if we accept postmodernism as the only current legitimizing narrative. Because this is still centered on European modernism, it is really post-European modernism.[23] Recognizing that there have been other modernisms and other colonialities, then, "post-coloniality" can read as "post-European(-colonial)ity." In that way, all the many colonialities and resistances to them throughout history can at least be addressed.

This particular chapter therefore begins with a critique of "post-coloniality" in order to address some of the assumptions of "postness" and question some of its elisions and postponements as it addresses the re/male/ing of post-colonial discourses. It examines some of the ways in which feminists of color have been speaking outside of the post-colonial. These are preliminary strategies in order to clear the space for the necessary examination of the contributions of Black British women writers, who, living within the administrative center of the former British Empire, produce a variety of anti-imperialist or "uprising textualities," as they critique home and Empire.

For that reason, then, I want to assert unequivocally that I see few "Third World women," or "women of color" or Black women "doing post-coloniality" even when a few use the language of post-colonial discourse, or name themselves and their work as such. Instead, there is the repeated query from a number of the writers who are asked to locate their work and themselves within the post-colonial of: who deployed post-coloniality? Even more deliberately: when is post-coloniality going to end? (Lorna Goodison). I therefore get the same sense of unease when I hear "post-colonial feminist" as when I hear "Afrocentric feminist" because of the forced conjunction of these ideological/theoretical discourses.

From my readings, Third World/Black/women of color feminisms move the imagination away from dominating authorities and do not constantly accept their existence as a fact of life. Therein for me lies the need to liberate some of our discussion from this need to justify feminist articulations as expressed by Black women/women of color through some conjunction with or subsuming under another master discourse. Thus, Ketu Katrak's "Decolonizing Culture. Toward a Theory for Postcolonial Women's Texts,"[24] raises a number of questions which have to be held open much longer than even Katrak's titling and working principles. For example, her questions, "How can we, within a dominant Eurocentric discourse, make our study of postcolonial texts itself a mode of resistance?" and "What theoretical models will be most constructive for the development of this literature?"[25] are viable and important questions which demand developed discussion and not the early closure of the discourse of post-coloniality. Still, the spirit of her enterprise is one with which I find some common ground, as in her formulation "Decolonizing Postcolonial Theory" and her need to go back towards Fanon and Ghandi for theoretical guideposts. For, her formulation seems to effect that very destabilizing of the post-colonial to which I refer and has the implicit agenda of superseding colonial theory altogether. Katrak's work demonstrates significantly that a return to named father-figures like Ghandi and Fanon is also a return to the discourse of decolonization or anti-colonial struggle where, paradoxically, women are constructed as absent or silent. Her theoretical reversal in a way makes my point that we have too rapidly leapt over some of the difficult work of decolonization and the articulation of anti-imperialist discourses, including very pertinent questions on the position of women.

Finally, Katrak's accessing of the texts of working-class Caribbean women like the Sistren collective through decolonization theory carries its own contradiction. Given the limited vision of theorists like Fanon on the question of women, attempts to incorporate the theoretical contributions of the named father-figures have to simultaneously interrogate their positions on gender. So Katrak, in ending with Sistren, effects, to some extent, a critique of the master discourses. In this pattern, we can see a moving out of the boundaries of Western-style formulations of theory, to theorizing as it exists in multiple ways.

This leads to another major assertion, that the articulation of feminisms in non-Western contexts is the submerged discourse, as post-coloniality became re-maled for the academic mainstream and was produced as a gender-neutral discussion. This answers the question often asked about where the women are in the discourses of post-coloniality. As this work will show, they are somewhere else, doing something else. As post-coloniality was written in as a mainstream discourse, as had feminism and postmodernism, the non-Western women who are/were exploring their myriad identities outside of these discursive fields have produced/are producing a different range of wonderfully textured articulations. Definitely not operating out of any similar situatedness as post-coloniality, and perhaps for that reason, they continue to remain unaccounted for in most of the current theoretical discussions. Given the tendency of dominant discourses to absorb resistant discourses into their centers, outside may be not such a bad place to be. For this reason it is interesting to see Greenblatt and Gunn's *Redrawing the Boundaries*,[26] which has redrawn the boundaries to again leave Black/women of color/non-Western feminist criticism totally unaccounted for. It is as though Greenblatt and Gunn still have not heard about *All the Women are White, All the Blacks are Men, But Some of Us Are Brave*.

The women who are absent or have disappeared from the formulations of post-coloniality are doing something totally different. They participate as pieces in a growing collage of up-rising textualities. Their works exist more in the realm of the "elsewhere" of diasporic imaginings than the precisely locatable. Much of it is therefore oriented to articulating presences and histories across a variety of boundaries imposed by colonizers, but also by the men, the elders and other authorized figures in their various societies.

In other words, the assertion of many of the women *outside* the post-colonial could be reformulated as saying a definite and possible "yes" to operating outside of these very structures, conventions and constructions of dominance and thereby working on the side of those resisting injustices.[27] This is clearly an issue of rebellion against the early constructed master discourses.

One illustration may suffice: Jamaica Kincaid in "On Seeing England for the First Time,"[28] speaks of her initial, childhood encounter with England as one of maps, schooling, seeing colonial representatives and products and finally her adult perceptions of the colonial reality. Her first physical encounter with England is filled with loathing, disgust and hatred, not awe; hers is a moving away from the structures of dominance:

> The moment I wished every sentence, everything I knew, that began with England would end with "and then it all died" was when I saw the white cliffs of Dover . . . you would only call them that if the word "white" meant something special to you; they were dirty and they were steep, the correct height from which all my views of England, starting with the map before me in my classroom and ending with the trip I had just taken, should jump and die and disappear forever.[29]

Thus, Kincaid's work cannot be located primarily within the "post-colonial," for her work is, among other things, a literature of resistance on issues of race, gender, class, location and so on. Kincaid's generation is one which witnessed the transition, throughout the major Caribbean islands, from the colonial to the ideology of "independence." This writer is also of that generation who as children witnessed beginnings, grew up with the language of independence and new flags, anthems, etc., celebrated and then promptly recognized as adults that there were new colonial formations and American imperialism and how painful it had been to be put out in the sun with flags as children to wave at some member of the royal family as we marched to independence. So for us it is necessary to create "elsewhere" worlds and places and consciousness.

GAYATRI SPIVAK AND
THE INSTITUTIONALIZING OF
POST-COLONIALITY[30]

In terms of women deliberately articulating the discourse of post-coloniality, we come logically to the work of Gayatri Spivak. In fact many responses to the critique of post-coloniality indicate that Spivak's presence prevents a response singularly based on gender. Michèle Barrett asserts that while Gayatri Spivak's "work has been crucial for the development of understanding of post-coloniality . . . her interests and knowledge range across matters of technology, economics and so on."[31] Spivak has consistently challenged the tendency for Third World women always to be located as native informants. Indeed, her work traverses with confidence a variety of discursive fields and she has the capability of making connections with them or reading their disjunctions skillfully. Still, a critique of Spivak's formulations of post-coloniality is necessary since a major stream of the articulations of post-coloniality has been through Spivak.[32] In fact, as Gyan Prakash in "Postcolonial Criticism and Indian Historiography" argues, Spivak becomes a common figure in the articulation of both postmodernism and post-coloniality. Prakash identifies some of the ways in which "the deconstructive philosophical position (or postcolonial criticism)" is allied using Spivak's "saying of an impossible 'no' to a structure, which one critiques, yet inhabits intimately."[33]

It is this existing inside yet outside of the structures of dominance which becomes the post-colonial trap and signals some of its pessimism or the sense of "being stuck,"[34] as Robert Gooding-Williams (pp. 1–12) formulates it using Rodney King's words. Post-coloniality is thus much like being stuck after coloniality in some "hybrid place."

Let us look at some of Spivak's conceptions of post-coloniality. In an interview with Howard Winant, "Gayatri Spivak on the Politics of the Subaltern,"[35] under the category "the formation of the postcolonial subject," she talks autobiographically about her personal, colonial paths in India and subsequently the US. A question about feminist politics in her Indian experience elicits a "no" response and a bit of a discourse on the genesis of her left politics, reading *Capital*, etc. It becomes clear as one reads the rest of the interview that the formation of the "post-colonial subject" here is, therefore, definitely Winant's, but Spivak makes the important point during the discussion of subalternity that, while we are anxious to ascribe European parentage to each concept (Derrida for "difference" and Gramsci for "subalternity"), she locates some of what she is doing in Ranajit Guha's formulation of *Subaltern Studies*[36] (p. 90). Thus later we have Winant's formulation again, "Guha, Not Gramsci" (p. 93).

The discussion of "post-colonial culture," however, reveals some important information for our discussion here. Through a set of contradictory assertions, Spivak attempts a variety of positions on the post-colonial. First she asserts, "There's no 'space' that is postcolonial" (p. 94), and here one can assume a range of "spaces" from the physical or geographical space (given the parenthetical reference to nation-states) to the discursive. Then: "I see post-coloniality as precisely the trajectory which has brought us to planetary transnational capitalism, the break-up of space-based imperialisms" (p. 93). And, importantly,

> I see a *new colonialism* which is not space-based. We're moving toward planetary capitalism. . . . In that sense the whole world is postcolonial. Even this trajectory of non-metropolitan transnational capitalism is a postcolonial phenomenon. In postcoloniality, all the explanations are different. *But I don't see anything called postcolonialism*, and I don't see postcoloniality as a way of saying that there is a North-South difference or that there are cultural differences; I see it as a crisis-managing ensemble of cultural explanations.
>
> (pp. 94–95; my emphasis)

Later, she adds, "when I say postcolonial, I mean everything. I'm talking about decolonized space (so-called)" (p. 95).

Clearly, the terms and concepts, language and meaning, constantly slip, evade and are constantly deferred or transferred. There is the identification of colonialism and transnational capitalism, but a parallel naming of it as post-coloniality. Gayatri herself admits difficulty in articulation when she says, "I'm trying to learn how to say it, not succeeding, but I'll arrive again" (p. 95). This tentativeness is for me not a failure, in fact it is desirable.[37] It is a caution in the articulation which does not, for example, exist in the Ashcroft, Griffiths and Tiffin definitions. For Spivak, here, it is a way of naming transnational capitalism, and not so much an "after-colonialism."

A definite articulation of post-coloniality as "after-coloniality" appears in response to Benita Parry's article in which Spivak quotes herself from an earlier piece, saying, "When Benita Barry takes us to task for not being able to listen to the natives, or to let the natives speak, she forgets that the three of us, postcolonials, are 'natives' too."[38] The post-colonial assertion, comes, unfortunately, in defense against a certain important critique launched by Parry. In the rest of the piece, she talks of "post-coloniality" as a strategy, process, as a naming by others and so on: "We are always *after* the empire of reason, our claims to it always short of adequate. In the hands of identitarians, alas, this can lead to further claims of marginality. 'We are all post-colonials'" (p. 228).

I am seeing a few things going on here: first, the post-colonial subject being defined by some Euro-American scholars and others from the "Third World" for management purposes; second, the same "subject" being forced to respond to the formulations already constructed, as often takes place in patriarchal-style interview contexts; third, the anti-colonial intellectual having difficulty with, and expressing caution in, constructing definition and meaning that is Western-derived so attempting to produce distinctions; fourth, the post-colonial intellectual expressing a kind of academic agency by attempting to create a matching respectable theoretical field; fifth, a deferring of the direct identification of present realities in circumlocution and the search for less weighty synonyms; sixth, the sometimes wry, sometimes ironic assertions of Spivak taken at face value or literally; seventh, no indication from Spivak's work of wanting to see post-coloniality as a fixed, theoretical entity, which takes the place of anti-imperialist struggles; yet eighth, the parallel fixing of the term and its meaning at the institutional level.

For example, Spivak makes it clear that she cannot identify a "post-colonialism," though she would speak to the post-colonial or the aspects of post-coloniality. In her collected interviews, *The Post-Colonial Critic. Interviews, Strategies, Dialogues*,[39] similar slippages and graspings for precise articulation occur. While the "post-colonial critic" is named titularly and captured and framed from the outset, I find the interview in New Delhi with Bhatnagar, Chatterjee and Rajan very important in that the Indian scholars at home deliberately critique and disrupt some of the formulations that Spivak works with, one being that of the "post-colonial diasporic Indian who seeks to decolonize the mind" (p. 6). With very elaborate question structures which assert positions as they question and locate issues such as exile, Western theories, pedagogic practice and "native intellectual" as well as indigenous theory, the at-home Indian intellectuals problematize some of the categories that are exported to them from the West even though dispatched from other Indian intellectuals abroad. Spivak responds necessarily that she also constitutes the local scholars "equally with the diasporic Indian, as a post-colonial intellectual" (p. 67). The questions in this context speak more deliberately of a kind of home-assertion as in: "what are the possibilities of discovering/promoting indigenous theory?" (p. 69), to which Spivak responds that there can be no indigenous theory which ignores all the centuries of Western theorizing.

One could as easily return the question rhetorically: can the West construct its indigenous theory and ignore the centuries of non-Western theorizing? But for the purposes of this discussion, the follow-up question on the "structure of postponements" in her work is most relevant. It ends particularly on the question of gender. The deferring of the woman question, it seems to me, is central to the "male-ing" of post-colonial discourses:

> Why does your theory lever the woman question via homologies and analogies? Why is it necessary to have a series of discontinuous displacements of the concept – to metaphors from, say, Marx's text to, say a text of Mahasweta Devi's? Why is there a structure of postponements in your work which you have yourself noticed in Derrida and Foucault? So we have read and assented to your cautionary narratives for a readership of First World feminists. What is it you now say to us?
>
> (p. 70)

This series of questions is telling, particularly in the context of home-based and displaced foreign intellectuals talking to each other. Yet, in all of these responses Spivak seems to be saying, rather uneasily, that all she is doing is attempting to clarify herself. She therefore identifies the predicament of the non-Western/Western-trained intellectual who is technically the "post-colonial." Yet Spivak's inability, *in this exchange*, to formulate any theoretical positions which account for gender[40] identifies a major gap in the theorizing of "post-coloniality" as it misrecognizes the space that the women are occupying outside the post-colonial.

In this context the "post-colonial critic" remains outside of

current struggles at home. The "post-colonial critic," then, becomes a self-conscious position, a self and identity which articulates
itself in the West through writing and speaking and a series of
provisional definitions of which "post-colonial" is just one, but
more importantly through alienation. It is the kind of position
which leads logically to the conclusions offered by her important
interrogative: "Can the Subaltern Speak?"[41] We are therefore
observing, in process, the weight of having to define and advance
a theoretical discourse that can match, at least at the level of
language, that of postmodernism, for example.

The essay "Poststructuralism, Marginality, Postcoloniality and
Value," seems to be pivotal in this shift to the articulation of
post-coloniality. Her essays collected in *In Other Worlds. Essays
in Cultural Politics*[42] pursued a variety of issues of subjectivity,
culture, gender, identity and interpretation, outside this formulation. Even so, I find this essay useful when it moves out of the
self-conscious need to define the post-colonial. Its discussion of
the "Third World" and issues of marginality and its section on
"Woman and Engels" which locates issues of "sexual possessive-
ness" and paternity with the vanquished "mother-right" are helpful. Nevertheless, the inability to consistently and simultaneously
pose gender as a fundamental ingredient in any/all theoretical
speculations on current conditions, often leads to a disempowered
space.[43]

The fact remains, however, that Gayatri Spivak is a major
contributor to discourses on non-Western women and their inter-
pellation in imperialistic discourses. A great deal of her work,
therefore, operates on a different axis to the institutionalizing definitions of "post-coloniality." So, it is necessary to read the entire
trajectory of her work which is still unfolding[44] in order to come
up with any finite conclusions about her theoretical contributions.
Spivak's work is important for me when she articulates the
theoretical underpinnings of dominant discourses and provides
strategies of reading which mark startling connections. The
intellectual contributions of other women raise related issues but
seem to have another agenda and a variety of audiences in mind.
Mohanty, Russo and Torres in *Third World Women and the Politics of
Feminism* speak in their introduction to the deliberate titling of their
text: "While the term *third world* is a much maligned and contested
one, we use it deliberately, preferring it to *postcolonial* or *developing
countries*" (p. ix). The position of women and the critique of

patriarchy has to be stated deliberately, the editors of *Recasting Women* assert in their introduction:

> We feel that the implications of the reconstitution of patriarchies in the colonial period bear significantly upon the present, and this, in fact, is the justification for this venture . . . the social and political developments of the past two decades have shattered the post-colonial complacency about the improving status of women and with it has gone the legitimacy of nationalist models of reform and "development." It is now apparent that far from enjoying the benefits of so-called development, the majority of women have in fact been pushed to the margins of the production processes.[45]

My reassertion, then, is that post-coloniality is Western-oriented and formulated to manage a wide series of disjunctive realities. It does duty in some academic contexts as a marking of the creativity of all the geographically and racially distant others outside of Western literatures and theories.[46] For that reason it has to be called into question as it becomes entrenched. Post-coloniality, then, while it has the specific meaning of marking a certain historical period and political condition, becomes dangerous when it avoids the recognition of colonial transition from European to US and a variety of other recolonizing, imperialistic processes. Ama Ata Aidoo maintains on the question of the "post-colonial": "colonialism has not been 'POST'-ed anywhere."[47]

A number of writers share similar responses. Merle Collins speaks of the danger of a category which tries to lump together too many different histories in sweeping fashion and that then asks writers to fit themselves into it so that one has to say, "Oh, this must be what I am doing."[48] Véronique Tadjo of Côte d'Ivoire suggests that post-coloniality is not useful as a category for her as it does not capture the realities of the people who live outside of Western formulations and that she cannot, as a writer, see things in terms of pre-colonial and post-colonial but of Africa today. And Lorna Goodison asks in bold, rhetorical fashion: "When is post-coloniality going to end? How long does the post-colonial continue?"[49]

BLACK WOMEN WRITING THE ANTI-IMPERIALIST CRITIQUE

The decentering of home and exile advances the critique of labelling, place, origin, home/lands. It is a recognition that because of their history, Black women themselves have to redefine the contours of what identity, location, writing, theory and time mean, and thus redefine themselves against Empire constructs. In this context, when the colonizer has an epistemic position in defining "post-colonial" dynamics, this work recognizes the persistence of struggle. Black British women writers then become crucial in this articulation, for, positioned as they are, they are able to launch an internal/external critique which challenges simultaneously the meanings of Empire, the project of post-coloniality as well as the various nationalistic identifications of home.

A variety of redefinitions begin this process. This study, therefore, begins by asserting their relevance to larger understandings of anti-imperialist discourses. A collection edited by Shabnam Grewal, Jackie Kay, Liliane Landor, Gail Lewis and Pratibha Parmar, *Charting the Journey*,[50] is very strong in its identification of the idea of new journeys, new identifications, multiple locations of home. The opening section entitled "Alien-Nation. Strangers At Home," begins with lines from June Jordan's poem "Notes Towards Home," using it as a riff to engage the shifting meanings of home for Black women. In their poetic opening statement, home is foregrounded as a series of contradictory statements: for example, "home is where you live – home is where you can't live." In the rest of the introduction, the contradictory meanings of home are expressed as a reality:

> For black women, there is an inherent contradiction in the very word "home." . . . Where is home for starters? Can you call a country which has systematically colonized your countries of origin, one which refuses through a thorough racism in its institutions, media and culture to even recognize your existence and your rights to that existence – can you call this country "home" without having your tongue inside your cheek?[51]

They move from there to talk about a variety of homeless conditions in South Africa, India and the Caribbean. Questions of deportation from Britain make a mockery of the safety of home.

Attacks on Black people in their own homes challenge the myth of security that accompanies home. The dreamings of a nostalgic home back in the old country is beset with problems, for "back home" becomes an idealized, romanticized place of origins which often turns out not so glossy when the "migrant" returns. They conclude therefore that "Until we can be both visible and belong, the word "home" will remain for us ambiguous, ironic, and even sarcastic. We will still be 'Strangers at Home'."[52]

The introduction to *Charting the Journey* identifies well the terms for most of the deliberations on home and exile, the colonized and Empire which one finds in Black British women's literature. Much of the empirical grounding for their assertions comes through Valerie Amos and Pratibha Parmar's important work in this area, which addressed the issues of gender and migration and significantly linked "patriarchal immigration legislation" to the ways in which the exploitation of women's labor benefits racist, patriarchal and class structures, across boundaries, without neglecting the agency embedded in resistance. For example, "Many Voices, One Chant. Black Feminist Perspectives," a special issue of *Feminist Review*, documents Black women's organizing in London and opens with an essay by Valerie Amos and Pratibha Parmar, "Challenging Imperial Feminism," which says, "true feminist theory and practice entails an understanding of imperialism and a critical engagement with challenging racism – elements which the current women's movement significantly lacks, but which are intrinsic to Black feminism. We are creating our own forms and content. . . ."[53] The creative work in *Charting the Journey*, then, is grounded in the practical examinations of migration. Thus, the section "Frontiers" engages some of the issues of constructed boundaries and borders which have to be challenged.[54] Still it leaves room for the personal/political as "The Whole of Me" talks about the many identities which have to be accounted for and "Turning the World Upside Down" speaks to necessary resistance. In each section, the contributing writers engage, in a variety of modes, the various issues that have to do with the Black women's experience in Britain. Similarly, *Black Women Talk Poetry*[55] is organized into sections like "England, this land that had been no mother to her . . .," "Ask me where home is . . .," "Where do I go who do I turn to . . .," "Being a lesbian . . ." and so on.

Black women's experience in England has its genesis in British colonialism (their migrations for exploitation) and the disruptions which followed their earlier involvement in the forced migration, indenturing and enslavement of African and Asian peoples. The subsequent migrations to England for economic, political and other well-documented reasons are all by-products of this earlier series of displacements. The creative response has been documented in a variety of places such as Paul Gilroy's *There Ain't No Black in the Union Jack*[56] and Amon Saba Saakana's *The Colonial Legacy in Caribbean Literature*.[57] These, however, do not account in any significant way for Black British women. David Dabydeen and Nana Wilson Tagoe's *A Reader's Guide to West Indian and Black British Literature*[58] offers a detailed identification of some of the principal texts and writers in the Black British experience. In the section on "Women Writers," they comment that although Black women have been in England from at least the sixteenth century,

> the overwhelming experience of black women in Britain has been less glamorous than that of courtly entertainment. In the seventeenth and eighteenth centuries, the records point to employment as domestic servants, seamstresses, laundry-maids, children's nurses, fairground performers and so on. Many were forced into street prostitution. . . .[59]

Dilip Hiro's *Black British. White British*[60] examines a range of communities and conditions in the categories of "West Indians," "Asians," "White Britons," looking at history, migration, social and economic conditions, consciousness, urban conditions, resistance, organization, policing and so on. In that context, the state has been known to be outward in its hostility to the developing Black community as expressed in *Policing Against Black People*[61] which contains numerous cases of police brutality and repression. On its cover is a very revealing photograph of a mature Black woman on the ground, recoiling in a position of submission, as a white policeman stands over her with his baton raised. The evidence compiled by the Institute of Race Relations paints a grim picture of sustained police harassment and miscarriages of justice.

More developed discussion, specific to women, can be found in *The Heart of the Race. Black Women's Lives in Britain*[62] which goes into detail on issues of labor, the relationship to state systems – education, welfare, health – and the ways that Black women had to organize. *Strangers and Sisters. Women, Race and Immigration*[63] contains the proceedings of the conference, "Black and Immigrant Women Speak Out and Claim Our Rights." It is a practical product including the voices of the many women who participated and the themes, concerns and strategies for claiming those rights. Another helpful work for me was Marsha Prescod's *Black Women: Bringing It All Back Home*,[64] organized as it is, in a similar way, around women seeking empowerment, identifying why and how they got to Britain and how they plan to negotiate and demand more from the system. It is a text which carries a great deal more agency for Black women than many of the other works which speak for Black women. Here Black women speak for themselves.

A more recent work, *Young, Female and Black*,[65] looks at how Black girls make the transition to adulthood in Britain. "Young black women," Mirza concludes, "bear all the hallmarks of a fundamentally inegalitarian society. They do well at school, contribute to society, are good efficient workers yet, as a group, they consistently fail to secure the economic status and occupational prestige they deserve."[66] In other words, for Mirza nothing much has changed.

The articulation of the women's voices themselves, which is central to *Strangers and Sisters*, is echoed in Amrit Wilson's *Finding a Voice. Asian Women in Britain*.[67] This book is organized around women's responses to migration, their family and community relations, education, marriage and struggle. In each case the women's voices are privileged and their life-stories together create the larger story of migration and living conditions in the seat of Empire. It is a project which within the context of the life-story genre gives a variety of women a chance to tell their stories.[68]

In the context of telling one's story, one's self, Beryl Gilroy's *Black Teacher*[69] had earlier recorded autobiographically the experience of a Black woman, immigrant from Guyana, trying to make her way with integrity and efficiency as a teacher in the British school system of the 1950s. It documents the journeys of a Black woman who experienced then the entrenched prejudice, racism, sexism and foreign bias that subsequent generations of Black professional women have had to face. Beryl Gilroy calls it "a fight for survival and dignity" (p. 10). Steeped in the culture of 1950s colonialism, Beryl Gilroy struggles through jobs such as filing clerk, uniformed maid to a Lady Anne and so on. Looking on with 1990s consciousness and eyes, it is easy to feel impatient at the postures of servility that Black women had to adopt at that time in order to survive and even in the end to find some benefit from the experience. Beryl Gilroy explains it as at least an opportunity to study upper-class British culture, but, even more so, to define herself over and beyond their expectations: "Above all, during the months spent with her I found my own identity – learning how important to the development of my personality and my future purpose was a knowledge of both family and country."[70]

Beryl Gilroy, of course, became a successful teacher, head-mistress of a North London School, a reading specialist at the University of London Institute of Education, a writer of children's stories, novelist, poet, psychologist and generally a creative writer with an impressive record of work in a variety of genres. In my view, it is necessary to understand Black women writers like Beryl Gilroy in order to put into some historical context the creative achievements of younger writers. It also allows us to see some of the generational dynamics in the anti-imperialist critique. For it is against this background that a number of Black British women write today and assertively critique Empire-building and its displacements.

The interrelations of home and exile, personal history and location in their multiple meanings operate as necessary conditions for the problematizing of these easily conflated, flattened or homogenized categories. A collection of essays by Black women writers in Britain, *Let It Be Told. Black Women Writers in Britain*,[71] has an introduction by Lauretta Ngcobo, its editor, which outlines well the many issues, writers, their texts and their range. It also includes discussion on a variety of women writers (Amryl Johnson, Maud Sulter, Agnes Sam, Valerie Bloom, Grace Nichols, Marsha Prescod and a collective of Beverley Bryan, Stella Dadzie and Suzanne Scafe and Lauretta Ngcobo), with commentary on their work by other writers. In general, much of the work on Black British women's writing has emphasized creative production and the scholarly inquiry into their work is beginning.[72]

Unbelongingness

Joan Riley's novel, *The Unbelonging*, best captures the issue of displacement, which is its central theme. It is perhaps the most well-known of the writings that engage the question of home and identity. Her character is a young girl, Hyacinth, who makes the journey from her Jamaican home to London to live with her father after living with her Aunt Joyce in the Caribbean. Her childhood becomes a series of traumas which include physical and sexual abuse by her father and the British school system. She becomes a displaced figure caught between a family that cannot organize itself to love and protect her and an outside system which does not seem to care and which even turns against her in violent ways.[73] Between the cold and dinginess of London, her bed-wetting and struggles to grow up are her idyllic dreams of "back home." Her dismay is expressed at her initial encounter in the airport in London,

> She had been feeling lonely and small, and wishing for Aunt Joyce, for Jamaica and her friends, hating the father who had insisted on sending for her. Well she had thought she hated him then, but boy, had she been wrong. There had been a sea of white faces everywhere, all hostile. She had known they hated her, and she had felt small, lost and afraid. . . .[74]

Significantly, her father had learned to utilize this double fear and need against her (the fear of white racism and her desire for home) in order to maintain his control of her. And paralleling this fear is her own growing self-hatred which located beauty always in European features and physical characteristics:

> She often wished that she had nice hair, that her skin was lighter. She was sure they would not pick on her then. The more she suffered, the more she clung to thoughts of Jamaica, sinking further into her world of dreams.[75]

Hyacinth's entire life becomes, then, a manifestation of this sense of "unbelonging," a sense of feeling "unwanted" which parallels the dream of going back home to Aunt Joyce. Images of homelessness, desire, dreaming, strangeness permeate the entire text. Her escape at one point becomes the plots of cheap romance books which further distance her from her practical experiences. Finally, running for her life from her father's house (he himself is victimized by British racism) because of his unrelenting abuse, she enters the system, and while it holds her at arm's length, she is able to make her way, develop her own interests and claim some things for herself.

A series of small, drab and lonely rooms in foster homes, reception homes, institutional homes, dormitories help make the statement of displacement come alive. A similar mood and condition is created by Maureen Ismay's "The Bed-Sitting Room,"[76] where the character "had lived in tiny rooms, it seemed forever," rooms whose walls begin to close in on her (p. 48) in a mood of greyness and images of peeling wallpaper, isolation and imprison-ment. The young Black woman in this story never leaves, seems to have no home to go to. The landscape outside similarly does not embrace her as she negotiates between inside and outside.

Rooms in this context become metonymic references for reduced space and the references to homes are therefore often within the context of alienation and outsideness. Homes here are contrasted with "home," as in back home for Hyacinth. At university, she resists the demystification of her dreams of home which she encounters through the progressive politics of the university students whom she meets.

All her movements therefore lead to returning to the flat, stereo-typic and over-romanticized "home" as the culmination of all the desires she carried over the years. When she returns, however, predictably, the reality and dream converge in a nightmarish sequence with the dying old aunt whom she had not really written to, a run-down housing situation, neglect and poverty and people hostile to "foreigners" and particularly those like Hyacinth who, with all her dreams, had never written or sent anything to help. The importance of "writing home" (p. 140) is thus foregrounded over the flat constructions of "dreaming of homeland." "She could not remember living in this hovel, could not recall this decay and neglect" (p. 138). The refrain which she hears, "Go back whe yu come fram" (p. 142), highlights her sense of unbelonging and identifies the critique of the false constructions of "belonging."

Thus, migration produces a sense of this "unbelonging" which then triggers memories of England, its own pain and the identical cries of "Go back where you belong" (p. 140). Hyacinth's sense of displacement is juxtaposed with the tourists who seem to be more located and, because of whiteness, seem to her to be always "at home" wherever they go. In the end Hyacinth thinks of her friend Perlene and misses the fact she had not identified with her sense of a need to construct new worlds borne of resistance. Still, she returns to the world of her childhood, but it is no longer a romanticized dream of home, rather one of a childhood of powerlessness and loneliness from which she had to recuperate.

Joan Riley has written a number of other works which engage the Black British experience. *Waiting in the Twilight*,[77] begins with a disabled, middle-aged Black woman who mops public spaces with one good arm and revels in the lies of England that were sold to her and caused her to exchange her life in the Caribbean for one in the

"Motherland" where she struggled to provide for her children. It also speaks to the generation of Black British, born in England, who did not really know "back home" (p. 10). For her England is still a grim place in which she struggles with an irresponsible husband, Staunton, buys a run-down house and works to claim something of her own, but dies in the end with her dreams intact. The author indicates that this book was written to put

> a small part of the record straight where the West Indian woman in Britain is concerned. To show that the tremendous act of Bravery in leaving their home countries and stepping into a society of alien values will not readily be forgotten.[78]

The theme of returning home is further explored in Vernella Fuller's *Going Back Home*,[79] and it also runs through work such as Claudette Williams, "Gal . . . You Come From Foreign,"[80] which deals reflectively with migration, affirming that it (migration) will not "silence our voices and kill our spirit" (p. 145). Williams reflects on the difficulties and pleasures of life both at home in the Caribbean and in London: "I still possess a strong emotional attachment to the concept of 'back home'; England has never emotionally become my home, even though I've lived here some twenty years now" (p. 151). Life in Britain made itself clear to her through the educational system, the Eurocentric and paternalistic racist systems and finally through Black consciousness groups and Black women's organizations.[81] The result is, as for African-American women, an understanding of the multiple locations and politics of Black female identities. Still, her sense of being a "stranger" in Britain does not mask the fact that on returning home she is also a "stranger-outsider," but nevertheless one who brings a history and knowledge which extends beyond the limited identifications with which she began her journey.

Still, in this context of deconstructing home, Beryl Gilroy's longer vision ends *Boy-Sandwich*[82] with a final decision to return home. This novel which charts the lives of an aging couple in London, living with difficulty in retirement homes, and their relationship to their grandson, has its narrative voice which sees coming home, not as a situation of joy, but rather as a "service for old folk seeking a familiar graveyard" (p. 122).

"She Lives Between Back Home and Home" is how Sindamani Bridglal sees the contradiction, identifying how the shifting meanings of "home," its nowhereness and everywhereness, captures the mood of migratory subjectivities:

> She lives between back home and home
> Frantic
> Desire mingling with unease as she
> Carved a space for you
> Kindled a spirit that would guard against
> The despair of her life
> And the desire for you to be
> What she could not be . . .[83]

Black British writing experience deals in interesting ways, poetically and narratively, with concepts of Empire and self-articulation in the midst of Empire. In a variety of poetic expressions, the anti-imperialist critique is articulated. The poetic texts in many ways carry the direct urgency of the critical response along with the desire to create in spite of the existence of stifling experiences. In a poem titled "Birth Certificate," Maya Chowdhry sees her identity in the following terms:

> My birth certificate says
> born in Edinburgh, Scotland, 1964
> but I was born in the world
> and the year doesn't matter.[84]

In "Diary of Home," she explores many of the meanings surrounding her identity as a Black British woman, her origins, relation to home place, parentage, colonialism, boundaries. It is a simultaneous telling of her father's story and hers – his of migration to the colonial center, hers of the need to return – and it is also a re-mapping of her identities:

> I get out some old maps of India, trace the Mogul
> Empire in 1605, from Kabnul to Bengal my finger weaves
> in and out of the provinces. I turn to 1836, India
> was a patchwork of territories striped with colonial
> boundaries, the whole world had to go to war twice
> to change this map. The map was changed by a line
> which looked for the religion of the population
> which followed rivers not reason.

> I put the maps away and think about the lines of
> Hindus and Moslems crossing this line.

1 October 1992
I examine my bank balance, this is the best
month to travel to India, post hot season,
post monsoon climate just right for someone
brought up on snow and North Sea winds. No good
it's in the red, maybe next year.[85]

A special issue of *Feminist Art News* (London)[86] says it was organized after "countless conversations which took place in the course of daily living – especially with many different Blackwomen, unpicking the nuances of how imperialism and patriarchy hold hands to bulldoze their borderlines through our homes" (p. 1). The link between patriarchy and imperialism is central to the anti-authority discourses of Black and Third World women's feminisms. So in "Ethnic Monitoring or a Geography Lesson," Kamila Zahno begins

> Black, Asian, White, FAR EASTERN, Other!
> The boxes on the tear-off slip remain blank
> I never thought there'd be a space for Indo-Swiss!
> but my mind turns its attention
> To the mind between the confusion
> behind those mixed-up boxes.
>
> Is there a line between middle-east and far east?
> And where's nearly east?
> And can't someone be black, asian *and* far eastern?
> In my colonial style geography books
> With whole areas coloured empire pink
> There was a line . . .[87]

And Lesley Saketkoo adds in an emotive dismantling of colonizing boundaries:

> life affirming beyond the power of any passport
> vital beyond the OK of any immigration officer
>   that I live within the boundaries of a nation
>   which is not mine
>   that I live outside the boundaries of the nation
>   into which I was born
>
> . . .
>
>   these are certainly not denotations of sterile–mapped–out
>   borderlines. . . .[88]

Another poem by Shahida Janjua, entitled "Will You," affirms the need for women to love each other beyond the boundaries which societies impose:

> Women loving women
> Is the hardest place to be
> Experiencing, learning them knowing
> The games of patriarchy
> Don't deliver us from our colonisation as women,
> So easily
> Each colony gaining Independence
> Became a military dictatorship
> Or took on the values
> Of the colonizers
> Each independent woman
> Find herself policed,
> Policing herself and others of our kind
> Lest we stray too far
> Spilling over the boundaries
> Into Truth —
> Such a frightening place to be
> Alone – outside the colony,
> Will you come with me?
> I'm sick of living lies.[89]

A clear recognition of all the colonizations, both externally and internally imposed, is communicated along with the desire to dismantle the untruths and create new worlds. Many of these works have begun the intellectual task of dismantling colonial boundaries and establishing journeys across difference. They therefore move even beyond Gloria Anzaldua's formulations of *Borderlands*, searching for reconnections beyond the boundaries imposed by colonialism and imperialism.

Merle Collins is similarly conscious of the colonial boundaries in "The Sheep and the Goats," which talks of various immigration posts as places where the sheep and the goats of her mother's cryptic folk sayings are manifested:

> Standing in the queue
> at the airport terminal
> London
> Heath-
> row

> I tried to decide
> which were the sheep
> and which
> the goats
>
> (p. 11)

In fact the entire collection *Rotten Pomerack*[90] is a series of meditations on home and exile and the meanings of displacement and dislocation. Snatches of remembered colonial verses are mixed with folk-songs in the consciousness of a London domestic as she rides the train. A woman ponders where is home in the poem "Seduction": "Twenty years, she said,/ in this cold confinement/ and every winter I am packing/ to leave. . . . But that's changing/ this place is the home of my children/so the picture is shifting again" (pp. 14–15). The title poem, "Rotten Pomerack," uses the formulaic "Crick Crack" to pursue the myth and history, truth and lie of Columban/Western discoveries (pp. 60–63).

The directions these works take are revolutionary in the sense of renewed struggles rather than post-struggles. Narratives such as Leena Dhingra's "Breaking Out of Labels,"[91] eschew patronizing labels of various kinds and instead articulate resistance. Meiling Jin's "Strangers in a Hostile Landscape"[92] offers a story to explain the oft-asked question about her presence in England. It is a historical narrative in poetic form which breaks down key words like indentured laborers, colonial-ization, in-Dee-pendence, Imperial-ization, Invisible-Ness. It is a poem that tracks similar historical ground as Merle Collins's, "No Dialects Please,"[93] which challenges the British on their convenient acceptance, "African Slaves Please!," and rejection, "No African languages please!," all the while missing the fact that the formerly colonized and enslaved are mastering the language of the master as they redefine their own. This I would assert moves us beyond the uneasiness or hesitancy of naming at the theoretical level. For it necessitates a move to a new kind of optimism and struggle for change rather than a pessimism and postness or belatedness. Black British women writers have already moved beyond the "posts."

Uprising textualities

The inability to unequivocally name current conditions is a central feature of our current theoretical/academic condition/s. This need not be read as a lack, but as space for doing important work without the constraints of circumscribing definitions. Kumkum Sangari speaks of "The Politics of the Possible"[94] and Stuart Hall, in *The Road to Renewal*, speaks of the difficult work of "rethinking" everything including the ways to rethink.[95] Paula Gunn Allen in *The Sacred Hoop* frames it as "recovery."[96] The institutions in which academics work demand theories and theorizing. Feminist criticism was similarly pushed (and pushed itself) to develop a theoretical respectability. The new Western-trained, Western-academy-bound intellectual, outside "uprising textualities," can "get stuck" in this mandate to theorize. The "[w]hat are you saying now to us?", as the earlier questioner of Gayatri Spivak had concluded, is that open question which begs the response of a reversal, a listening by the Western intellectual to some of the movements among the various populations.

Uprisings in the many meanings of the word represent one of those discourses that link reasoning to action: i.e., no justice, no peace. The Los Angeles Riots in 1992, as the press dubbed it, was called by grass-roots activists internationally, an "uprising" in the sense of the people rising up from oppression. I propose to identify the meaning implicit in "uprising" to reformulate a host of textualities which seek to destabilize the established knowledge/authoritarian bases. It is a new resistance to imperialism which eschews colonial borders, systems, separations, ideologies, structures of domination. In that context, then, the intellectuals who stay behind the "posts" reveal an unwillingness to look at these new movements for social change and their specific naming of imperialism. We are clearly operating within hegemonic US imperialist time which imposes its agenda as synonymous with world time. Resisting colonialities, in this context, means resisting dominations of discourse and a parallel advancing of anti-imperialist discourses. I would therefore want to re-engage the spirit of a number of resistant articulations as expressed by a range of theorists and writers within the context of formulating some understanding of "uprising textualities."

The "uprising textualities" of Black women writing in England[97] capture some of the creative movement upward and outward from constricted and submerged spaces. It signifies resistance, reassertion, renewal and rethinking. This energy allows a movement outside the pessimism of Western intellectuals. It addresses that condition of "unheardness" to which dominant discourses (patriarchal and imperialistic) relegate a range of voices. It allows some movement toward the unnamed/unmarked "elsewhere" of rearticulated worlds, operating on the same poles as "maroon societies," "slave rebellions," "underground railroads." "Uprising textualities" similarly responds to the language, innovation and energy of Rastafari, which identifies action and meaning with a certain poetic intent, on the one hand, and a literalization structured in words, on the other.[98] The ideology implicit in "uprising textuality" is also available in certain streams of "rap music," as in Sister Souljah's lyrics and certain forms of urban popular culture. Finally "uprisings" in this context resist theorizing and cannot really be "read" or defined in totality, for while they come across as spontaneous, they are the products of mounting resentment to oppression and are always, as Mutaburaka would say in "dis poem," "to be continued."

Since Black writing in England deals in interesting ways with concepts of self-articulation in the midst of Empire, the voice of creative "uprising textualities" which also voice the anti-imperialist critique comes in this context from Black women. In a poem titled "Black Women Uprising," Stephanie George captures the movement with active verbs like "rising," "leaving," "running," "coming," "fighting back."

> From the bed of the Black man
> We are rising
>
> From the factory of the white man
> We are leaving
>
> From the whip of oppression
> We are running
>
> From our being and soul
> We are coming . . .
>
> In this dirty, marked sheet of unequal society
> We are fighting back
> For equality for your children, our people, our future
> Black women rise![99]

Thus, these uprising discourses of Black women writers in England carry some of the energy with which I think we need to address some of the questions raised by post-coloniality. An uprising consciousness moves us out of post-coloniality and the state of "postness" or "afterness" and into a more radical consciousness of our creativity.

Grace Nichols in her poem "The Return," invokes the memory of legendary Black women freedom fighters like Nanny of the Maroons, as she listens and questions her ability to hear the "Abeng voice echoing its warcry through the valleys."[100] But resistance for Black women can be the determination to be lazy in the context of expropriated domestic labor, as Grace Nichols affirms in her *Lazy Thoughts of a Lazy Woman*,[101] which revels in "Grease" and "Dust" having their existence independently of her compulsion to "not clean" them. In "The Body Reclining," she says, "Those who dust and dust/incessantly/also corrupt the body/And are caught in the asylum/Of their own making/Therefore I sing the body reclining" (pp. 4–5). In the same collection, though, is the poem, "Spell Against Too Much Male White Power" (p. 18): "How can I remove the 'Big Chiefs'/ from the helm/How can I put them to sit on beaches/quiet, sea-gazing, retired old men" (p. 19). Her *Fat Black Woman's Poems*[102] similarly critique, by the oppositional existence of the fat Black woman persona against the socially-embedded norm, what constitutes appropriateness, beauty, location, identity. Nichols's work in general is a celebration of body, magic, sexuality, power, resistance. It is the kind of self-celebratory poetry which is bold enough to say, on the question of home and exile, "Wherever I hang me knickers – that's my home" (p. 10). Still, it is a conclusion which is arrived at after charting the journey from home to England and the many adjustments to her new world-self along the way: "I get accustom to de English life/But I still miss back-home side/To tell the truth/I don't know really where I belaang" (p. 10). The deliberate fracturing of the English word disrupts from outside the contained identity of Englishness as expressed in its language.

A number of writers make the transition from the poetic page to other media – photography, film, art, performance. Grace Nichols's collection, for example, has been reinterpreted as a filmic piece with the same title, produced by Frances Anne Solomon.[103] Similarly, Maud Sulter, a photographer, has a collection, *As a Blackwoman*,[104] which speaks to all the things about her that she loves – her passion, her work, creativity, her politics – but also her pains. Her artistic installation booklets, such as "Hysteria,"[105] carry the poetic texts as well as the photographic. Sulter has also edited *Passion. Discourses on Blackwomen's Creativity*,[106] which is a wonderful collection of photography art, poetry, reflections, essays, stories. It is a sense-challenging, norm-breaking work which moves outside the boundaries established for the written and the visual.

But "uprising textualities" can also refer to the growing body of creativity by Black lesbian writers or Zamimass in London who take their name from Audre Lorde's reidentification of the Caribbean creole term, and who creatively and politically assert a presence and leadership in a variety of contexts. Many of the poets in the collections I have identified speak to this identity, in overt and subtle ways, as one of their many identities. The context of women loving themselves, as in the earlier identified poem by Zahno, then articulates itself in resistance as it does in affirmation, as Carmen Tunde's "Dreadlocks Lesbian" asserts: "Have you seen dreadlocks lesbian/I tell you/she is one powerful woman/she no bother 'bout no man/inna heartache fashion."[107] Shabnam similarly says in "The Women Loving Women": "They are/ Everywhere/Bearing no names/wearing no badges/an underground army/with no uniforms/and no weapons/except love/for women/Beware."[108] Barbara Burford who had earlier published the Black lesbian novel, *The Threshing Floor*,[109] has also jointly edited a collection of love poems by women called *Dancing the Tightrope*.[110]

The performative/activist basis of much of the creativity of Black British women writers frees the creative to exist outside of the academy and instead in the practical, pedagogic and experiential community contexts. Thus a great deal of the work is produced in workshops, small groups and community organizations,[111] and as such constantly escapes institutional and publication-oriented identifications. In a more directly assertive stance, Rasta/dub/ performance poet, Sister Netifa, in "We are Revolting,"[112] takes an intended insult heard on a train in London and hurls it back in the lines

> We resisted. We were revolting
> call it what you like
> babylon
> riots, mobs, uprising, rebellion
> we are revolting!

> still you have the wrong words
> we are not revolting
> we revolt still

(p. 16)

For me, therein lies the response to one of the guiding questions with which I began this chapter: where are the women in post-coloniality?

Critical responses to this work have been slow in coming.[113] A great deal has been written about Buchi Emecheta's work within the context of African/women's writing. Her two early works, *In the Ditch* and *Second Class Citizen*,[114] are well-recognized for engaging the British welfare system as they critiqued the cultural/familial practices which attempt to subordinate women.

The Black women who are writing out of their experience of Britain, articulate temporalities and locations outside the paradigms set by men, white society, British literary establishments. In the middle of the former colonial heartland, they create different spaces for women's work or for women speaking outside the given boundaries, standing outside some of the dominant discourses. Creative activity therefore takes place within and outside contexts of publishing and sometimes more as an affirmation of creativity and existence as Black women in Britain. Thus, much of what exists may never see the published forum nor have any desire to be thus exposed. Black women writers in England are therefore articulating assertive presences, rather than belatedness – voicing creative uprisings.

5

WRITING HOME

Gender, heritage and identity in Afro-Caribbean women's writing in the US[1]

Migration creates the desire for home, which in turn produces the rewriting of home. Homesickness or homelessness, the rejection of home or the longing for home become motivating factors in this rewriting. Home can only have meaning once one experiences a level of displacement from it. Still home is contradictory, contested space, a locus for misrecognition and alienation. Home, conflated here as a move toward a "myth of unitary origin" as is nationalism, becomes radically disrupted in the writings of Afro-Caribbean women in the US. The woman as writer then doubly disrupts the seamless narrative of home and so of nation. Further, her location in a variety of social and political contexts allows internal critiques of new inscriptions of coloniality and imperialism.

In "Notes Towards Home,"[2] June Jordan offers "home" as a place of departure. Yet, in an age of ceaseless migrations of people seeking refuge at various border places or adrift on different oceans as "boat people," detained on island-prison camps or blockaded, as were the Haitian refugees, or homeless on streets and sidewalks or parks, in cardboard cities, home has multiple significations for identity. On the practical level, we can hold up the many exploitative disruptions of people's lives as end results of colonialism, wars, ecological disasters, the destruction of natural environments, drought and famines which produce an unending cycle of homelessness.[3] On personal levels as well are the many old and young people seeking refuge in shelters, displaced from their homes because of abuse, cycles of poverty and dispossession, economic exploitation and personal disasters.

The figure of the displaced, homeless person is the most poignant, tragic representation of the transnational, capitalist, postmodern condition. Both physical and psychic homelessness exist on a continuum which has as its extreme physical disruptions and outsiderness and a variety of nodal points of displacement through exile, migration, movement. The writers of "Alien–Nation. Strangers at Home," one of the introductory sections of *Charting the Journey*, locate homelessness in the context of exploitation:

> When white people come to your Home, steal your land and impose their language, culture and religion, force you to live in ghettoes, shanty-towns or reservations, can you still call your country Home? Black people in South Africa have been made homeless in their own country.[4]

Similarly, they assert, "when a white person asks a Black woman where she comes from, the implicit assumption is that she does not belong here."[5] Further, the term "immigrant," with which many Black people in large European centers are marked, is a term which, Stuart Hall asserts, "places one so equivocally as *really* belonging *somewhere else*. 'And when are you going back home?' "[6] is the completing rhetorical gesture.

The word "home" remains therefore for many, "ambiguous, ironic and even sarcastic" because it also produces the notion of "Strangers at Home." This contradictory or disruptive meaning of home is also expressed in the work of Afro–Caribbean women writers in the US. It is significant that June Jordan, like many of the writers I will discuss here, was born into the home of a Caribbean woman, living in the United States. But as a Black woman living in the US, the sense of displacement based on race, gender, sexuality remains, as her latest work, *Technical Difficulties*,[7] reveals. But June Jordan is acutely aware in "Finding the Way Home,"[8] of being homeless with the privilege and ability to move in relation to being homeless because of abuse, oppression or exploitation. In other words, homelessness itself cannot be trivialized or essentialized into a flat, monolithic category. For some writers, exile is a desired location out of which they can create.[9]

In "Dreams of Home. Colonialism and Postmodernism,"[10] Ian Baucom offers an interesting reading of the variety of discourses around nostalgia and home. Baucom, with Bhabha and Jameson, distinguishes between a postmodernist nostalgia and a colonialist nostalgia, the latter created by colonialists in the process of producing narratives of conquest and cultural traditions which constructed their Englishness in exile; the former which "maps onto its space a culture from which the subject cannot, even mythically, claim to have originated. Postmodernism does not reinscribe the 'touch-stone' culture, it reinscribes multiple cultures, a dazzling eclectic array of defining absences."[11]

The creative writer, located centrally in these colonialist re-inscriptions, is nevertheless privileged. For the writing of home exists narratively – in conversation, letters to family, telephone conversations, stories passed on to children as family history or to friends as reminiscences. Thus, the rewriting of home becomes a critical link in the articulation of identity. It is a play of resistance to domination which identifies where we come from, but also locates home in its many transgressive and disjunctive experiences.

The question of identity for Afro-Caribbean/American women writers involves a self-definition which takes into account the multifaceted nature of human existence and of female identity. So, in all cases, it is a futile task to try to separate heritage/identity questions from say gender/identity issues. For the Caribbean-American woman writer, cultural politics have to be worked out and articulated along with sexual politics.[12] This chapter deals with the ways in which identity is mediated and redefined in the works of Caribbean-American women writers of African descent. It examines work of a number of writers who, because they live in the United States of America, did not reproduce the anti-(European) colonial text of the earlier generation of mostly male writers who wrote of the experience of British colonialism. While the evocation of Caribbean geography is strong, there is a re-mapping of the terms of that landscape. In many ways, it is a cultural geography and "cognitive mapping" of one's experience and location. Historical links to Africa are re-examined and relo-cated. Significantly, many of these writers are critically engaged in an anti-hegemonic discourse with the United States.

Although these are all current writers, it is important to place them in historical context, in relation to each other and to the variety of writing traditions which they exist in and disrupt. Paule Marshall and Audre Lorde were of the same generation, but Marshall's first novel, *Brown Girl, Brownstones* (1959),[13] is steeped in the culture of the second wave of migration between the two world wars in a climate of Garvey Pan-Africanist activism. Thus she addresses the conflicting world of a Caribbean people trying to control their new environment and construct a Caribbean com-munity in New York. Audre Lorde, in contrast, published her autobiography, *Zami. A New Spelling of My Name*,[14] two decades later than Marshall's first book, although Lorde had been publishing poetry consistently. This marked her identification as an Afro–Caribbean writer. Although her explicit lesbian and Black identification had been clear in her earlier works, this text functions almost as a re-/clamation (a biomythography as she calls it) of her many selves, living in the "house of difference."

These migrations between identities, or the articulations of a variety of identities, are central to our understandings of the ways in which these writers express notions of home in their works. Michelle Cliff, for example, creates the world of the bourgeoise, the Caribbean white vacillating between the metaphoric yard and the big house. And for her, migration issues are also critical and central to the definition of identity, because she becomes racially somebody else, an "other" within the contexts of migration and US racial politics.[15]

Jamaica Kincaid's work deals solidly with the Caribbean working–class/peasant experience and the interaction with both British colonialism and American imperialism. Both Kincaid and Cliff were born in the Caribbean and then migrated to the United States. Marshall and Lorde were born of Caribbean parents in New York and came to awareness of their identities within the Caribbean households which their parents created, through subsequent migrations and through their own political awareness of the meaning of personal geography and the politics of location. For me, these writers capture all the varying issues connected to migration, writing and identity which this book addresses. In particular, writers like Lorde and Marshall challenge the very meaning of specific identity and placement. For all of these writers tend, for varying reasons and to different degrees, to exist marginally in all the literary traditions to which they belong: namely, African-American literature, Caribbean literature, Caribbean women's writing, African-American women's writing, women's writing, Black writing.[16]

I am asserting consistently that all the postmodernist questions of redefinition of the meaning of identity, of home, of linear history, the metanarratives of the self and identity are destabilized in the writing of Black women's experiences. For the Caribbean woman, confronting racial discrimination and foreign bias, Caribbean male phallicism and American imperialism, the relationship to Caribbean identity has to be problematized. It cannot be a flat, unidimensional relationship or experience.

The acceptance of Caribbean heritage does not come easily, as Lorde reveals in *Zami*. For her, it is a tortuous passage through adolescence, a rejection of the authoritarian family, the cultivation of female friendships and the assertion of independence. Finally, a reintegration of the meaning of heritage is achieved through a fuller knowledge of her Caribbean female ancestry and the articulation of all the aspects of identity or all the identities recognized along the way. Further, the recognition of *zami* (literally "the friends" in Caribbean French patois), love between women, as a submerged conceptual and physical reality of Caribbean life, is a critical factor in that reintegration of Caribbean self and its broader acceptance.[17]

The heritage/ancestry relationship is similarly at the center of struggle in Paule Marshall's *Brown Girl, Brownstones* (1959) and *Praisesong for the Widow* (1983). In the former, the conflict of the girl, Selina, arises from continual tension between her mother's rigidity and serious immersion into the American enterprise model and her father's emotionalism and casualness to work in the capitalist machineries; between the conflicting worlds of Afro-Caribbean society in New York and her separate American experience. Selina's understanding of culture is shaped by the many conversations of the Caribbean working women in her mother's kitchen, the "nation language" from which she learns rhythm and poetry and friendships with other Caribbean women like Suggie, who luxuriates in sensuality and her body.

The autobiographical aspects of these novels are identified by Marshall, who as a child spent vacations in the Caribbean. Her adult relationships with the Caribbean family are also definite. In a story, "To Da-Duh in Memoriam," she dramatizes the contradictory spaces between ancestry and youth, tradition and modernity, African civilization and Western civilization, old and new worlds. The child in the story is taken on a journey back to the Caribbean, to one of those "vacations" home which have to do more with family identification and history than they have to do with holidaying. In the story, the child's identity is a source of the debate which Marshall unfolds. Da-Duh is in a losing battle, pitted against the skyscrapers of New York and the war-planes that swoop over Barbados toward the end of her life. For her part, Da-Duh wants to expose her granddaughter to the features of *her* Caribbean, to draw the child into *her* history. But the child has numerous examples of bigger and better things to counter Da-Duh's canefields. Yet, because the canefields are so wedded to Caribbean slavery and oppression of Africans, the child's rejection of them is an important departure from that particular experience and history. Still, her acceptance of North America's technological might is another form of slavery which she cannot yet resist.

Importantly, Da-Duh is presented as a migration figure, a displaced African in the Caribbean. Marshall captures the falling away that takes places between generations. For, whereas the grandmother's experience is of slavery and British colonialism, the insidious and also colonial relationship of the United States to the Caribbean is implicit in the child's acceptance of American dominance. Da-Duh's sense of resignation at the end catches her understanding of this new master/slave dialectic:

> The next morning I found her dressed for our morning walk but stretched out on the Berbice chair in the tiny drawing room where she sometimes napped during the afternoon heat, her face turned to the window beside her. She appeared thinner and suddenly indescribably old.
> "My Da-Duh." I said.
> "Yes, nuh," she said. Her voice listless and the face she turned my way was, now that I think of it, like a Benin mask, the features drawn and almost distorted by an ancient narrow abstract sorrow.[18]

> (p. 104)

The struggle to maintain a version of an African heritage in the path of encroaching Western values is pursued relentlessly in all of Marshall's works and is crystallized in *Praisesong for the Widow*.[19] Eugenia Collier, in "The Closing of the Circle. Movement from Division to Wholeness in Paule Marshall's Fiction,"[20] reads this novel as a move to heritage in terms of reintegration. I would want to read it instead as dramatizations of the conflicting demands of personal identification. In *Praisesong*, Avey is in a dream battle with her Great-Aunt Cuney, another of those ancestral figures who represent continuity with an African past. Avey, who has gone too far into the acceptance of things Western, must balance that out with a journey into Caribbean history, religion and cultural politics.

In terms of textual migration, it is important to track how the oral narrative of "Ibo Landing" which Marshall employs in *Praisesong* (pp. 37–40) also informs Julie Dash's *Daughters of the Dust* in a way related to Grace Nichols's *I Is a Long Memoried Woman* becoming the launching point for the film which Frances Anne Solomon makes and similarly titles.[21]

There is a Pan-Africanist focus in the relationships to heritage which Marshall identifies which makes Brathwaite call her work, for example, "literature of reconnection."[22] While accepting these ways of reading these works, I see multiple journeys taking place. I have read *Praisesong*[23] as activating at least two journeys: one journey into female identity, another into Black identity. Neither journey ought necessarily to attain supremacy over the other for, as a Black woman, these multiple journeys embody critical aspects of her being. One could also offer that an understanding of her sexuality is also a significant journey in the text. And the issue of migration is critical to any understanding of how these characters pursue these various identities. In other words, what it means to be American or Caribbean or woman or wife or somebody's notion of an "older woman" and the traffic between these various identities are pursued narratively here.

This sense of journeying between identities had already taken place for the younger woman, Selina, in *Brown Girl, Brownstones*. This novel ends with the protagonist about to embark on her journey back to the Caribbean. *Praisesong for the Widow* has a mature protagonist whose entire development is centered around journeying. All of these journeys, from the walks with her Great-Aunt Cuney to the tourist ship journeys and her journey to Carriacou and her subsequent journey back to the US are central to her being able to place her various identities in context. Avey, beyond the impetuousness of youth, has to be more fully engaged in the rituals of identification. These identifications are of gender, nationality, heritage, race, age, sexuality, class.

The traffic between United States and Caribbean identities is a large part of the focus of Marshall's latest novel, *Daughters*.[24] Here, the marriage of a United States Black woman to a Caribbean politician stages many of the dynamics of connection and separation implicit in these identities. The product is a daughter, Ursa, who is born in the Caribbean but is raised to live in the US. Throughout her life she journeys in different directions across class, race, sexuality and gender identities as she does physically between the Caribbean and the US. Trains and taxis and cars of various sorts convey her to different localities for schooling, work, family situations, friendships, relationships where some of her interactions are staged. Her mother, Estelle's participation, separation and alienation from the Caribbean island which becomes her home and its people, establish a particularity in difference which is often lost in monolithic cultural subsuming of identity. At a certain level she maintains an aloof distance from the people. This arises from her class position as the Prime Minister's wife but also from her own inability to fully become part of the island. And in other ways as well, her opposition is based on political grounds which come out of a consciousness honed in US race relations and Black political struggles which force her to reject servility. Because of this, she carries a more acute resistance to US imperialism than her husband. His interest in building a tourist-based facility runs diametrically opposite to the people's needs and, in the end, the information which she provides facilitates his eventual rejection by the people. The mother and daughter's joint recognition and rejection of his politics as they support him is one of the contradictory themes of this novel. The legendary warrior figures of Congo Jane and Will Cudjoe, whom she still must write about, are consistently in the background.[25]

The struggle to define a self amidst the overpowering Caribbean culture of her parental household is addressed in Audre Lorde's *Zami* in a way which reminds one of Selina's own fights in *Brown Girl, Brownstones*. But, in its intent, the rejection is more explicitly posed. The conventions of autobiography allow for a centering of a self caught in the conflicts of Caribbean and United States cultural demands. In her Caribbean household, any thought of individual, private space is eschewed: "a closed door is considered an insult" (p. 83). Still, she engages with Caribbean folk culture through the recalling of rituals of healing, food, song-making, the notion of "home" (p. 13). Above all, she is able to make explicit connections between her lesbianism and the fact that Carriacou women have a tradition of "work(ing) together as friends and lovers." *Zami*, as a Caribbean concept, allows her, like Michelle Cliff, to enter the process of "Claiming an Identity" she was taught to despise. The definition of *zami* is a bold epigraph to the work, as is its deliberate marking as title. A word spoken in silence or hurled as abuse, or identified as transgressive sexuality, or invoked to control women's power, attains public creative/discursive exposure and power and reclaimed meaning.

The tension in accepting a version of Caribbean identity seems finally to be expressed in this work and resolved by its writing. Her journeys throughout the North-Eastern United States, the West

Coast and Mexico, and finally back to New York as she pursues and critiques the meaning of home and of enforced heterosexuality provide her with the space to come to her own identification as Zami.

But the issues of sexuality are only one aspect of this public reclamation. Her essay, "Grenada Revisited,"[26] for example, is one of the best evaluations of the implications of the United States invasion of Grenada and, as I see it, a fitting conclusion to the journeys embarked on in *Zami*. Buttressed by concrete images of Grenada pre- and post-revolution, she concludes with a tribute to the strength and resilience of the Grenadian people:

> I came to Grenada my second time six weeks after the invasion, wanting to know she was alive, wanting to examine what my legitimate position as a concerned Grenadian-american was toward the military invasion of this tiny Black nation by the mighty U.S. I looked around me, talked with Grenadians on the street, the shops, the beaches, on porches in the solstice twilight. Grenada is their country. *I am only a relative*. I must listen long and hard and ponder the implications of what I have heard, or be guilty of the same quick arrogance of the U.S. government in believing there are external solutions to Grenada's future.
>
> I also came for reassurance, to see if Grenada has survived the onslaught of the most powerful nation on earth. She has. Grenada is bruised but very much alive. Grenadians are a warm, resilient people (I hear my mother's voice: "Island women make good wives. Whatever happens they've seen worse"), and they have survived colonizations before. *I am proud to be of stock from the country that mounted the first Black english-speaking People's Revolution in this hemisphere*. . . .
>
> (pp. 188–189; emphasis added)

Thus, the heritage/identity question is definitely established in the Grenada essay, as is the Caribbean/woman/sexual identification established in the acceptance of *zami*. The name *zami* becomes a renaming of the self as "Black lesbian" (i.e., lesbian as a white-identified, Greek-originated term has to be qualified with the adjective "Black" or latina or Asian, for example, or renamed). The deploying of the etymology and meaning of *Zami* is a similar move to find new language and new starting-points from which to express a reality, as is, for example, Alice Walker's definition

121

of "womanist" as another term of meaning for "Black feminist" or "*khush*" as a starting-point for gay identity in Indian cultures.[27]

The identification as Grenadian-American specifies an identity, narrowed beyond the broader Caribbean-American identification. Lorde's connectedness to the Caribbean has its impetus in revolutionary Grenada (not colonial Grenada) and the sense of possibility and challenge which it held. For Lorde, cultural identification has to be addressed along with an overtly anti-hegemonic discourse. She therefore moves the discussion beyond a Pan-African identification as in say Marshall, to a fuller acceptance of a gendered relationship to history and an ideological consciousness of the meaning of Grenada's thwarted revolution within the context of power, powerlessness and empowerment.

The implications of identity are centrally located in Michelle Cliff's *Claiming an Identity They Taught Me to Despise*.[28] The expressive titling of the book with the issue of identity reclamation, as well as its suggestion that identity is not a singular thing, confronts questions of subjectivity in a discursively lyrical manner. It is a somewhat autobiographical exploration of identity, with gender, heritage, sexuality and the sense of place defining that identity. Landscape, family, historical events, places, relationships, all become features in her exploration. The movement of the book mirrors the migratory pattern, beginning in the Caribbean and childhood and moving to the United States and adulthood. The sections entitled, "Obsolete Geography" and "Filaments" particularly typify the thematics of identity. In the first, we get an extended catalog of Caribbean fruits, vegetation, details of day-to-day experience like the waxing of the parlor floors, the burying of umbilical cords, the slaughtering of domestic animals. Much of the identification with "home" comes from the rural grandmother who maintains continuity with homeland and whose entire being conveys the multifaceted composition of Caribbean society. We see our narrator, however, caught up in the conflict of being privileged, yet poor, white-skinned but culturally Caribbean. Her mother is a distant, intangible, liminal presence in her life. The contradictions of surface appearance versus multi-textured reality, of camouflage and passing are explored. For this reason she feels affinity with Antoinette of *Wide Sargasso Sea* as she does with Tia.[29] The creoleness that is essentially Caribbean identity is the necessity of accepting all facets of experience, history and personhood in the definition of the self. Here, Cliff integrates these into a consciousness of her own identities. Personal history, family history and a people's history and culture all converge.

Even more explicit in her connections are her polemical essays like "If I Could Write This In Fire, I Would Write This in Fire,"[30] where she is definite about the politics of Caribbean identity. Color and privilege are held up and examined. British colonialism and American colonialism are juxtaposed (pp. 67–68). Novels of Black female experience, like Toni Morrison's *Sula*[31] in the African-American context or Ama Ata Aidoo's *Our Sister Killjoy*[32] in the African context, are recalled and deployed. So too are W.E.B. Dubois's concept of double consciousness and Bob Marley and the Rastafarian assertions on identity questions. Cliff admits intertextual interrogations at many levels. For Cliff, as for Lorde and Marshall, connectedness to Caribbean homeland becomes a reality. Filaments toughen and expand:

> The Rastas talk of the 'I and I' – a pronoun in which they combine themselves with Jah. Jah is a contraction of Jahweh and Jehova, but to me always sounds like the beginning of Jamaica. I and Jamaica is who I am. No matter how far I travel – how deep the ambivalence I feel about returning. And Jamaica is a place in which we/they/I connect and disconnect – change place.

> (p. 76)

One distinction that can be made, however, is that for Lorde and Marshall, both Afro-Caribbean/American in terms of parentage, the re-connection with home occurs in at least three levels – first, the parental home, the Caribbean homeland occupying the secondary level, and at the tertiary level the African identification. This tertiary level is one at which Cliff gets sustenance, but has no possibility of direct connection as the other writers do. Further, for her, sexuality is explored as part of the consciousness of the growing sensuality of the girls. These issues unfold in her subsequent works, as in *Abeng*,[33] for example.

The exploration of the multiple identities of the growing Caribbean woman–child are intrinsic to the narratives of Kincaid's *At the Bottom of the River* and *Annie John* and, more recently, her novel *Lucy*.[34] Kincaid seems to present an early engagement with Caribbean identity, located at a different point on the continuum than Lorde, Cliff and Marshall. The fact that she was born and raised in the Caribbean allows a different kind of engagement with the homeland and Caribbean cultural community which provides the impetus for the internal critique. Hers is never an uncritical, unproblematized acceptance of Caribbean identity. In fact, as *A Small Place* shows, she rejects almost everything that had negatively shaped this homeplace and its people: colonization, corrupt politics, neglect, pettiness. But it is the rejection of a critical insider/outsider who sees with an eye for detail the many idiosyncracies, anomalies and perversions wrought on a Caribbean slave society and their legacy on today's people. It is in this context that she explores her woman self in "Girl," which resonates outward to diverse experiences of growing up female in many cultural communities. "Wingless" and "Blackness," also in *At the Bottom of the River*, are not only about racial Blackness as one expects, but relationships of light and dark and to the inner self stripped of all the outward trappings of identity. Her relationships to the landscape and its folklore are explored in "In the Night," "Holidays" and "At the Bottom of the River." The female self is explored in the context of landscape and Caribbean folk culture and as expressed in *Lucy* in the context of migration. Central to all of these is perhaps the best presentation of conflicted mother–daughter relationship in Caribbean literature so far. And the mother is a symbolic figure here because she can also be read as the Caribbean, as well as all Lucy rejects in female subordination.

Female sexual identities are multiply-explored as "Girl" begins the catalogue of rules of conduct for the growing Caribbean girl/womanchild. These merge into surrealistic images of the Caribbean supernatural world, but conclude with her woman-to-woman motif which runs through the text. In *Annie John* a similar landscape is created. Here, the maternal grandmother, Ma Jolie, clearly an ancestral presence, is characterized as a mysterious healer who appears at a time when her granddaughter is experiencing a terrible psychological dislocation which is manifesting itself in physical illness. Much of this dislocation is located in Annie's attempts to define herself against her mother and in the context of Caribbean colonialism. *Annie John*, as an autobiographical narrative, functions as a decoder of much that is unexplainable in the mysterious world of the first book, *At the Bottom of the River*. But in both, the necessity to identify with, yet separate oneself from, the mother is a central issue. "My Mother," in *At the Bottom of the River*, pursues this maternal identification/separation fully. There is a need for bonding as there is a need for separate space. The ability of each to separate and thus grow ensures a different resolution of things. But it is only in *Lucy* that we understand some of the history of this mother–daughter relationship. During the early years, the girl is incapable of delineating a separate self and it is the mother who has to initiate and force this break: "You can't go around the rest of your life looking like a little me"; "Of course in your own house you might choose another way" (*Annie John*, pp. 26, 29).

The mother's seemingly brutal way of instituting this break produces emotions in the daughter which border on hatred, but actively produce an intense love/hate sequence with much pain and rejection for both women. In *Lucy*, we learn that the mother's privileging of the male children she had later also precipitates the separation. Separation and loss throughout these texts follow a pattern of repetition which produce her migration at the end of *Annie John* and the subsequent departures that are central to *Lucy*. In this latter work, the daughter institutes the separation, refusing to write and respond to her mother's letters, yet recalling her continually through her stories in the text.

Annie John is a *bildungsroman*, chronicling the girl's growth from childhood to womanhood, and only at the end of the work do we realize that she and her mother share the same name. The representation of exile and departure are strong and remind us of other Caribbean texts like G's departure in Lamming's *In The Castle of My Skin* (1953) or Tee's departure in Merle Hodge's *Crick Crack Monkey*.[35] Idyllic yet often difficult, explorations of childhood and coming of age seem to be one of the stock features of Caribbean literature, and may be explained partially by the meaning of "writing home" for, in writing of home, one is often putting oneself in the position of child *vis-à-vis* the Caribbean or African homeland/household. Descriptions of experiences in colonial schools link this work to other Caribbean novels of childhood.

Perhaps more centrally than in the other works explored is the relationship between girls as they encounter Caribbean worlds. Lamming similarly explores boys' relationships, but for Kincaid, the adolescent girls' feelings of sameness and coming of age to sexuality and place permeate the works. The several allusions to the Gwen/Annie and Annie/Red Girl friendships provide a variety of possibilities. Gwen, and the path she chooses to conformity, becomes a rejected persona as is Red Girl and her wildness and freedom which is a preferred identification for Annie. The same woman-love image is central to both books: "Now I am a girl, but one day I will marry a woman – a red skin woman with Black bramble bush hair and brown eyes, who wears skirts that are so big I can easily bury my head in them" (*River*, p. 11). In the surreal landscape of *At the Bottom of the River*, it is easy to see the fluidity between maternal identification and woman-love. *Annie John's* solid autobiographical narration is allowed free poetic explorations into emotions of self in *At the Bottom of the River*. What I am seeing here, then, is a self immersed in a Caribbean consciousness which it both accepts and rejects, engages and struggles with. This is made even clearer in her more polemical exploration of tourist culture and Caribbean identity, *A Small Place*. It is a hard look at colonial and neo-colonial culture and its reductiveness, violence and destructiveness. Kincaid seems to be asserting that the relationship to home is not innocent and idyllic; it is fraught with conflict, tension, bitterness and struggle.

The representation of the house as source of self-definition occurs with some frequency in the literature of Afro-Caribbean/ American women writers. The house and its specific rooms become metaphors of self and loci of self-identification in many of the works examined in this chapter. Kincaid's narrator says, "My mother and I walk through the rooms of *her* house. . . . As we walk through the rooms, we merge and separate, merge and separate; soon we shall enter the final stage of our evolution."[36] At the end of her own explorations, of self and meaning in *At the Bottom of the River*, she constructs another house, the house of writing: "I looked in, and at the bottom of the river I could see a house, and it was a house of only one room, with an A-shaped roof . . . "(pp. 74–75).

These same metaphors of house and rooms are present in a variety of modes in the Marshall works. In *Brown Girl, Brownstones*, particularly, the mother's struggle to acquire a house is what drives the narrative. But it is a house she controls and defines and from which the girl must leave. In *Praisesong*, Avey had to move beyond the superficiality of the White Plains home and come to an acceptance of herself in sparer circumstances in Rosalie Parvay's, the healer's, house.

Separation from the mother and the mother's house in Audre Lorde's *Zami*, means temporarily rejecting ties to the culture in which she was raised. But it is this separation which allows her the expansiveness she needs in order to survive:

When I moved out of my mother's house, shaky and determined, I began to fashion some different relationship to this
country of our sojourn. I began to seek more fruitful return
than simple bitterness from this place of my mother's exile,
whose streets I came to learn better than my mother ever had
learned them. . . . And there I found other women who
sustained me and from whom I learned other living. How to
cook the foods I had never tasted in my mother's house. . . .

(p. 104)

In a mature reappropriation of the Caribbean culture of her mother,
however, a wider space is identified; the confines of the mother's
house are deliberately transgressed and so her world is expanded.

The connection between gender and heritage is never really
severed by Lorde, as we learn in *Zami*. The legendary women of
the extended family become sources of reidentification and allow
her to make specific personal and political connections. The politics
of Zami-life is seen on a continuum between her female ancestors
and the women who sustained her during her departure from her
mother's house:

Their shapes join Linda and Gran' Ma Liz and Gran' Aunt
Anni in my dreaming, where they dance with swords in their
hands stately forceful steps to mark the time when they were
all warriors. In libation, I wet the ground to my old heads.

(p. 104)

In the spatial meaning-expansion of home, female elders are crucial
links in its rewriting. In all of the works discussed here, one can
identify a female ancestor (from Great-Aunt Cuney to Ma Jolie to
Da Duh to Gran' Aunt Anni) whose presence or absence evokes a
very specific identification and redefinition of the meaning of home.
They become specifically gendered ancestral links in terms of
knowledge of healing arts, survival skills for Caribbean women,
nurturing, re-membering.

As significant to the contradictory meaning of home are the
consistent departures between mother and daughter. This is also
represented by Michelle Cliff in a piece called "Separations," in
Claiming an Identity They Taught Me to Despise, in which the
emotional and physical gap between mother and daughter is
replayed: "we hold few memories in common: our connections are
limited by silences between us" (p. 33). Mother-daughter tensions

are right at the center of the rewriting of home. In any writing of home by women writers in patriarchal or matriarchal cultures, the challenge to the meaning of the mother attains symbolic importance in terms of definition and redefinition. And it is in this context that I would like to place the mother-daughter struggles which recur here.

★

Migration and the fluidity of movement which it suggests or the displacement and uprootedness which is often its result, is intrinsic to New World experience, fundamental to the meaning of the (African) diaspora. Rigid compartmentalizations based on geography and national identity, convenient for some critics and politicians, are rendered meaningless when confronted by many of these writers. Migration and exile are fundamental to human experience. And each movement demands another definition and redefinition of one's identity. One of the benefits of this Black feminist approach is a cutting across geographic boundaries in order to present a much more trans-cultural/trans-local awareness of Black women's writing communities. Beyond language, locale, genre, medium, we question what it is that creative Black women are saying everywhere. It becomes easier, then, to study Black women writers, outside of the male academic categories. On the part of the writers, this ongoing cross-examination is an identified reality. So, for those readers literate in various allied traditions, all sorts of connections can be made.

An important point of reference in charting the ambiguous relationship between the Caribbean-American woman writer and the United States, lies largely in that female migration to the United States documented by Dolores Mortimer and Bryce Laporte.[37] This was produced through labor migration, according to Sassen, a "transnational space within which the circulation of workers can be regarded as one of several flows, including capital, goods, services, and information."[38] In "For the Poets in the Kitchen," Paule Marshall makes explicit the relationship that these women had to American capitalism, on the one hand, and to their own creativity on the other.[39] Determined, hard-working women, primarily employed in service industries, struggled to make a way in great difficulty and without many of the support systems they could count on at home. This migration and their work produced daughters caught in between the cultural demands of home and the larger society, producing a profound multiplying of experiences and the construction of new identities, as my own personal biography attests. At times, there is no connection to the mother's place of origin; often it has to be relearned and reappreciated from a mature location. Always, there is little idealization of these mothers. Still presented with all their failings, they nevertheless remain heroic (sometimes anti-heroic). Caught on the borders between two culture areas, and between exile and home, movement and fixity, these daughters who nevertheless listened, evoke the landscape, food, people, stories of the Caribbean. Writing home means communicating with home. But it also means finding ways to express the conflicted meaning of home in the experience of the formerly colonized. It also demands a continual rewriting of the boundaries of what constitutes home.

6

MOBILITY, EMBODIMENT AND RESISTANCE

Black women's writing in the US

That's the freight train blues, I got box cars on my mind
I got the freight train blues, I got box cars on my mind
Gonna leave this town, cause my man is so unkind.[1]

Re-conceiving the theoretics of movement

The question of journeying in Black women's writing in the United States offers a variety of possible understandings of internal migrations, historical displacement, captivity and agency. The specific conditions of US slavery and the (im)possibility of escape, including the mythical meanings of the North and freedom, embedded movement in the consciousness of a variety of narratives and cultural products, from sorrow songs to jazz. The debate around slave narratives by men and by women, suggests that by adopting the paradigm of the male slave narrative, with physical flight and physical resistance often embedded textually, the specifics of women's resistance to slavery are often not addressed.[2] Valerie Smith would say (with Mary Helen Washington) that

> By mythologizing rugged individuality, physical strength, and geographical mobility, the narratives enshrine cultural definitions of masculinity. The plot of the standard narrative may thus be seen not only as the journey from slavery to freedom, but also as the journey from slavehood to manhood.[3]

In her early essay, "New Directions for Black Feminist Criticism,"[4] Deborah McDowell, like Claudia Tate, had asserted that though one can find the motif of the journey in Black male writers' works as well, it is often expressed differently, and his

130

journeys may take him physically underground or elsewhere, but for the Black female writer,

> journey, on the other hand, though at times touching the political and social, is basically a personal and psychological journey. The female character in the works of Black women is in a state of becoming 'part of an evolutionary spiral, moving from victimization to consciousness.'[5]

Claudia Tate would take this position further, asserting that "because of the restrictions placed on the black heroine's physical movement, she must conduct her quest within close boundaries," often within a room or within the borders of two nearby towns. Further, "her quest does not terminate with her arrival at a new destination; in fact she remains stationary. Her journey is an internal one and is seldom taken on land."[6] While McDowell's discussion identifies a number of representative texts like Alice Walker's *Meridian*, Toni Cade Bambara's *The Salt Eaters*, Zora Neale Hurston's *Their Eyes Were Watching God*, in which characters make internal journeys, she cautions in this very preliminary articulation of the issues of Black feminist criticism that we should be aware of generalizing based on too few examples.

It may be that this is where we are today, at that point of redefinition and a recognition of tentativeness. For the growing availability[7] of a variety of narratives and texts, with new ones being produced all the time in the "black woman's renaissance" as Braxton and McLaughlin would put it, is changing and will continue to change the examinations of Black female experience as it relates to mobility. This will require new and thorough examinations and retesting of a variety of hypotheses on the nature of Black (women's) writing. Further, advances in textual criticism are offering a variety of modes of reading these texts which changes some of the flat assumptions and meanings generated by new critical approaches.

For now, however, this particular chapter wants to assume tentativeness as it engages a variety of texts in which the questions of migration and agency are visible. In "On the Road Again. Metaphors of Travel in Cultural Criticism," Janet Wolff[8] examines recent theoretics on travel in order to pursue "the ideological gendering of travel," which she would suggest "both impedes female travel and renders problematic the self-definition of (and response to) women who *do* travel."[9] The point is that women *do travel*, and the issue is to find ways of understanding these negotiations of the road, since we do not all have "the same access to the road."

Georgia Douglas Johnson, for example, would title a poem "Escape," but write escape as protection:

> Shadows, shadows,
> Hug me round
> So that I shall not be found
> By sorrow:
> She pursues me
> Everywhere,
> I can't lose her
> Anywhere.[10]

Escape for Black women/men has necessarily involved the seeking out of protective spaces, or concealment at some points, as the logic of "underground railroad" implies and particularly the darkness of night during which time freedom/flight was often undertaken.

But any physical escape does entail physical movement, so distance may be more the issue than the contradiction of movement and containment. Clara Smith concludes her "Freight Train Blues" with the contradiction embedded in the lines:

> When a woman gets the blues, she goes to her room and
>   hides
> When a woman gets the blues, she goes to her room and
>   hides
> When a man gets the blues, he catches a freight train and
>   rides.[11]

The lyrics here suggest a closure which would seem to give men agency and movement and women containment. But, again, this is only a scribal version of an oral form. Blues songs, like most oral performance pieces, allow a variety of riffs and retellings in their improvisatory contexts and audience-oriented presentations. So meaning is not contained in fixed lyrics. Thus the rest of the song implies a great deal of desire for this movement only seemingly contained in the end by blocked access, the brakeman's "Clara, you know this train ain't mine."

This sense of the language of movement often being positioned as male, as Janet Wolff suggests, would seem to be validated in Houston Baker's discussion in *Blues, Ideology and Afro-American*

Literature. A Vernacular Theory.[12] Baker importantly concludes that "if one is dedicated to discovering such vernacular faces, one must acknowledge . . . that all fixed points are problematical" (p. 200). Further, "the 'placeless,' by contrast, are translators of the non-tradition . . . their lineage is fluid, nomadic, transitional" (p. 202). Baker would therefore employ the crossing sign as representation of movement rather than fixity.[13] Still, much of Baker's discussion at this point is particularly gendered, addressing primarily Black male subjectivity and agency. I find the entire text helpful, nevertheless, and in particular "To Move Without Moving," the examination of "Ellison's Trueblood Episode," an interesting disruption of the notions of mobility. But, again, physical mobility does not necessarily mean emotional growth or internal movement.

So, reading Baker's discourse on Black mobility and subjectivity against Daphne Harrison's work on women's blues, particularly the section "Wild Women Don't Have the Blues," offers ways of re-examining blues signs with the issues of gender specified. What is revealed is a series of versions of "travelling blues" with women having a great deal of agency in movement, sexuality and struggles to negotiate the various exploitative conditions they encountered. It is often suggested that women blues singers became a representation of freedom of mobility, while the other women seemed to be more "at home" or "left behind." Documentation of migration suggests, however, that escape and travel were not necessarily gendered, as in only men having access to the road. Clearly, if the meaning of Harriet Tubman's life is at all iconic, then the notion of a woman making multiple journeys back and forth in difficult situations has to stand for some form of agency and resistance. Hazel Carby, in "It Jus Be's Dat Way Sometime. The Sexual Politics of Women's Blues,"[14] speaks in "Movin on" of the mass migration from urban areas and cities of the North which forced a questioning of the imaginary version of "the people." She concludes that

> Men's and women's blues shared the language and experience
> of the railroad and migration but what that meant was differ-
> ent for each sex. The language of the blues carries this conflict
> of interests and is the cultural terrain in which these differ-
> ences were fought over and redefined.[15]

So we may need to look more closely at modes of migratory representations in a variety of cultural forms, cross-culturally, in order to understand the dynamics of mobility and agency. Daphne Harrison's work, together with Carby's and Baker's are important contributions to this discussion. What becomes clear from examining these discussions is that for women and for men, the struggle over the signs of captivity is consistently expressed in rejection of current conditions, physical and emotional movement, assertiveness and a variety of migrations to "elsewhere."

In a variety of Black women's texts in the United States, escape/flight/movement is embedded in various ways. A number of scholars would suggest, as Carby does in discussing *Quicksand*, that slave women who could not abandon their children had to forego escaping to freedom and the cities of the north. This point is often made with reference to Harriet Jacobs's *Incidents in the Life of a Slave Girl*,[16] in which the protagonist, Harriet Jacobs, escapes but remains in confinement in the attic of her grandmother's house so that she can watch, voyeur-like, her children and the community pass by. Valerie Smith shows how Jacobs "repeatedly . . . escapes overwhelming persecutions only by choosing her own space of confinement. . . ." As well, the confined space of the garret "renders the narrator spiritually independent of her master, and makes possible her ultimate escape to freedom."[17] Still, in the rest of the narrative, she undertakes a series of journeys which get less attention than her period of dramatic confinement. For example, she escapes in the classic conventions, using disguise, cross-dressing and so on. It is my assertion that the idea of the contained woman who does not migrate, and who primarily grows internally or makes emotional/mental journeys instead, is perhaps not as applicable to the Black woman in any generalized way. If, as the research shows, the meanings of situatedness of womanhood for white women did not necessarily apply to Black women,[18] then we need also to re-think the situation of mobility for Black women. Further, if we open up the category "Black woman," from its monolithic assumptions, then this identity may contain multiple narratives of confinement, but it could also leave room for other narratives of escape and agency. Similarly, the monolithic category "white woman," would have to be problematized with issues of class, origin and so on. If we continue to read Black women only as doubly contained because of the implications of race and gender oppression and therefore further distanced from the possibilities of flight, then whatever agency is implied in physical movement is too easily erased.

But since we know that Black women did travel and that they perhaps negotiated movement in different ways, we need to read escape/flight critically against a series of modalities – time, age, space, education, language, ability, family, location and so on.

The mark of motherhood is often ascribed to women's inability to travel. I want to look therefore more closely at two texts which address the issue of women being marked as mothers and as "enslaved" in order to readdress this issue of mobility and women. Since one of the impediments to women having the ability to travel is their children and/or societal constructions of biological motherhood, then it is important to examine how some of these conventions are either supported or rejected by some texts.

CAPTIVITIES: MOTHERHOOD, ENSLAVEMENT AND MOBILITY

The historical construction of the Black woman as the "great mother", negatively embedded in the "mammy" figure of Euro-American imagination, is confronted with practical realities of mothering in recent Black women's writing. As consumers of hegemonic popular and literary culture, we are recipients of these contradictory narratives of motherhood. But now, the selflessness of the "mammy" is positioned against or along with a series of deliberate self-constructions by Black women. Motherhood and/or mothering thus become central and defining tropes in Black female reconstruction. A conflicting set of possibilities have to be negotiated in reading African-American motherhood and this is the source of the beautiful-ugliness[19] of its presentation in Toni Morrison's *Beloved*.[20] I propose to read *Beloved*, one of the most deliberate problematizings of motherhood that I have encountered, against Sherley Anne Williams's *Dessa Rose*,[21] which subverts many of the societal constructions embedded in *Beloved*.

The theoretical implications of mothering for Black women are being advanced in a growing number of ways. Gloria Joseph's "Black Mothers and Daughters. Their Roles and Functions in American Society"[22] and Patricia Hill Collins's "The Meaning of Motherhood in Black Culture and Black Mother-Daughter Relationships,"[23] move beyond the solitary biological imperative to a notion of shared responsibility for caring. Examinations of Black womanhood have also pursued the meaning of motherhood. For example, Hazel Carby, in *Reconstructing Womanhood*,[24]

identifies how "within the discourse of the cult of true womanhood, wifehood and motherhood were glorified as the 'purpose of a
woman's being' . . . ." Sojourner Truth's "Ain't I a Woman"
speech (1852)[25] had asserted her specific experience of womanhood,
which included motherhood but also motherhood as loss and
thereby a critique of the experience assumed for white women: "I
have born thirteen children and seen most all sold into slavery and
when I cried out a mother's grief, none but Jesus heard me."[26]

Black women defined in opposition to the terms of motherhood
accorded to white women, and with a different set of historical
realities, developed their own discourse of womanhood. This is
addressed, at a certain level, in "Mothering and Healing in Recent
Black Women's Fiction,"[27] in which I identified a cluster of novels
in which the mother construct seemed to be foregrounded and
linked to the social and emotional reconstitution of Black women
in their communities. Further reflection on the literary history of
Black women writers – from Harriet Wilson's *Our Nig* (1859)[28] to
Alice Walker's *The Temple of My Familiar*[29] – reveals that reconstructions of mothering have been continuous. For, when explored
in relation to motherhood in African societies and when examined
in materialist/feminist contexts which read-in the exploitative
nature of motherhood in male-dominated societies, the rewriting
of "mammy" offers its own theoretical excursions.

In a 1985 conversation with Gloria Naylor,[30] Morrison identifies
the project which has dominated her own imaginative world as
bringing to life the "dead girl," the Black girl that society has willed
out of existence. For Morrison, this ongoing literary reconstruction
of Black female identity has been part excavation, part recreation,
"rescuing her from the grave of time and inattention . . . bringing
her back into living life" (p. 593). Clearly, Morrison uses her
creative writing as a way of engaging a variety of theoretical issues
concerning friendship, mothering, history, family, including tensions between community and individual. She says, for example, in
discussing *Beloved*, that she was trying to find a channel for the
negotiating which women have to do, between the imperatives of
nurture/love for its own sake and the desire to be a complete
individual. As well, she was looking at the ease with which women
sabotage these efforts.[31]

Beloved, in my view, simultaneously critiques exclusive mother-
love as it asserts the necessity for Black women to claim something
as theirs. It is a work which resists single, unitary, laudatory

readings. The text, therefore, speaks double-voicedly to those twin imperatives, each position continuously subverting the other. It speaks multiply, answering the meaning and practices of mothering, voicing the positions of daughters, grandmothers, fathers, male friends, neighbors, community and, of course, the mother herself. Sethe's action is measured and weighed against *numerous atrocities and destructions* and the possible responses to them. The text, therefore, deliberately centers the historical fact that there were Black women during slavery who terminated their babies' lives rather than allow them to be offered up to the destruction of slavery. Morrison clearly does not bring a singular position to this issue; rather, she poses several arguments. In other words, the specter of Beloved, the living embodiment of Sethe's mother love and the painful past of enslavement she represents, never is really destroyed. Instead, it dissolves into the mythology and the history of the community. Read as Morrison's bringing to life of "the dead girl," then perhaps she will manifest herself elsewhere. Issues of reading and writing in the making of the text are importantly implicated in *Beloved*. This work demands that the reader hold open a range of possibilities. An unquestioning endorsement of Sethe's action cannot reveal the text's complexity. This reading of Black motherhood and its representation also speaks to the need for feminists to racialize and historicize their definitions of motherhood. Questions of "maternal splitting" (Suleiman) and "maternal thinking" (Ruddick) and critiques of the "perfect mother" (Chodorow and Contratto)[32] become empty and limited understandings if they do not configure the issues of race and history.

MARKING, BODY AND THE "ABIKU" CHILD

In "Motherhood. The Annihilation of Women,"[33] Jeffner Allen sees child-bearing as a definite "marking" or "stamping" of women. In this perspective, "the mark of motherhood" inscribes the domination of men into women's bodies:

> Stamped, firmly imprinted on women's bodies, is the emblem that our bodies have been opened to the world of men: the shape of the pregnant woman's stomach. From conception to abortion, acts which are biologically different and yet symbolically the same, our stomachs are marked MOTHER.
>
> (p. 322)

Hortense Spillers, in an essay appropriately titled "Mama's Baby, Papa's Maybe. An American Grammar Book,"[34] identifies the Black female body as the site of a series of visible markings, mutilations, distortions and violations during the period of slavery. Being an African at that historical juncture was to be marked for enslavement and physically lacerated against resistance. The enslaved African woman, with child, has to be seen then as multiply marked. It is important to make some distinctions between "marking" and "naming" (re-marking) as used here. "Marking" is the product of abuse and is linked to societal inscriptions on the body of the "other." Naming or (or re-marking) has to do with redefinition. In *Beloved* and *Dessa Rose*, the visibility or invisibility of marking has multiple significations.

All of these multilayered markings of the Black female body in *Beloved* create their own independent textualities. Sethe is physically marked, a marking which exudes blood and later scarring. The evidence of physical brutality which is this marking is identified as a "chokecherry" tree by Amy Denver (p. 79) and by Sethe herself, as the decorative work of an ironsmith too passionate for display by Paul D and as a revolting clump of scars, also by Paul D. Sethe, then, is a marked woman, marked physically by abuse, pregnancy, motherhood and other societal inscriptions by white female, by Black male and by the white male inflicter of the abuse which marks her initially. The marking which is reidentified as the branches of a tree itself sometimes resonates as life, with myriad reference points. For when looked at differently it also becomes the signifier for captivity.

The marking is also indicated, following Jeffner Allen, in the physicality of child-bearing, a marking which similarly produces visible, physical results and bodily products. One correlative of racial marking, then, for people in racially stratified societies, is child-bearing for women in male-dominated societies. Motherhood becomes, literally, embodiment – in both cases the body as *read* text. One has to read Sethe, as a particular Black woman, as the concentration of female identity, not as its aberration. Sethe is the convergence of these multiple bodily markings: "Sethe could not move. She couldn't lie on her stomach or her back, and to keep on her side meant pressure on her screaming feet."[35]

The feet, for the slave, are the ultimate agents of flight, but here, because of their swollen condition, caused by pregnancy, they take her only a part of the way. Sethe's body is represented as multiply captive. And, significantly, while she can flee slavery, she cannot flee motherhood or the body that has been captured by the needs of her children. That Morrison is using marking as a multiple signifier of captivity is indicated in an encounter that Sethe recalls between herself and the woman identified as her mother who had been denied physical contact with her child because of the demands of slave labor. One day she showed Sethe her "mark."[36]

It is important that in the end the mother's self-identification is erased by the mutilation of slavery. Deliberate self-marking as is seen in African scarifications, one thesis holds, was engaged in during the period of slave trafficking, in order to inscribe ethnic identities on faces and bodies.

The notion of marking is carried over to the child Beloved and the way she is marked by Sethe like the legendary *abiku*[37] children of Yoruba cosmology or the *ogbanje* in Igbo culture, who die and are reborn repeatedly to plague their mothers and are marked so that they can be identified when they return. The marks of the saw on Beloved's neck[38] become the one visible sign to Denver and subsequently to Sethe that this is the physical manifestation of the dead child. Beloved then functions as an *abiku* to Sethe, and to author and reader in the "coming to life of the dead girl." The *abiku* concept provides another strategy for reading *Beloved*. Sethe's violent action becomes an attempt to hold on to the maternal right and function. In a society in which the Black mother's rights and existence are already delimited, Sethe's persistent desire is to bring *her* milk to *her* children. In the face of that inability and the possibility of returning to the debased status and captivity she had left, she says, "I stopped him . . . I took and put my babies where they'd be safe."[39] Sethe, as an African–American mother in and out of bondage, becomes the fictional embodiment of Spillers's theoretical assertion:

> The African–American woman, the mother, the daughter becomes the powerful and shadowy evocation of a cultural synthesis long evaporated – the law of the Mother – [so that] . . . 1) motherhood as female bloodrite is outraged, is denied at the very same time that it becomes the founding term of a human and social enactment; 2) a dual fatherhood is set in motion, comprised of the African father's banished name and

body and the captor father's mocking presence. In this play of paradox, only the female stands in the flesh, both mother and mother-dispossessed.[40]

The horror of Sethe's central act then resides within this social construction. Sethe is a marked daughter of a marked mother, who herself had appropriated the "law of the Mother" by deciding to let Sethe (the only child that was conceived with some aspect of participation) live. Sethe herself acquiesces in the only legality which the society paradoxically imposes. The two women, like Baby Suggs, stand as both "mother and mother-dispossessed." I am arguing nevertheless that the African-American mother does not stand outside of traditional symbolics of gender, as Spillers concludes. Instead, she becomes the most clarifying representation of society's expectations and contradictions surrounding gender.

There is no abandonment of the tensions of gender identification in *Beloved*. Amy Denver's role in Sethe's difficult delivery of her child is representative of the paradoxical separations and commonalities among women. The child of an indentured servant and a victim of abuse attains a parallel dispossession. Her journey is in search of some softness, some velvet, the North (p. 80). There is an intertextual relationship between *Our Nig* and *Beloved*, then, in the construction of the white female without the protection of the patriarchal power. Amy Denver massages Sethe's legs and reads and renames her marking so that it suggests life and not death, though the fact that Amy is not relieved of her racial baggage is seen in her casual acceptance of racial constructions and difference. Nevertheless, in a society stratified along race, class and gender lines, the narrator asserts, there are a lot of "throw-away people" and, while a "slave and a barefoot whitewoman with unpinned hair" (p. 85) may form a temporary alliance around the need to give birth, inevitably they take divergent paths to freedom. It is significant, then, that Sethe had run away while pregnant and had sent another child ahead of her. Thus, her giving birth on the way provides the semiotic linkage of the child with travelling/flight or existence in between bounded spaces, and therefore rewrites the notion of limited spaces because of mothering.

Marking, re-marking and their links to slavery and motherhood similarly inform Sherley Anne Williams's *Dessa Rose*. Here the tendency toward total immolation, seen in *Beloved*, is completely

destabilized. In fact, the entire text articulates the subversive potential in each oppressive situation. Nehemiah sees "the darky's pregnancy as a stroke of luck" (p. 29), allowing him increased access to
information through her containment. Dessa uses her pregnancy
to her benefit, to stay her impending execution and gain for herself
the space and time to defy all expectations, particularly to escape
on the verge of childbirth. All of his attempts to write her existence
are foiled. Instead, she persistently inserts *her story* and her child
conceived out of her love for Kaine into his text. Throughout,
she offers her double-coded oral narratives, songs, gestures and
(re-)markings, which he cannot decipher (pp. 29, 40–41).

Significantly, Dessa, with childbirth imminent, escapes through
the coded messages in the song. Earlier she had rejected the idea
that a pregnant woman could not lead a slave rebellion. Marking,
the physical scarring of the body, and the marking of childbirth are
present but are renamed or erased at every turn. A variety of textual
strategies of resistance and reversal organize this novel. For
example, the erasure of Dessa's marking in this text is the point of
final liberation. The old Black woman called in to identify Dessa's
scars (which would have ensured her return to enslavement) calls
out: "I ain't seed nothing on this gal's butt. She ain't got a scar on
her back" (p. 231). Williams also permits Dessa a great deal of
physical mobility. Through a series of confidence tricks and multiple journeys, she and Rufel and the others in their community
engage in challenges to the located meanings of racial and gender
identities. Still, in the end, they go in multiple directions.

Deborah McDowell, in her study "Negotiating Between Tenses.
Witnessing Slavery After Freedom – Dessa Rose,"[41] shows how
the text destabilizes and resists a series of misnamings and mis-
representations. In fact, McDowell concludes that Dessa has
"avoided public exposure as fiercely as she has hidden her bodily
scars. . . . Here, Dessa's body is her text and owning it, she owns
the rights to it" (p. 154). Thus a link is made between Dessa's
ownership of her body and her control of her own story and its
writing.

Two distinct reconstructions are offered. Both novels are
grounded in historical record: *Beloved* in the Margaret Garner
story[42] and *Dessa Rose* in the story of a woman who led a slave
rebellion.[43] But, in my view, *Beloved* is more in the tradition of the
protest novel, recalling atrocities in order to challenge the vicious-
ness of oppression and explain racist practices which survive. (I am

using James Baldwin's critique of the protest novel for accepting white society's denial of humanity.) The text essentially implies that slavery and racism wiped out resistance except at a very personal level. It offers a community which censures the mother after not coming to her aid. Baby Suggs, the mother-healer, gives up all ability to resist and confines herself to bed in philosophical explorations of the meaning of color – a valid response, perhaps, but definitely not empowering.

The position on mothering in *Dessa Rose* validates some of Patricia Hill Collins's conceptions of motherhood (for example, as power) in African-American communities in "The Meaning of Motherhood,"[44] but it also resists them. The community of ex-slaves is organized for its liberation. Since the entire text seems to be constructed to identify perpetual resistance to enslavement, at personal and communal levels, then, within these boundaries, mothering is more liberatory than "motherhood" in *Beloved*. Still, it is necessary to hold open the other side of the argument and restate that mothering is not always power, it can also be destruction for many women. Its very definition in patriarchal culture provides a complex mixture of meanings, ranging from annihilation, to creation, to changing given statuses. Audre Lorde, in "Man Child. A Black Lesbian Feminist Response,"[45] sees raising Black children "in the mouth of a racist, sexist, suicidal dragon as perilous and chancy" (p. 74). Yet mothers must teach children to love and to resist simultaneously. Mothering for Lorde is a cooperative venture which allows the formation of a variety of new and healthy responses to the world. Williams's rewriting of mothering is more in line with the Lorde formulation. A variety of reversals in the mothering function are effected. This strategy allows a greater degree of journeying between patriarchal conceptions of motherhood and women-defined patterns of mothering, in and out of its biological mandates and social constructs.

BREASTS, MILK AND BLOOD

Breast-feeding, as a reference to biological motherhood and maternal identification and nurturing, is central in the two texts being examined here. True to its consistent subversion of the societal limitations of motherhood (as an institution), *Dessa Rose* reaches for a definite disalignment of biological motherhood (as experience) from non-biological mothering. In a definite reversal of the arrangement in Euro-American slave societies, where the Black woman historically served as wet-nurse, Rufel, much to Dessa's consternation, breast-feeds Dessa's baby along with hers: "The white woman, her shoulder still bare, the curly black head and brown face of a new baby nestled at her breast, faced her now" (p. 88). Breast-feeding, as Williams poses it, is an expression of responsibility for raising the children and is not assigned racially in *Dessa Rose*. Dessa and Rufel consistently exchange maternal functions, depending on need. Rufel as white female, a more developed version of Amy Denver of *Beloved*, grows consistently in the process of her interactions with the marooned African-American community. It is a characterization, however, that is not without its contradictions. Rufel has to learn, for example, the true identity of the woman she identified as "Mammy"; "the comfortable, comforting image of Mammy" (p. 147), which she held, had to be destroyed. The white woman, oblivious to her status as simultaneously privileged because of race and subordinate because of gender, has to recognize herself and others. Beyond that, the reified, monolithic, socially constructed "whitewoman" is dismantled by Dessa and the community in a series of symbolic acts. The structure of slave society, held in place by its characterization of the white woman, is decentered in a series of unmaskings which begin when Rufel breast-feeds Dessa's baby.

In this context, it is important to de-romanticize the symbolics of milk in the construction of motherhood. Anna Davin, in "Imperialism and Motherhood,"[46] shows how – in a series of manipulations of state apparatuses – white women were instructed in maternalism as a means of maintaining Empire. Racist assumptions were allied to class and gender discourses on motherhood. Similarly, Spivak's translation of Mahasweta Devi's "Breast Giver"[47] and her Marxist-feminist analysis of milk and motherhood in "A Literary Representation of the Subaltern. A Woman's Text from the Third World,"[48] help elucidate the textual emphasis on milk and breasts in the construction of motherhood. Inserting the "free/domestic" labor provided by women, Spivak argues,

> The milk that is produced in one's own body for one's own children is a use-value. When there is a superfluity of use values, exchange values arise. That which cannot be used is exchanged. As soon as the (exchange) value of Jashoda's milk emerges it is appropriated.[49]

She goes on to make a number of assertions about the idealization of the products of a woman's body and identifies how the erasure of gender in Marxist analyses allows this product of women's bodies to escape specific constructions of labor.

This allows us to problematize more definitively textual references to "milk" as a signifier for motherhood, breast-feeding as containment for women. This is particularly important given that poor/Black women's milk and breasts were appropriated in order to raise healthy white upper-class children. As well, Black women, in and out of slavery, often did not have the luxury of caring for their own children. Reaching for the complex economic and social meanings of "milk" and "breasts," Morrison offers a variety of associations with motherhood in exploitative contexts. The core response of Sethe in *Beloved* is to the appropriation of her milk, and therefore to her reduction to animal status that is entailed in appropriated motherhood (clearly "schoolteacher's" intent in his research measurings). Sethe's assertion throughout the text is that she was trying to get her milk to her children and, paradoxically and uncritically, that she had milk for *all*.

Angela Davis has identified the critical gaps in scholarship around the abuses of women in slavery:

> The designation of the black woman as a matriarch is a cruel misnomer. It is a misnomer because it implies stable kinship structures within which the mother exercises authority. It is cruel because it ignores the profound traumas the black woman must have experienced when she had to surrender her child-bearing to alien and predatory economic interests.[50]

So, it is around issues of milk, breasts and bloodlines that Sethe is complexly caught. Her response to the exploitation of the material products of her body leads her to a process of holding on, which cannot allow cooperative care-giving as it does in *Dessa Rose* or in the Lorde formulation.

This is where, in my estimation, a critique of the text's unfolding on the issue of maternity is valid. Morrison fails to overturn the symbolics of breasts. The alignment of cows (with all the associations of milk-giving) with women in *Beloved* speaks eloquently to this issue. In the absence of women, the narrator asserts, the Sweet Home men were "fucking cows," "taken to calves" (pp. 10–11). Beginning when Sethe allows Paul D the responsibility for her breasts, Morrison fails to free them from their negative and exploitative representations. Morrison, it seems, in reaching for what Mary Helen Washington identifies as the "romantic text" and Deborah McDowell as the "family romance,"[51] shifts the responsibility for Sethe's final empowerment away from Sethe herself and her daughters and leaves it to Paul D to define in the final "Me? Me?" which Sethe is allowed in the text.

Marianne Hirsch's reading in *The Mother/Daughter Plot*[52] sees the questions ("Me? Me?") as the beginnings of (or openings for) the construction of beyond her identity as a mother. In particular, Paul D, who knew her before she was so over-determined by her status as mother, allows her to liberate her story. However, what is installed in the process is heterosexual dominance, the woman operating without a certain clarity and agency in creating her own subjectivity and therefore about how she came to be so contained by situations, and so marked as mother.

The link of milk to blood to ink in both texts provides a series of associations that have to do with mothering and writing. Each text, in its way, engages with, affirms, subverts, challenges or decenters the boundaries of motherhood which keep sex/gender or racial systems in place and so women from travelling.

This approach has been more to problematize the mother rather than to romanticize her, and thereby to examine the issues of subjectivity that constrain mobility or liberate the Black female subject to travel. This problematizing has included a necessary removal of mothering from its biological mandates, which in turn empowers women's migratory potential. This is made quite clear in the various migrations of children and mothers from urban to rural areas as identified in Maya Angelou's *I Know Why the Caged Bird Sings*,[53] for example.

There has been, it seems, a need in Black cultures to affirm Black motherhood and/or to construct an essentialized, "outraged"[54] mother as a strategic response to racist constructs. Strategically valid on some fronts, on others this affirmation becomes too defining and limiting for women. Even a radical suggestion in Black mother theory that women mother cooperatively assumes that all African-American women want to participate in this activity.

The attempt to construct Sethe as resisting mother is highly charged, but also problematic. We identify with her attempt to resist the appropriation of her body and its products for the slave-holding class's benefit. But her mother-love is definitely "too thick," as Paul D says, because it too fully accepts the given paradigm of motherhood as exclusive responsibility of the biological mother. But how do we account for this "thickness" during a slave period designed to deny any family bonding? Spillers's position is legitimately recalled here. A slave mother is not supposed to demonstrate deep love for her children. Sethe defies that injunction. Yet her heroic response to enslavement paradoxically becomes the kind of mother-love which the society enforces for women. Sethe shuttles back and forth between enslavements and constraints, exchanging one for the other, unable to be freed from both at once. The unity of preservation, growth and acceptability, posited by Ruddick's maternal thinking, is rejected in Sethe's action. She defines preservation as taking her children out of the reaches of the slave-holding system. But, paradoxically, in her situation this means that she has to function as their executioner, effecting the opposite of growth. Denver, finally, is able to break out of the narrowly-defined, self-destructive circle of family relationships of house No. 124. One can read the entire narrative as Denver's reading of Sethe's stifling mother-love. Denver moves back a generation as she recalls her grandmother Baby Suggs's voice, and then forward as she allows the community to participate in nurturing her family and dismantling exclusive motherhood. Importantly, Denver makes her link to the community through writing, which she had learned from the Black woman teacher, as well as by reading the notes left with the food. Denver, as resisting daughter, writes herself out of this limiting construction.

Psychoanalytic readings of *Beloved* actualize theories of the child in the mirror stage. Although adult, Beloved's needs are for oral gratification and the locking-in of the mother's gaze. We can also see how desire drives the text. The women of the house had willed Beloved's presence as much as Beloved had willed herself to return. In a more discursive reading, of the return of the ghost of the past, the narrative becomes the ritualistic act which stays the returning of the *abiku*, the "return of the repressed." The African mythological pretext may offer a more textured understanding, a sign of the mother possessed and dispossessed, than the vaporous context of the Western ghost. Beloved therefore cannot be fully "re-membered" or brought into flesh and sustained in present form. In Yoruba cosmology, the *abiku* child eventually stays, when certain rituals and necessary passages have been accomplished. But the *abiku* can also be read as the woman haunted by societal demands that she be a mother.

Rather than adopting an open and single critique of a society which creates such violence, *Beloved* also engages the internal narrative, the meanings which create specific responses: "I had to deal with this nurturing instinct that expressed itself in murder," Morrison says.[55] Tensions, then, exist around struggles to tell a difficult story; to place on record those things silenced or repressed, such as problematical responses to motherhood; to speak the "unspeakable."

Providing a differently textured strand in this continuing discourse on mothering, *Dessa Rose* ends with her writing/righting her own story for her grandchildren and allowing Dessa a great deal of mobility. As she braids their hair, another non-scribal way of storytelling, she maintains history. She also ensures that the children know the story and that it is written down and then "re-oralized." Her articulations at closure are much more empowering gestures, with more human agency, than is Sethe's. The move from being the-mother-as-she-is-written to being the-mother-as-she-writes is one of the text's most radical strategies. She becomes the speaking Subject, while the authorial or narrating "I" is submerged. The re-oralizing move also decenters the text's narrative control.

LONG DISTANCES AND MOVING THROUGH HOMES

A variety of newer texts are dealing in interesting ways with issues of migratory subjectivities. Marita Golden's *Long Distance Life* is a narrative of an old Black woman who had left a rural home and secure but boring marriage to make a new life in Washington, DC on her own. Finding her 1920s, Southern, small-town existence too limiting (and significantly after the crib death of her infant daughter), she propels herself outward in search of a more fulfilling life "elsewhere." Letters from her cousin Cora who had "written home" provide the space for the imagination of a different life: "Cora had wrote me in one of her letters that soon as she got on the train to leave North Carolina she felt free. Said she felt like she was being born all over again" (p. 33). But "home" has special significance and when Naomi is about to have her second child, she returns there:

> When I got pregnant, then I had everything I'd always wanted. I went back home to Spring Hope to have my baby. Back then, no matter where you lived – in New York, Chicago, Philadelphia, wherever – home was where you come from, and it was natural to go home to do something as important as having your child.[56]

Both Naomi and her daughter Esther struggle with the dialectics of home and the migratory meanings of placement and identity, Esther finally rejecting many of the understandings of her mother's home. Esther later returns South for political involvement in much the same way as Meridian of Alice Walker's work[57] of the same name makes a trans-South journey of education, politics and involvement. Marita Golden had tackled another trans-cultural, transnational migration in her first and autobiographical novel, *Migrations of the Heart*,[58] in which she, a young African-American woman, had married and migrated to Nigeria, attempting to negotiate a different cultural location and eventually had given up an untenable situation to return home. This text can also be read intertextually with Marshall's *Daughters*, addressing the dynamics of Estelle's move to the Caribbean as wife. Migration as wife, a number of texts such as *Juletane*[59] have shown, does not carry power in cross-cultural contexts. After a number of difficult marital scenarios which had produced an untenable situation, the narrator in *Migrations of the Heart* returns to the US. Interestingly, a series of conversations which she had with other African-American women living in Africa produce a version of an "underground railroad" from wifehood. Nevertheless, this migratory process clarifies the various subject positions – African, African-American, woman, African-American woman, migrant – which are often overlooked in cross-cultural re-connections.

The notion of travelling women is not as obscure in African-American women's fiction as it may seem on the surface. Morrison's several novels all are embedded with tropes of movement. In an earlier work, "Black Woman's Journey into Self,"[60] I addressed the ways in which Marshall employs the journey theme in *Praisesong*. In a variety of the Marshall works, the sense of physical and ideological examinations of identities is always posed.[61] In Morrison's earlier work, a series of departures and returns are important textual references in the characters' lives. *Song of Solomon*, for example, has Pilate making the journey South for reclamation and flight. Earlier, she had posed her as a migrant figure who sojourned elsewhere before being located in that community. Similarly, Sula's[62] journeys take place outside the specific narrative moment of the text but have a lot to do with her self-definitions and her pariah relationship to the community. And *Tar Baby*[63] deals with the transnational, Jadine, a contemporary model figure moving between the United States, the Caribbean and Europe, yet having to come to terms with various cultural locations and meanings.

Perhaps the strongest statement of a "migratory subjectivity" is expressed in Janie in Hurston's *Their Eyes Were Watching God*. Janie travels south to Eatonville with Jody and then further south with Tea Cake to the Florida Everglades. Her grandmother's text is also one which describes escape with her infant daughter, Leafy, hiding in swampy places in the dark, and then coming out and getting on the road to join the now free African-Americans migrating to places of re-connection: "So Ah got with some good white people and come down here in West Florida to work and make de sun shine on both sides of the street for Leafy."[64] Gates and roads are important tropes of movement in *Their Eyes Were Watching God*. One early image is of Janie as she "hung over the gate and looked up the road towards way off."[65] In Hurston the South to North journey is reversed as Janie develops her subjectivity and agency in migrancy and redefinition. But she returns home alone and to a different sense of space, a newly redefined home which bell hooks would argue,[66] in "Zora Neale Hurston. A Subversive Reading," is a new site for the imaginative: "interiority is not depicted as a space of closure. It is not restrictive or confining. Janie opens windows letting in air and light. Transformed interior space is expansive."[67] The sense of homeplace that hooks identified as a necessary place of recognition, healing and resistance, is applicable here. But there are other understandings. We may also want to look at how Barbara Smith, in her introduction to *Homegirls*,[68] speaks of the meaning of home. In the definition of "homegirls," she identifies that home for her was a secure place of learning and growth precisely because it was a woman-centered space which nurtured. But, she is also conscious that everyone's home does not offer the same ease. When she travels South to her grandmother's home she is nevertheless impressed with the grandeur of the landscape as she is conscious of the racial and economic inequities which forced her grandmother to travel to the North. One gesture which captures the migratory meaning of home is in her taking a piece of the red Southern soil to carry with her on her own wanderings. A variety of helpful explorations of the many meanings of being "not-at-home" in the United States are expressed in June Jordan's *Technical Difficulties*,[69] in which discussions range from the meanings of family, to displacement, sexuality, war, anger, motherhood, racism, democracy and American dreamings.

The migration between historical locations and consciousness is effected well in Octavia Butler's *Kindred*.[70] Employing the science fiction mode,[71] Butler has her character make large journeys of time and into slavery to understand and experience how the past affected the future. It becomes in a way a kind of reverse journey to the one effected by Beloved, who comes from the past into the future and also crosses corporeal boundaries. The issues of body, space, meaning and mobility are captured well in the text's closure where Dana comes back into the present, scarred and minus an arm: "I touched the scar Tom Weylin's boot had left on my face, touched my empty sleeve" (p. 264).

The questions of movement and migratory subjectivities and captivities are all interlinked in any consideration of African-American women's writing in the US. For example, novels of "passing" can be read within the context of migratory positionalities that have to do with identity and race and personal politics in conjunction with racially oppressive hegemonies.[72] For passing exists on a variety of levels ranging from the physical to the psychological. This opens, I propose, interesting ways to re-engage a host of texts and confront new ones. For it is not just the physical movement, but the ways through which various subject positions are negotiated. In all of this, I am asserting much more mobility for Black women and in Black women's texts than is often assumed.

Joyce Hope Scott has an interesting essay which takes off from Houston Baker's notion of commercial deportation to explore this issue as a trope in Black women's writing. In it she defines the migration to the North within the context of "commercial deportation" and the economics of the American version of chattel slavery.[73] Chinosole, in "Audre Lorde and Matrilineal Diaspora. Moving History Beyond Nightmare Into Structures for the Future,"[74] uses Lorde's words to speak to the "internalized conflict created by being caught between cultures inside and outside the United States." Chinosole's "matrilineal diaspora" concept is "the capacity to survive and aspire, to be contrary and self-affirming

across continents and generations."[75] It is with a consciousness of
the various external and internal migrations, personal and social,
that have already taken place and still have to be approached that
this understanding of the notions of travelling in Black women's
literature in the United States is reconsidered.

A fitting circularity, with difference, concludes this examination
with the words of Black women rappers who operate in a mode of
uprising textualities identified earlier. Cheryl Keyes, in "'We're
More Than a Novelty, Boys.' Strategies of Female Rappers in the
Rap Music Tradition," cites Sparky Dee's lines which are a fitting
counterpoint to the blues line with which I began: "I don't sound
soft at all. I'm hard/I wake up and I go [hard] hello. . . ."[76]
Similarly, M.C. Lady "D" says, in a sense echoing Maya Angelou's
"Still I Rise" poem,

> Women are rising
> We've finally hit our stride
> It's not surprising we're rolling in like tide
> We're talking peace we're talkin' unified
> All to the beat of a new black pride
> We're talkin' loud
> 'cause we've found our voices
> We're walkin' proud
> makin' positive choices
> we're hittin' hard oppression is no joke
> 'Cause in the words
> That Sojourner Truth spoke
> Ain't I woman too even if I'm strong
> In the '90's I shouldn't
> haveta sing this song. . . .[77]

7

OTHER TONGUES

Gender, language, sexuality and the politics of location

It's not everything you can talk, but . . .

"*It's not everything you can talk*," the Caribbean women of my childhood would say even as they expressed their feelings around difficult life situations. My godmother would bustle in from a distant town, knowing that in our female-centered household there was space to cry, to talk about difficult marital situations, about having made a terrible choice of a mate, that there was no possible way of leaving with seven children or leaving seven children with an abusive, alcoholic husband. "*It's not everything you can talk, Maccomay,*[1] *but* . . ." became a formula or a code for talk even as it negated complete expression of feelings and of pain. The placement of the conjunction, "but," after the negation of the possibility of full speech signalled a determination to articulate, to challenge, to reveal, to share. For the word *but* is more than a conjunction, it is also a subtle mark of opposition.

The statement "*it's not everything you can talk*," locates the ways in which speech for the dispossessed is received, for it also identifies its opposite: it's not everything people will hear. The ways in which certain forms of speech are erased, the way in which the "rational discourse" of the dominant culture (as in senate speech or parliamentary language) reverses itself, expropriates certain forms of speech, discredits critical speech for political necessity. "*It's not everything you can talk*" is the pretext of Spivak's assertion on the impossibility of the subaltern woman's speech to be fully articulated or represented given all the already embedded constructions and "spoken-fors." Yet the full version, "*It's not everything you can talk, . . .*" with the ellipsis, challenges that very construction of non-speech.[2] Instead it recognizes safe spaces where Black woman's speech can be heard. A certain kind of opposition and reopening is represented in the conjunction "but" and the elliptical space that signals the speech outside of the closure suggested by "*It's not everything you can talk*." It is this "excess," the "supplement," the "left-over" that is always there that I want to activate in my understanding of "other tongues." It is also the contradiction embedded in the very formulation of the sentence that I want to address, feeling already that in the desire to do so, the possibility escapes me. I would want to assert unequivocally, however, that what in the mainstream culture is deployed as the definition of specific identities has no meaning until the "other tongues" have spoken. "Meaning continues to unfold, so to speak, beyond the arbitrary closure" Stuart Hall asserts in an insightful discussion.[3]

It is this tension between articulation and aphasia, between the limitations of spoken language and the possibility of expression, between space for certain forms of talk, and lack of space for Black women's speech, the location between the public and the private, that some Black women writers address. My titling of these assertions of speech, between the speaking and not-speaking space, as "other tongues" locates speech within the context of gender, identity, sexuality and the politics of location. For it is location which allows one to speak or not speak, to be affirmed in one's speech or rejected, to be heard or censored.

The politics of location brings forward a whole host of identifications and associations around concepts of place, placement, displacement; location, dis-location; memberment, dis-memberment; citizenship, alienness; boundaries, barriers, transportations; peripheries, cores and centers. It is about positionality in geographic, historical, social, economic, educational terms. It is about positionality in society based on class, gender, sexuality, age, income. It is also about relationality and the ways in which one is able to access, mediate or reposition oneself, or pass into other spaces given certain other circumstances.

Audre Lorde, for example, identifies the "mythical norm" in society which assigns authority to certain people based on certain qualities that Euro-American society gives value to, i.e., one is valued if one is white, thin, male, young, heterosexual, Christian and financially secure. Yet, we already know that each of these categories of authority can be destabilized, or enhanced, by an oppositional positioning, i.e., one has less value if one is fat, Black,

153

female, old, homosexual, etc. We are therefore talking of one's physical and social space, but also the oppositions embedded in each identity when we talk of positionality or location. Following Lorde a bit further,

> Those of us who stand outside that power often identify one way in which we are different, and we assume that to be the primary cause of all oppression, forgetting other distortions around difference, some of which we ourselves may be practising.[4]

One's location may therefore be a site of creativity and re-memory; exploration, challenge, instability. Or it may be a site of further repression. But positionality assumes not necessarily fixity, but movement: "there is no fixed subject except by repression."[5] Trinh Minh-ha talks as well of "re-departure: the pain and the frustration of having to live a difference that has no name and too many names already."[6]

Trans-lations, trans-locations, trans-formations, migrations are also implicated as resistance to fixity. In Stuart Hall's words, "boundaries of difference are continually repositioned in relation to different points of reference"[7] – place, time, history, different questions. Further, even among the "marginal, the under-developed, the periphery, the 'Other' . . . we do not stand in the same relation of 'otherness' to the metropolitan centres. Each has negotiated its economic, political and cultural dependency differ-ently."[8] Examination of the whole process of location as re-creation allows us to identify sites of resistance. The interesting thinking which is taking place on the "politics of location" provides the space for developing new theoretical approaches which chal-lenge traditional verities, methodologies, assumptions, arguments. Thus they expand the epistemological bases which have limited our ability to explore the cultural texts in which we are implicated. These in turn produce what can be identified as a "new space, an area of transformation and change where we can no longer accept a factual or natural account of history and culture, nor simply seek to retrieve a hidden authentic identity." Further, we can "begin to unravel the ordering and structuring of dominant cultural codes so that we may better utilize the locations we occupy as sites of resistance – spaces where critical positioning, or a process of identi-fication, articulation and representation can occur."[9]

bell hooks asserts "a radical standpoint, perspective position. The

politics of location necessarily calls those of us who would participate in the formation of counter-hegemonic practice to identify the
spaces where we begin the process of revision."[10] It is in this
context of resistance that I examine the works of two women
writers, Marlene Philip and Jamaica Kincaid, who challenge
definitions of space and location by their writing presence. I
propose to work with two basic formulations of language:
first, Demythologizing the Power of the Tongue; and, second,
Repositioning of Women in/and Language. These writers offer
ways of resisting the "othering" and "silencing" installed in the
dominant discourses.

DEMYTHOLOGIZING THE POWER OF THE TONGUE

> Ah don't mean to bother wid tellin' 'em nothin', Pheoby.
> 'Taint worth de trouble. You can tell 'em what Ah say if you
> wants to. Dat's just de same as me 'cause mah tongue is in
> mah friend's mouf.
>
> (Zora Neale Hurston, *Their Eyes Were Watching God*)[11]

The epigraph from Hurston with which I begin again captures
some of the dynamics of language, place, sexuality and identity
which are expressed in the demythologizing of the tongue. Janie,
after three failed marriages of varying types, returns alone with the
speculations of the community surrounding her. "Ah don't mean
to bother wid tellin' 'em nothin'" restates my opening Caribbean
women's assertion, "*It's not everything you can talk, but . . .*,"
because the text itself speaks out of that silence which her resistance
to talking to the community indicates. The narrative which
Janie gives to Pheoby becomes the speech after Janie's closure, the
closure which itself opens. It is speech which is located in the
context of female identification, a created female space, and their
shared discursive power. Hurston demythologizes the power of the
tongue, of language, by having Janie locate her tongue in her
friend's mouth. This "mah tongue is in mah friend's mouf," is as
much itself a critique of heterosexuality as it is the privileging of
language, as it is a recognition of how articulations for the dispossessed can take place.

In a similar move, Jamaica Kincaid in "The Tongue," in *Lucy*,
begins her demystification of the tongue with "At fourteen I had

155

discovered that a tongue had no real taste."[12] It is a deliberate link of the tongue to sexuality and not to language exclusively, but also to language. In other words, what is all this anxiety of the tongue? It is an organ like others, of speech, of pleasure, of stimulation. "As I was sucking away, I was thinking, Taste is not the thing to seek out in a tongue; how it makes you feel – that is the thing" (p. 44). The tongue is eventually linked to pleasure. And in the rest of the discussion of the tongue, Kincaid pursues a variety of ways in which the tongue gives feeling, does not have flavor, reminds her of "cow's tongue" which some people eat. She also pursues the sensuality of its stimulations: the appropriate and inappropriate responses to tongues on cheeks, necks, breasts.

Significantly, the entire text and this piece on "The Tongue" is a studied critique of white, middle-class, suburban manners. It is also a critique of her mother as a representation of all she resents in female subordination and male privilege. It is also an identification of imperialism as visible in the material practices of uncritical, white, middle- and upper-class behaviors: "Like her, all of the members of this organization were well off but they made no connection between their comforts and the decline of the world that lay before them."[13] Kincaid makes these leaps and links as she pursues all of these questions in her examination of this white family/white privilege/male dominance. And just as she begins the text talking about adolescent tongue-suckings, she ends with a more mature sexuality with another man, an informed traveller who was able to see difference: his "[w]here in the West Indies are you from?"[14] which asks for specificity as it assumes the Columban error, opposes the "So you are from the islands?" (p. 56) of Dinah and other white women who are friends of the family and who perceive her only as "the girl." But she is not overwhelmed by Hugh.

The insertion of her friend Peggy in the text challenges a number of the heterosexual assumptions of the families around them. Peggy is the loner, the best friend, the one who also repudiates her family. Significantly, our narrator ends her affair with Hugh as she reflects on all the other tongues:

> We were so disappointed that we went back to my room and smoked marijuana and kissed each other until we were exhausted and fell asleep. Her tongue was narrow and pointed and soft. And that was how I said goodbye to Hugh, my arms

and legs wrapped tightly around him, my tongue in his mouth, thinking of all the people I had held in this way.[15]

I believe that Kincaid offers Peggy as another possibility in the text. In this way she offers a critique of patriarchal assumptions and a commentary on heterosexuality at the level of readership and societal normatives. This she had similarly effected in her novel *Annie John*.[16] On one occasion, after choosing to spend the night with a man she had just met, she and Peggy quarrelled about her choice and her objectification as island girl by Paul. A number of gaps and silences concerning her relationship with Peggy are offered at this point:

> I had never chosen the company of a man over her. I had never chosen anyone over her. . . . I immediately imagined our separately going over the life of our friendship, and all the affection and all the wonderful moments in it coming to a sharp end. I made no reply.[17]

Immediately following this scene, the next memory she brings forward is of a little girl, Myrna, in her neighborhood who was sexually molested by Mr Thomas, a fisherman, an otherwise respectable man. It seems a deliberate demystification of the fisherman of Caribbean literature and mythology and a critique of her own choices in relationships. For she remembers herself as a little girl who wondered how come Mr Thomas had not done the same thing to her too. Her friend Myrna's story, which occupies this portion of the text, is one of sexual abuse, adolescent sexuality and dangerous adventure which comes close to personal tragedy. And this our narrator links again to Paul, the man she spends the night with as: "And so it was that hands I would come to know very well – Paul's hands, moving about in the fish tank – reminded me of some other hands lost forever in a warm sea" (p. 109). The juxtaposition of the Peggy relationship here makes the point clear.

> Because Peggy and I were now not getting along, we naturally started to talk about finding an apartment in which we would live together. It was an old story: two people are in love, and then just at the moment they fall out of love, they decide to marry.
>
> (p. 109)

Kincaid's linked critique of heterosexuality and of language is a long way from the anxiety over language and decolonization of the African and Caribbean male writer. The struggle over language which is central to African and Caribbean male letters pursues in myriad ways questions of which language in which to write. (This I summarize as: Oh God! This tongue is not mine. It gives me hell and angers me but I cannot part with it.) These struggles over language and colonized male anguish are located in all the discourses around Caliban of Shakespeare's *Tempest* and the responses by Césaire, Lamming, Brathwaite, Retamar and others. Still, different options and analyses which centrally locate gender have been offered by Abena Busia's "Silencing Sycorax. On African Colonial Discourse and the Unvoiced Female,"[18] and Sylvia Wynter's "Beyond Miranda's Meanings. Un/Silencing the 'Demonic Ground' of Caliban's 'Woman'"[19] both offer critiques of the erasure and silencing of the "native woman."

The dismantling of the colonial anxiety over language is best reflected by Ngugi wa Thiong'o, who begins his *Decolonising the Mind. The Politics of Language in African Literature*[20] with the statement:

This book . . . is my farewell to English as a vehicle for any of my writings. From now on it is Gikuyu and Kiswahili all the way. However, I hope that through the age old medium of translation I shall be able to continue dialogue with all.

(p. xiv)

The rest of the Ngugi text examines some of the historical movements, arguments and issues in the use of language in African literatures. In the Caribbean, the question of language for the male writers also has a long history, culminating in Brathwaite's *History of the Voice*[21] in which he defines "nation language" as

the kind of English spoken by the people who were brought to the Caribbean, not the official English now, but the language of slaves and labourers, the servants who were brought in by the conquistadores. Finally we have the remnants of ancestral languages still persisting in the Caribbean.

(pp. 5–6)

It is an important exploration of submerged languages in the Caribbean, an assertion that nation language is that which ignores the pentameter of European language, that underground language which was constantly "transforming itself into new forms." My assertion is that, for Caribbean women writers like Jamaica Kincaid, the assumptions about language are already embedded textually. Thus, the theory comes, not from the externalized exploration of what is taking place with language, but from the very deconstruction of the meaning of "tongues" and taste and language and ultimately of self.

Marlene Philip, in "Discourse on the Logic of Language,"[22] pursues this examination within the text of the poem itself. The entire series of poems becomes an answer to the questions: "what is language? what is English? what is speech?"

> English
> is my mother tongue
> A mother tongue is not
> not a foreign lan lan lang
> language
> l/anguish
>   anguish
> – a foreign anguish.
>
> (p. 56)

The stutter over land and language also speaks its opposite about English being a mother tongue in which one has fluency. Yet it is the poet's mother tongue. The link to the maternal and speech is made deliberately in the myth of birth, speech, language and mother–daughter transferral of the power of speech which occupies the outer left margin of the text once we turn the text around. The accompanying edicts about the erasure of native speech and the textbook-like definition of Broca and Wernicke of the right brain/left brain and its controls of the functions of language, line up with English and "father tongue," "a foreign language," and "not a mother tongue" (p. 56).

It is in between the assertion that English is both/and that the writing exists, that the normalizing of the tongue and the acceptance that for English to work the writer has to recognize that in it she will have to be "dumb, dumb-tongued, dub-tongued, damn dumb tongue," for English is "another tongue." It is simultaneously an entreaty for the return of the mother tongue in the midst of this anguish and a reduction and dismemberment of language as in parsing. And it is here that the "tongue" takes on the other, the critique of dominance, the father tongue with a variety of riffs which camouflage as they assert a female identification around the issue of tongues: "tongue, mothertongue/tongue mother/tongue me/mothertongue me/mother me touch me /with the tongue of your/ lan lan lan language/l/anguish anguish/english is a foreign anguish."[23]

Abena Busia, in her "Caliban" poem, ends "I speak this dispossession/in the language of the master."[24] Afua Cooper titles her latest collection of poetry, *Memories Have Tongue*,[25] in which the title poem speaks to a grandmother who claims she has bad memory but who nevertheless articulates all the significant events in her life. A related advance on this position is captured in Grace Nichols's epilogue to her book *I Is a Long Memoried Woman*:[26]

> I have crossed an ocean
> I have lost my tongue
> From the root of the old
> one
> a new one has sprung

And Jennifer Rahim, a young Trinidadian poet, in her first book of poems, *Mothers are not the Only Linguists and Other Poems*, devotes two sections to issues of speech, exploring in the rest of the collection themes such as departure, revolution, travel and home.[27] One can see no colonial agony at all here; rather a statement of migration, of loss of one language, but a recognition of a new mode of discourse, a new language, new birth. It is significant that Grace Nichols's poem in particular would serve as the basis for Frances Anne Solomon's[28] film which in turn becomes an independent text, incorporating language, dance, art, the technology of film. In this way, then, the poetic text moves out of the written to the oral, the performative, the filmic.

In "Declension and the Logic of Language," Marlene Nourbese Philip offers multiple choice questions with the all correct answers which further make the point about the multiple choices between the tongue, the penis, about what the tongue is in man. The empowered nature of the tongue and of speech and its link often to phallic mastery has to be deconstructed. In particular, when women use the tongue, then, it gets removed from its primary male identifications.

An intertextual reading of *Lucy* with *She Tries Her Tongue* further clarifies difficult questions of language and migration that have continued to haunt theorists of decolonization. These along with other discourses on speech articulate the demystification of the tongue that is so central to finding a voice.[29] How does one really speak? Philip asserts rhetorically: through the anatomical organs of speech, through the cultural histories embedded in a "mother tongue," through an oppressive force; through all of these in their collectivity and multiplicity. Philip's "The Absence of Writing or How I Almost Became a Spy," which also introduces *She Tries Her Tongue*, offers a forward-thinking exploration of language which says that:

> Subversion of the language has already taken place. Much more must now be attempted. If we accept that some of the earlier premises, that at the heart of the language lies the image, metaphorical and otherwise, and that to the artist falls the task of articulating and presenting this image to the people, then the attack must be made where any true change is ever possible, at the heart of language, the image and the simultaneous naming of it.[30]

Repositioning women in/and language

> My past was my mother; I could hear her voice, and she spoke to me not in English or the French patois that she sometimes spoke, or in any language that needed help from the tongue; she spoke to me in language anyone female could understand. And I was undeniably that – female. Oh it was a laugh for I had spent so much time saying I did not want to be like my mother that I missed the whole story: I was not like my mother – I was my mother.[31]

In an article entitled "The Politics of Language. Beyond the Gender Principle," Nelly Furman[32] articulates some issues around women and language which I find helpful. She asserts that "not only are we born into language which molds us, but any knowledge of the world which we experience is itself also articulated in language."[33] Margaret Homans, in *Bearing the Word* and her introductory chapter, "Representation, Reproduction and Women's Place in Language," offers an important intervention into the Lacanian conception of the place of the phallus as interrupter in the mother-child dyad:

For a daughter, sexual difference and the difference that underlies the functioning of the symbolic order are not the same in the way that they are for a son. The daughter discovers that she is the same as her mother and different from her father, so her relationship to her mother contradicts, rather than reinforces (as in the case of the son), the dependence of the symbolic order on the absence of the mother. . . . The daughter might seem to desire the mother as much as does the son, so that the law would be as meaningful for the daughter as it is for the son. But because difference does not open up between her and her mother in the same way that it does between mother and son, the daughter does not experience desire in the Lacanian sense, that is as differentiated from a preoedipal merging with the mother.[34]

Homans continues that this alternative understanding has consequences for daughters and the ways "women re-write the story of language."[35]

Still, the assumption in much of Lacanian reference, out of which the Homans discussion revises the earlier French feminist *l'écriture feminine* rewritings of some of the Lacanian positions on language, still has the function of privileging the phallus which I reject on principle. Cecilia Konchar Farr, in "Her Mother's Language," suggests that "by treating Lacanian language acquisition theory as a cultural model, we escape the oppression of its linguistic determinism and disrupt (and eventually destroy) its phallocentric foundation."[36] Konchar Farr would opt instead for identifying the multiplicity of languages which she sees in women's writing.

Writing by Black women, I think, offers ways of viewing speech as it links with storytelling and performance as I suggested earlier. Leslie Marmon Silko, in "Language and Literature from a Pueblo Indian Perspective," identifies the spider web as a conceptual model for articulating and arriving at meanings. This approach to storytelling has paradigmatic and cosmological affinity with the "web" as sign in Caribbean and African mythologies. Meaning is constructed out of multiplicity of voices and positions: "As with the web, the structure emerges as it is made and you must simply listen and trust, as the Pueblo do, that meaning will be made."[37]

Kincaid, in the extract which begins this section, seems to be articulating some of the principles of the "silenced female talk," or "unheard mother-daughter language" as well as its suppression in a variety of languages. Thus she interweaves stories of the mother within the narrative of Lucy's life. The play between the articulation of language, silence and other modes of expression weaves its way through women's writing. It seems to me that writers like Kincaid and Philip are in many ways attempting to access these various forms of language, the presymbolic language or "literalizations," the possibilities of the performative embedded in the language which move outwardly beyond any closures. As, significantly, Grace Nichols's poem is an "epilogue" which nevertheless opens, so Kincaid's narrator walks around with letters from her mother all unopened which suggests an interrupted, surface communication, but also a more significant cultural and personal conjunction. The mother, then, stands as the figure of dispossession in patriarchal culture, but also the figure of language and articulation. Of the unopened letters, she says,

> I thought of opening the letters, not to read them but to burn them at the four corners and send them back to her unread. It was an act I had read somewhere of one lover rejecting another, but I could not trust myself to go too near them. I knew that if I read only one, I would die from longing for her.[38]

The repositioning of women in language occurs when we reverse, interrupt or dismantle the cultural mythologies which position women in language in negative ways; when we challenge how the feminine in language is addressed. It may therefore include reducing the language to its barest and most elemental, or it may access other modes of articulating or even other languages. The language reduced to its barest, most elemental, "literalizes" at every turn. Mae Henderson, in "Speaking in Tongues. Dialogics, Dialectics and the Black Woman Writer's Literary Tradition,"[39] offers another intervention which revises the previous intervention by Homans through the relocating of Black women's speech. She argues instead for an

> internal dialogue with the plural aspects of self that constitute the matrix of black women's writing. The interlocutory character of black women's writings is, thus, not only a consequence of a dialogic relationship with an imaginary or generalized "Other," but a dialogue with aspects of "otherness" within the self. The complex situatedness of the black woman as not only the "Other" of the Same, but also the

163

"other" of the other(s) implies, as we shall see, a relationship
of difference and identification with the "other(s)."

(p. 18)

This phenomenon accounts for the multiple ways of voicing that
reside in Black women's textualities. They range from the presymbolic "baby talk" of the mother tongue, to an understanding of the
complex references of mother tongue in African and Native
American contexts, to the politically challenging critical speech
which "talks back" (hooks)[40] and all of the other modes in which
gestures, expressions, language are voiced.

So, in "Universal Grammar," Marlene Philip goes into the structures of language to pull out again a more definite response, taking
Lorde's identification of the mythical norm and calling it for what it
is: an alliance to dominance, destruction and violence, thus challenging its authority:

Man is
The tall man is
The tall, blond man is
The tall, blond, blue-eyed man is
The tall, blond, blue-eyed, white-skinned man is
The tall, blond, blue-eyed, white-skinned man is

        shooting   (p. 63)

        . . .

        an elephant
        a native
        a wild animal
        a Black
        a woman
        a child

somewhere[41]

A significant version of a theory of language[42] is therefore embedded in the poetry of Marlene Philip and, as I am finding, in a
significant amount of creative work by Black women writers. They
offer ways of reading a range of signifying practices which give
voice to material and historical specificities of Black female experiences. The words name, stand alone, relate, reduce themselves and
build as they speak critically, signify, oppose dominance. Philip
seems to be effecting a similar process in her exercises in parsing.
So, in "The Question of Language is the Answer to Power," she
says, in "Lessons for the Voice,"

word it off
speech it off
word in my word
word in your word
I going word my word
                        begin
the in of beginning   OO as in how die they "lose" a
                                    language. . . .[43]

In each case, she engages in a series of dismantlings of meaning, language, using dictionary formulations which question themselves, reproducing the lessons of grammar with her examples. Thus she subverts received meaning, rewriting catechisms and other Eurocentric patriarchal texts such as the Anglican prayer book, which she calls *The Book of unCommon Prayer*, and the litany for communion which asks unquestioning self-negation and submission to an unknown father-figure, which ends,

> *Is it in the nature of God to forgive himself –*
> *For his sin?*

(p. 95)

That language can be linked with dominance, but also can be resisted is expressed in her piece from "Mother's Recipes on How to Make a Language Yours or How Not to Get Raped" which positions the language learner in a subordinate position to the language as phallic power – thus:

Slip mouth over the syllable; moisten with tongue the word.
Suck Slide Play Caress Blow – Love it, but if the word
gags, does not nourish, bite it off – at its source –
Spit it out
Start again.[44]

All of this identifies positionality: political location, social and historical identification and the reclamation of one's own language as one resists imposed/dominant language.

ANTI-CLOSURE PARTING

It's not everything you can talk, but . . .

NOTES

1 INTRODUCTION: MIGRATORY SUBJECTIVITIES

1 This narrative is inspired by Alexis De Veaux's poem, "Rooms," from her portfolio collection of drawings and poems, *Blue Heat*, 1985, p. 8:

> My mother
> manipulated space
> what you call
> change the house
> around
> that is, the contents
> ever so often
> taught me this skill:
> try on these rooms
> one has got to fit.

2 There is a growing body of research and literature in the social sciences on migration. See, for instance, Saskia Sassen, *The Mobility of Labor and Capital. A Study in International Investment and Labor Flow*, London and New York, Cambridge University Press, 1988 which has, for example, a chapter on "The Feminization of the New Industrial Work Force" (pp. 107ff.). A great deal of work on migration has taken place at various centers in England. This study acknowledges their existence but deals more with the affective meanings of migratory subjectivities.

3 Nawal el Saadawi has an interesting discussion on the history and function of the veil in *The Hidden Face of Eve*, London, Zed Press, 1979. But one can also include some consideration of the multiple use of the veil during the Algerian revolution as in Frantz Fanon's "Algeria Unveiled," in Ibrahim and Hopkins, *Arab Society in Transition*, Cairo, American University in Cairo, 1977, pp. 149–172. Some Islamic/North African feminists, like Fatima Mernissi in her piece, "Virginity and Patriarchy," in Aziza al Hibri, ed., *Women and Islam*, Oxford, Pergamon Press, 1982, pp. 186, 189, see the veil as

166

NOTES

class-based, locational and even a protective weapon. Rafika Merini in her "The Subversion of the Culture of Voyeurism," Ph.D. diss., SUNY Binghamton, 1992, pp. 190–195, sees the veil as weapon or mask against the voyeurism of the Western/male "gaze" which permits one to see without being seen. Many see its mandatory deployment as women's proper external dress as oppressive. Read semiotically, the veil has multiple significations. See also Lama Abu Odeh, "Post-Colonial Feminism and the Veil. Thinking the Difference," *Feminist Review*, 43, Spring, 1993, pp. 26–37.

4 Thanks to Deborah Britzman, author of *Practice Makes Practice*, Albany, NY, SUNY Press, 1991, for this formulation and for supporting my decision to intersperse the "horror stories;" also for reading this introduction and offering useful suggestions.

5 See the work of Mayra Santos Febres of the University of Puerto Rico, particularly her dissertation for Cornell University, 1990, a chapter of which was presented at the "Decentering Discourses" conference at Binghamton, 1989, which articulates an understanding of Puerto Rican identities between the US and Puerto Rico as within the trans-local.

6 *Women's Studies International Forum*, 14, 4, 1991, pp. 249–263.

7 Edward Kamau Brathwaite, "The African Presence in Caribbean Literature," *Daedalus*, 103, 2, Spring, 1974, pp. 73–109, describes Paule Marshall's work as "literature of reconnection."

8 See, for example, Margaret Busby, ed., *Daughters of Africa. An International Anthology of Words and Writings by Women of African Descent from the Ancient Egyptian to the Present*, London, Jonathan Cape and New York, Pantheon, 1992; and Carole Boyce Davies and 'Molara Ogundipe-Leslie, eds, *Black Women's Diasporas. Writing New Worlds*, London, Pluto Press, 1994.

9 There have been internal and external migrations, voluntary and forced because of radical changes in climate, wars, natural disasters, oppression, radical breaks for change, in search of food, better conditions, land and other circumstances throughout the history of human life on the planet. For African peoples, dispersed into many widespread geographical regions, these migrations were often forced and disruptive and at the expense of familial connections and linked to the demands for labor in international marketing contexts. See Eric Williams, *Capitalism and Slavery*, New York, Russell, 1961, for an early formulation of this. Some would argue that more recent migrations are a variety of combinations of the above, moving more radically to "refugee" as the current condition of many people.

10 Because I was studying Brazilian culture and politics, I was mindful of the problem of assumptions of race based on US categories and also of the nature of language, description and the problem of race in Brazil.

11 Ama Ata Aidoo, "Conference Presentation," in Philomena Mariani, ed., *Critical Fictions. The Politics of Imaginative Writing*, Seattle, Wash., Bay Press, 1991, pp. 151–154.

12 Stokeley Carmichael and Charles Hamilton, *Black Power. The Politics of Liberation in America*, New York, Vintage, 1981.

13 An important history of the dynamics of the black presence in Britain is Peter Fryer's *Staying Power. The History of Black People in Britain*, London, Pluto Press, 1984. But see also the work of the Centre for Contemporary Cultural Studies, *The Empire Strikes Back. Race and Racism in 70's Britain*, London, Hutchinson, 1982; and Paul Gilroy's *There Ain't No Black in the Union Jack*, London, Hutchinson, 1987.

14 *I Love Myself When I am Laughing . . . A Zora Neale Hurston Reader*, New York, The Feminist Press, 1979, pp. 152–155.

15 "White Woman Listen! Black Feminism and the Boundaries of Sisterhood," in Centre for Contemporary Cultural Studies, *The Empire Strikes Back*, pp. 212–235. See, for comparison, Richard Wright's *White Man, Listen*, New York, Anchor Books/Doubleday, 1957.

16 *Nothing But the Same Old Story. The Roots of Anti-Irish Racism*, London, Information on Ireland, 1984.

17 See James Arnold's *Modernism and Negritude. The Poetry and Poetics of Aimé Césaire*, London and Cambridge, Mass., Harvard University Press, 1981; and Ellen Conroy Kennedy, ed., *The Negritude Poets*, New York, Thunder's Mouth Press, 1989.

18 See Biodun Jeyifo's work on Negritude as nativist discourse or the neo-Tarzanism critiques of the Ibadan/Ife critics in this area which, like Omafume Onoge's "The Crisis of Consciousness in Modern African Literature," are represented in Georg M. Gugelberger, ed., *Marxism and African Literature*, Trenton, NJ, Africa World Press, 1986. Wole Soyinka's famous essay, "And After the Narcissist," *Africa Forum*, 4, Spring, 1986, is credited as an early critique of Negritude, itself critiqued by Chinweizu of *Toward the Decolonization of African Literature*, Washington, DC, Howard University Press, 1983.

19 See, for example, F. James Davis, *Who is Black? One Nation's Definition*, Philadelphia, Pennsylvania State University Press, 1991; and essays in Ronald Takaki, ed., *From Different Shores. Perspectives on Race and Ethnicity in America*, London, Oxford University Press, 1987; and essays in Henry Louis Gates, Jr, ed., *"Race," Writing, and Difference*, Chicago, Ill. and London, University of Chicago Press, 1985; and Jack D. Forbes, *Africans and Native Americans. The Language of Race and the Evolution of Red-Black Peoples*, Urbana and Chicago, Ill., University of Illinois Press, 1993, which discusses the various classifi-cations, for discussion of some of the complexity of the history of racial identifications.

20 Editor of *Nation and Narration*, London and New York, Routledge, 1990, citing Frantz Fanon, "The Fact of Blackness," from his *Black Skin, White Masks* at symposium on "Identity in Question," CUNY Graduate Center, New York, November 16, 1991.

21 As did Lauretta Ngcobo at the African Writers in Exile Conference, London, March 29, 1991.

22 See Paula Giddings, *When and Where I Enter. The Impact of Black Women on Race and Sex in America*, New York, Bantam, 1984.

23 *Gender Trouble. Feminism and the Subversion of Identity*, New York and London, Routledge, 1990.

24 I have found Michael Hanchard's work on this, especially his "Identity, Meaning and the African-American," *Social Text*, 24, 1990, pp. 31–42 and "Racial Consciousness and Afro-Diasporic Experiences. Antonio Gramsci Reconsidered," *Socialism and Democracy*, 3, Fall, 1991, pp. 83–106, and my several discussions with him in Brazil and in the US helpful and supportive examinations of my thoughts on this issue.

25 Her presentation, "The Invisible Afro-America," in which she discussed this was given at SUNY Binghamton University on April 1, 1993.

26 From a conversation with Prof. Akbar Muhammad, African historian, SUNY Binghamton, November 20, 1991. See also Christopher Miller's *Blank Darkness. Africanist Discourse in French*, Chicago, Ill., University of Chicago Press, 1985, pp. 6–14, and his "Theories of Africans. The Question of Literary Anthropology," in Gates Jr, *"Race," Writing and Difference*, pp. 281–300, which discusses a variety of African philosophical and literary positions on the meaning of "African" and concludes by asking that critics "reconsider the applicability of all our critical terms [and] looking to traditional African cultures for terms they might offer" (p. 300). See also V.Y. Mudimbe's *The Invention of Africa*, Bloomington and Indiannapolis, Indiana University Press, 1988, and London, James Currey, 1988.

27 *Social Text*, 24, 1990, pp. 57–84.

28 See, for example, Maurice Barbotin, *Archéologie Antillaise. Arawaks et Caraïbes*, Parc Naturel de Guadeloupe, 1987; and D.J.R. Walker, *Columbus and the Golden World of the Island Arawaks. The Story of the First Americans and Their Caribbean Environment*, Kingston, Jamaica, Ian Randle Publishers and Sussex, The Book Guild Ltd, 1992.

29 Roberto Fernandez Retamar, *Caliban: notas sobre la cultura de nuestra America*, Mexico, Diogenes, 1971, translated as *Caliban and Other Essays*, Minneapolis, Minn., University of Minnesota Press, 1989.

30 See Elizabeth Meese's chapter, "(Dis)Locations: Reading the Theory of a Third-World Woman in *I . . . Rigoberta Menchu*" in her *(Ex)Tensions. Re-Figuring Feminist Criticism*, Urbana and Chicago, Ill., University of Illinois Press, 1990, pp. 97–128.

31 A great deal of literature has come out in refutation of discovery claims and as part of a process of recuperation of their histories by First People. See, for example, Ward Churchill's, *Struggle for The Land. Indigenous Resistance to Genocide, Ecocide and Expropriation in Contemporary North America*, Monroe, ME, Common Courage Press, 1993.

32 See Louis James, *Islands in Between*, London, Oxford University Press, 1968; and James Livingston, *Caribbean Rhythms*, New York, Washington Square Books, 1974.

33 In Bhabha, ed., *Nation and Narration*, pp. 8–22.

34 See Susheila Nasta's introduction to *Motherlands*, London, Women's Press, 1991; Kumari Jayawardena's *Feminism and Nationalism in the Third World*, London, Zed Books, 1986; and Chandra Talpade Mohanty's "Cartographies of Struggle. Third World Women and the

Politics of Feminism," in Chandra Talpade Mohanty, Ann Russo and Lourdes Torres, eds, *Third World Women and the Politics of Feminism*, Bloomington, Ind., Indiana University Press, 1991, pp. 1–47, offers discussions of gender and nationalism.

35 *Caribbean Discourse. Selected Essays*, Charlottesville, Va., University Press of Virginia, 1989.

36 Morejon, "The Invisible Afro-America."

37 Particularly relevant, of course, is its origins in the Bandung Conference of non-aligned nations. There are a variety of debates on naming as described in Lucy Lippard's chapter on "Naming," in her *Mixed Blessings. New Art in a Multicultural America*, New York, Pantheon, 1990, pp. 19–56, which pursues extensively some of these questions. Ama Ata Aidoo's work, cited in note 11, addresses the issue of "Third World." Gayatri Spivak has an interesting discussion of the "worlding" of the Third World in her "Poststructuralism, Marginality, Postcoloniality and Value," in P. Collier and Gaya Rayan, eds, *Literary Theory Today*, Cambridge, Polity, 1990, pp. 220–223. Most scholars speak of both the political efficacy and the problematic hierarchization expressed in the naming of the "Third World." But consider its deployment as *Third Text* or *Third Cinema*.

38 Kelvin Santiago-Valles in a thoughtful reading of this chapter challenged my thinking on internal border posts.

39 *There Ain't No Black in the Union Jack*. See also his "Nothing But Sweat Inside My Hand. Diaspora Aesthetics and Black Arts in Britain", *Black Film/British Cinema*, ICA Document 7, London, Institute of Contemporary Arts, 1988, pp. 44–46, and "It Ain"t Where You're From, It's Where You're At. The Dialectics of Diasporic Identification," *Third Text*, 13, Winter, 1991, pp. 3–16.

40 "Identity, Meaning, and the African-American."

41 Stuart Hall, "New Ethnicities," *Black Film/British Cinema*, ICA Document 7, London, Institute of Contemporary Arts, 1988; and Kobena Mercer, "Diaspora Culture and the Dialogic Imagination. The Aesthetics of Black Independent Film in Britain," in Mbye Cham and Claire Andrade-Watkins, eds, *Blackframes. Critical Perspectives on Black Independent Cinema*, Cambridge, Mass. and London, MIT Press, 1988, pp. 50–61.

42 "Racial Consciousness and Afro-Diasporic Experiences."

43 *Third Text*, 10, Spring, 1990, pp. 61–78.

44 *Living as a Lesbian*, Freedom, Calif., The Crossing Press, 1986, p. 75.

45 San Francisco, Calif., Spinsters/Aunt Lute, 1987.

46 In *Yearning. Race, Gender and Cultural Politics*, Boston, Mass., South End Press, 1990, pp. 41–49.

47 I find this formulation in a way resonant of the *kumbla* as expressed by Erna Brodber in *Jane and Louisa Will Soon Come Home*, London, New Beacon, 1980, and employed as title in Carole Boyce Davies and Elaine Savory Fido, eds, *Out of the Kumbla. Caribbean Women and Literature*, Trenton, NJ, Africa World Press, 1990.

48 New York, Alfred A. Knopf, Inc., 1987.

49 In "Where I Come From Is Like This," in Paula Gunn Allen, *The*

Sacred Hoop. Recovering the Feminine in American Indian Traditions, Boston, Mass., Beacon Press, 1986, pp. 43–50.

50 In her chapter, "Grandma's Story," in *Woman Native Other. Writing Postcoloniality and Feminism*, Bloomington and Indianapolis, Ind., Indiana University Press, 1989, pp. 119–151.

51 See her "Coalition Politics. Turning the Century," in Barbara Smith, ed., *Homegirls. A Black Feminist Anthology*, New York, Kitchen Table: Women of Color Press, 1983, pp. 356–368 and lectures given at subsequent conferences and performances.

52 Albany, NY, Kitchen Table: Women of Color Press, Freedom Organizing Series, no. 3, 1985, p. 19.

53 In Betsy Warland, ed., *Inversions. Writings by Dykes, Queers & Lesbians*, Vancouver, Press Gang Publishers, 1991, pp. 249–263.

54 *New York Academy of Sciences*, 292, 1977, pp. 41–62.

55 Jean Bernabé, Patrick Chamoiseau and Raphael Confiant, "In Praise of Creoleness," *Callaloo*, 13, 1990, pp. 886–909.

56 Kamila Zahno, "Ethnic Monitoring or a Geography Lesson," *Feminist Art News*, 3, 10, p. 24.

57 Introduction to Mohanty, Russo and Torres, eds, *Third World Women*, pp. 1–47.

58 "Migrant Identities. Personal Memory and the Construction of Selfhood," *Cultural Studies*, 6, 1, January, 1992, pp. 27–50.

59 See Vèvè Clark's "diaspora literacy" concept in her essay "Developing Diaspora Literacy. Allusion in Maryse Conde's *Heremakhonon*," in Boyce Davies and Savory Fido, eds, *Out of the Kumbla*, pp. 303–320.

60 In Cary Nelson and Lawrence Grossberg, eds, *Marxism and the Interpretation of Culture*, Urbana, Ill., University of Illinois Press, 1988, pp. 271–313.

61 "Writing Off Marginality," pp. 253–255.

62 I develop this more in an unpublished lecture, "The Politics of Black Women's Voice in Contemporary Times," March, 1993.

63 London, Longman, 1982; but see Carole Boyce Davies, "Private Selves and Public Spaces. Autobiography and the African Woman Writer," *CLA Journal*, 34, 3, 1991, pp. 267–289, for further discussion of this issue.

64 New York, Random House, 1969, and *The Heart of a Woman*, New York, Random House, 1981. See also Joanne M. Braxton, *Black Women Writing Autobiography. A Tradition Within a Tradition*, Philadelphia, Temple University Press, 1989.

65 "Just Another Woman," *Feminist Art News*, 4, 2, p. 29.

66 In Boyce Davies and Savory Fido, eds, *Out of the Kumbla*, pp. 271–278.

67 See Elsa Barkley Brown, "Polyrhythms and Improvisation. Lessons for Women's History," *History Workshop Journal*, 31, Spring, 1991, pp. 85–90.

68 In Gloria Anzaldua, ed., *Making Face, Making Soul/Haciendo Caras*, San Francisco, Calif., Spinsters/Aunt Lute, pp. 390–401. I discussed this with Maria further in 1991 and she suggested that the tourist is often the one with arrogant perception. My sense of apprehension

comes not with her formulation but with the implications of the language and the inability of many to make such distinctions.

69 Aimé Césaire in his *Discourse on Colonialism*, New York, Monthly Review Press, 1972 (first published Présence Africaine, 1955), was definite about locating American colonialism when he said, "The hour of the barbarian is at hand. The modern barbarian. The American hour" (p. 59). I thank Monica Jardine for consistently reiterating this point.

70 Audre Lorde, *Our Dead Behind Us*, New York and London, W.W. Norton & Company, 1986, pp. 16–18.

71 I am speaking in a way to those of us who became African American Women In Defense of Ourselves and were asked to donate money for an ad. which articulated our opposition to Clarence Thomas's seating on the Supreme Court and the US government and media handling of the situation. A similarly activated silencing took place around Clinton's nomination of Lani Guinier as his administration's prime civil rights lawyer and his withdrawal of her nomination because he disagreed with her positions on racial inequities and representation. There was no organized response to this. Also there is no real machinery to activate a critique of these issues in a sustained way. Among newspaper captions about Guinier were ones which described her as "Strange Hair, Strange Name, Strange Woman," thus highlighting all her gendered/racial identity markers as non-normative and therefore "strange." I suppose I am challenging the nature of response in terms of ads in mainstream publications like *New York Times* and the lack of some organized efforts in multiple ways at local, national and transnational levels.

72 In Elaine Marks and Isabelle de Courtivron, eds, *New French Feminisms*, New York, Schocken Books, 1981, pp. 137–141. See also, her *Revolution in Poetic Language*, New York, Columbia University Press, 1984; and Toril Moi, ed., *The Kristeva Reader*, New York, Columbia University Press, 1986.

73 See Marilyn Strathern, *The Gender of the Gift*, Berkeley, Calif. and London, University of California Press, 1988.

74 "On Being the Object of Property," in her *The Alchemy of Race and Rights*, Cambridge, Mass., Harvard University Press, 1991, pp. 216–236.

75 *Signs*, 14, 1, 1988, pp. 119–262.

76 *Signs*, 13, 1988, pp. 419–436.

77 See, for example, Susan Hekman's "Reconstituting the Subject. Feminism, Modernism, and Postmodernism," *Hypatia*, 6, 2, Summer, 1991, pp. 44–63.

78 Issues such as rape, physical and sexual abuse, pay inequity, battery, sexual harassment, labor exploitations, sharing of household responsibilities, child care, participation in economic systems, the judiciary, political systems, education, the military and so on. My position is that Black women or women of color are generally the ones who really offer the reality of issues in startling clarity.

79 Audre Lorde, "Age, Race, Class, and Sex. Women Redefining

Difference," in her *Sister Outsider*, Freedom, Calif., The Crossing Press, 1984, p. 116.

80 Edited by Gloria T. Hull, Patricia Bell Scott and Barbara Smith, New York, The Feminist Press, 1982.

81 Patricia Hill Collins, London, Routledge, 1990.

82 bell hooks, Boston, Mass., South End Press, 1989.

83 One advance in this issue is Stanlie James and Abena Busia, eds, *Theorizing Black Feminisms*, London, Routledge, 1993, which began as a Black feminist seminar with a variety of Black women from different places. An earlier model of inclusionary Black feminist scholarship was Roseann P. Bell, Bettye J. Parker and Beverly Guy-Sheftall, eds, *Sturdy Black Bridges*, New York, Doubleday, 1979.

84 See my "Feminist Consciousness and African Literary Criticism," in Carole Boyce Davies and Anne Adams Graves, eds, *Ngambika. Studies of Women in African Literature*, Trenton, NJ, Africa World Press, 1986, pp. 1–23.

85 Claudia Tate's book was published in New York, by Continuum, 1983; and Adeola James's work in London, by James Currey, 1991.

86 New York, Greenwood Press, forthcoming 1994.

87 Mary Helen Washington, *Midnight Birds. Stories by Contemporary Black Women Writers*, New York, Anchor Press/Doubleday, 1980, and *Black Eyed Susans*, New York, Anchor Press/Doubleday, 1975, *Invented Lives. Narratives of Black Women, 1860–1960*, New York, Anchor Press/Doubleday, 1987.

88 New Brunswick, NJ and London, Rutgers University Press, 1989.

89 London, Verso, 1990.

90 Trenton, NJ, Africa World Press, 1994.

91 Many of these have been identified in Carole Boyce Davies and Elaine Savory Fido, "African Women Writers. Towards a Literary History," in Oyekan Owomoyela, ed., *A History of Twentieth-Century African Literatures*, Lincoln, Nebr., University of Nebraska Press, 1993, pp. 311–346.

92 Even so, Carby's definition of African-American women's literature remained located in the United States.

93 Rhonda Cobham and Merle Collins, eds, *Watchers and Seekers. Creative Writing by Black Women in Britain*, London, The Women's Press, 1987.

94 Shabnam Grewal, Jackie Kay, Liliane Landor, Gail Lewis and Pratibha Parmar, eds, *Charting the Journey. Writings by Black and Third World Women*, London, Sheba Feminist Publishers, 1988.

95 Lauretta Ngcobo, ed., *Let It Be Told. Black Women Writers in Britain*, London, Virago, 1988; *Talkers Through Dream Doors. Poetry and Short Stories by Black Women*, Manchester, Crocus Books/Commonword Ltd, 1989; Maud Sulter, ed., *Passion. Discourses on Blackwomen's Creativity*, photography by Ingrid Pollard, Hebden Bridge, West Yorkshire, Urban Fox Press, 1990, which offers a wonderful exploration into the creativity and cultural production of Black women in a variety of media. Two recent collections of *Feminist Art News*, 4, 1 and

2 and also 3, 10 include work by Black women writing in Europe. And there are a number of individual texts and works of specific groups.

96 Makeda Silvera (ed.) Toronto, Sister Vision Press, 1992.

97 Some of this work will be published in Boyce Davies and Ogundipe-Leslie, eds, *Black Women's Diasporas*, which also has an essay on the subject. Miriam Alves whom I interviewed has a collection of Afro-Brazilian women writers ready for publishing called "Enfim, Todas Negras Brasileras Contemporaneas." Leda Maria Martins in Belo Horizonte, whom I also interviewed, has about four collections of poetry. A number of her works and those of other Afro-Brazilian women writers have been published in various volumes of *Cadernos Negros* in São Paulo. See also the special issue of *Afro-Hispanic Review*, 11, 1–3, 1992, edited by Phyllis Reisman-Butler on African-Brazilian Culture, with article by Carolyn Richardson Durham, "Sonia Fatima da Conceiçao's Literature for Social Change," pp. 21–25.

98 New York, Pergamon, 1985.

99 See her *Feminist Theory. From Margin to Center*, Boston, Mass., South End Press, 1984, *Talking Back. Thinking Feminist. Thinking Black, and Yearning*.

100 I thank Teresa Ebert of SUNY Albany for this formulation.

101 *Cultural Critique*, 6, Spring, 1987, pp. 51–63. But see also bell hook's critique of the Christian position in her *Talking Back*, p. 38.

102 Edward Said makes this point in "Secular Criticism," in *The World, the Text and The Critic*, London, Vintage, 1991, p. 25, that criticism is located far away from the questions that trouble the reader of a daily newspaper.

103 Lawrence Grossberg, "Wandering Audiences, Nomadic Critics," *Cultural Studies*, 2, 3, 1988, pp. 377–391.

104 Minneapolis, Minn., and London, University of Minnesota Press, 1993.

105 Minneapolis, Minn., University of Minnesota Press, 1988.

106 See, for examples, essays by Mary Russo, Jessica Benjamin, Nancy K. Miller and Biddy Martin and Chandra Talpade Mohanty, in Teresa de Lauretis, ed., *Feminist Studies/Critical Studies*, Bloomington, Ind. Indiana University Press, 1986.

107 See Susan Hekman's discussion of female subjectivity in her "Reconstituting the Subject" pp. 44–63.

108 See bell hooks, "The Politics of Radical Black Subjectivity," in her *Yearning*, pp. 15–22.

109 Hanchard, "Racial Consciousness," p. 101.

2 NEGOTIATING THEORIES OR "GOING A PIECE OF THE WAY WITH THEM"

1 "How It Feels to Be Colored Me," *I Love Myself When I Am Laughing . . . A Zora Neale Hurston Reader*, ed. Alice Walker, New York, The Feminist Press, 1979, p. 152.

2 "The Commitment to Theory," in Jim Pines and Paul Willemen, eds,

Questions of Third Cinema, London, British Film Institute, 1989, p. 118.

3 "Age, Race, Class and Sex. Women Redefining Difference," in *Sister Outsider*, Freedom, Calif., The Crossing Press, 1984, p. 123.

4 In a paper presented at a symposium on Africanist discourse at Oxford University, Summer, 1989, which would become part of the introduction to one of his latest works, Houston Baker asserted that only Hortense Spillers, Hazel Carby and Barbara Smith did theory.

5 Catherine Lutz, "The Gender of Theory," unpublished manuscript, SUNY, Binghamton, 1990.

6 Hanover, NH and London, Wesleyan University Press, 1992, pp. 13ff.

7 Ibid., p. 13.

8 See essays in W.J.T. Mitchell, *Against Theory. Literary Studies and the New Pragmatism*, Chicago, Ill. and London, University of Chicago Press, 1985.

9 *Cultural Critique*, 6, Spring, 1987, pp. 51–63. But see also bell hooks' important critique of this position in her *Talking Back*, Boston, Mass., South End Press, 1989, pp. 38–39.

10 Work done by Martin Bernal, *Black Athena*, New Brunswick, NJ, Rutgers University Press, 1987; and Cheikh Anta Diop, *Precolonial Black Africa*, Conn., Lawrence Hill & Co., 1987 and others is gaining significant ground in challenging Western ownership of all knowledge.

11 "Political Semiosis in/of American Cultural Studies," *American Journal of Semiotics*, 8, 1–2, 1991, pp. 122–123.

12 See Elizabeth V. Spelman's *Inessential Woman. Problems of Exclusion in Feminist Thought*, Boston, Mass., Beacon Press, 1988.

13 *Hypatia*, 6, 2, Summer, 1991, p. 51.

14 See her *Talking Back. Thinking Feminist. Thinking Black*, Boston, Mass., South End Press, 1989.

15 Lorde, "Age, Race, Class and Sex," p. 114.

16 Ebert, "Political Semiosis", p. 115.

17 Ibid.

18 See her *Talking Back*.

19 In Essex Hemphill and/for Joseph Beam, ed., *Brother to Brother. New Writings by Black Gay Men*, Boston, Mass., Alyson Publications Inc., 1991, p. 230.

20 Henry Louis Gates Jr, *The Signifying Monkey. A Theory of African-American Literary Criticism*, New York and Oxford, Oxford University Press, 1988.

21 Geneva Smitherman, *Talkin and Testifyin. The Language of Black America*, Detroit, Mich., Wayne State University Press, 1986.

22 "Signifying as a Form of Verbal Art," in Alan Dundes, ed., *Mother Wit From the Laughing Barrel: Readings in the Interpretation of Afro-American Folklore*, Englewood Cliffs, NJ, Prentice-Hall, 1973.

23 *Woman Native Other. Writing Postcoloniality and Feminism*, Bloomington and Indianapolis, Ind., Indiana University Press, 1989, p. 42.

24 *Nation*, May 22, 1989, pp. 691–692.
25 *Critical Studies in Mass Communication*, 2, 2, June, 1985, pp. 91–114.
26 Stuart Hall, "On Postmodernism and Articulation. An Interview," *Journal of Communication Inquiry* 10, Summer, 1986, pp. 45–60, and reformulated by Lawrence Grossberg within the context of his article, "Wandering Audiences, Nomadic Critics," *Cultural Studies*, 2, 3, 1988, p. 377 within the context of travel (transformation) and travel as work (communication).
27 In *The World, The Text, and The Critic*, London, Vintage, 1991.
28 *Cultural Studies*, 7, 2, May, 1993, pp. 224–239. See also James Clifford, "Notes on Travel and Theory," *Inscriptions*, 5, 1989, pp. 177–188.
29 Bhabha, "The Commitment to Theory," p. 118.
30 Ibid., p. 119.
31 Giles Deleuze, "Nomad Thought," in David B. Allison, ed., *The New Nietzche*, New York, Dell Publishing Co., 1977, pp. 142–149.
32 Laurence Grossberg, "Wandering Audiences, Nomadic Critics," p. 387.
33 Janice Radway, "Reception Study. Ethnography and the Problems of Dispersed Audiences and Nomadic Subjects," *Cultural Studies*, 2, 3, 1988, pp. 359–376.
34 Deleuze, "Nomad Thought," p. 149.
35 In Mbye Cham and Claire Andrade-Watkins, eds, *Blackframes. Critical Perspectives on Black Independent Cinema*, London and Cambridge, Mass., MIT Press, 1988, pp. 62–79.
36 I was asked by a graduate student at a seminar at the University of London where I presented this chapter (January 4, 1992) to give a practical example of this. One case would be beginning to look at the psychoanalytic aspects of Toni Morrison's *Beloved* and becoming instead a Lacanian psychoanalyst and forgetting about the work that began the inquiry.
37 As expressed in my "Writing Off Marginality, Minoring and Effacement," *Women's Studies International Forum*, 14, 4, 1991, p. 260.
38 Gabriel, "Thoughts on Nomadic Aesthetics," p. 72.
39 *Genders*, 10, Spring, 1991, pp. 1–24.
40 Ibid., p. 11.
41 Ibid., p. 23.
42 New York, Farrar, Strauss, Giroux, 1988.
43 Marcos Becquer and Jose Gatti, "Elements of Vogue," *Third Text*, 16–17, Autumn–Winter, 1991, pp. 65–81.
44 Ibid., p. 72.
45 Ibid., p. 69.
46 *New England Review and Bread Loaf Quarterly*, 7, 1, Autumn, 1984, pp. 430–452.
47 *Feminist Review*, 35, Summer, 1990, pp. 24–41.
48 Biddy Martin and Chandra Talpade Mohanty, "Feminist Politics. What's Home Got to Do With It?" in Teresa de Lauretis, ed., *Feminist Studies/Critical Studies*, Bloomington, Ind., Indiana University Press, 1986, pp. 191–212.

49 *Borderlands/La Frontera. The New Mestiza*, San Francisco, Calif., Spinsters/Aunt Lute, 1987.

50 "Living Borders/Buscando America. Languages of Latino Self-Formation," *Social Text*, 24, 1990, pp. 57–84. In fact there is a growing body of work on this subject, including a variety of articles which use the borderlands formulation and books as Pat Mora's *Borders*, Houston, Tex., Arte Publico Press, 1986.

51 *Feminist Theory. From Margin to Center*, Boston, Mass., South End Press, 1984, p. 19. In a more recent work *Yearning. Race, Gender and Cultural Politics*, Boston, Mass., South End Press, 1990, bell hooks speaks of "homeplace" in somewhat more nostalgic terms, as a site of resistance, a place to which one returns for healing and self-renewal. hooks tends to speak of home in both ways. For while home as site of belonging is true at times, for many the reality is of not being able to return to that space or "homeplace" unless it is an internal center, or a newly constituted home.

52 Private communication, 1991.

53 Berkeley, Calif., University of California Press, 1990.

54 Ibid., p. 44.

55 In Susheila Nasta, ed., *Motherlands. Black Women's Writing from Africa, the Caribbean and South Asia*, London, The Women's Press, 1991 and New Brunswick, NJ, Rutgers University Press, 1992, pp. 3–23.

56 See, for example, Zainab Jama, "Finding a Voice. Somali Nationalist Women's Songs," *African Languages and Cultures*, special issue of "The Literatures of War," ed. Theodora Ezeigbo and Liz Gunner, SOAS, Department of African Languages and Cultures Publications, June, 1991, and a range of other texts of women's role in nationalist struggle are being produced by the women themselves.

57 *Michigan Quarterly Review*, 28, 1, Winter, 1989, pp. 1–34.

58 Stanford, Calif., Stanford University Press, 1992, p. 1.

59 "Feminism, Postmodernism, and Gender-Scepticism," in Linda Nicholson, ed., *Feminism/Postmodernism*, London, Routledge, 1990, pp. 133–156.

60 In de Lauretis, ed., *Feminist Studies/Critical Studies*, pp. 102–120.

61 Ibid., p. 106.

62 *Signs*, 13, 3, 1988, pp. 405–436.

63 *Cultural Critique*, Winter, 1993, pp. 5–50.

64 Laclau at a conference on Identity at CUNY Graduate Center in November, 1991, offered clarifications of their position on essentialism, rejecting even Spivak's suggestion of a tactical essentialism. But see their *Hegemony and Socialist Strategy. Toward a Radical Democratic Politics*, London, Verso, 1985.

65 See also Chandra Mohanty's "Feminist Encounters. Locating the Politics of Experience," in Michèle Barrett and Anne Phillips, eds, *Destabilizing Theory. Contemporary Feminist Debates*, Stanford, Calif., Stanford University Press, 1992, pp. 74–92.

66 See her "Cotton and Iron," in Russell Ferguson, Martha Gever, Trinh T. Min-ha and Cornel West, eds, *Out There. Marginalization and Contemporary Cultures*, New York, The New Museum of

Contemporary Art, and Cambridge, Mass. and London, MIT Press, 1990, pp. 327–336.
67 Ibid., p. 328.
68 Lectures given at Binghamton in 1990.
69 Chandra Mohanty, "Feminist Encounters, Locating the Politics of Experience," *Copyright*, 1, Fall, 1987, p. 40.
70 My workshop diagram February, 1991 which uses the braid model to identify the strands of identifications which can be woven together or unbraided as needed.
71 See Samir Amin's *Delinking. Towards a Polycentric World*, London and New Jersey, Zed Books, 1990.
72 See, for example, Lisa Duggan, "Making it Perfectly Queer," *Socialist Review*, 22, 1, January–March, 1992, pp. 11–31.
73 *History Workshop Journal*, 31, Spring, 1991, pp. 85–90.
74 I can see evidence that Audre Lorde has done transnational organizing on the theory and practice of Black feminism on an international scale that is similar in extent to the work that Marcus Garvey did. The extent of her work will be proven by careful research in a wide range of geographical areas.
75 Title of her collection of essays and speeches, Lorde, *Sister Outsider*.
76 *Third Text*, 10, Spring, 1990, pp. 61–78.
77 See the work of Cherrie Moraga and Juanita Ramos and Gloria Anzaldua, for example.
78 Georges Van den Abbeele, "Sightseers. The Tourist as Theorist," *Diacritics*, Winter, 1980, p. 12.
79 Minh-ha, *Woman Native Other*, and her *When the Moon Waxes Red*, London, Routledge, 1991. See also my review of *Woman Native Other*, *Hypatia*, 6, 2, Summer, 1991, pp. 220–222.
80 *In Other Worlds. Essays in Cultural Politics*, New York and London, Routledge, 1988, and *The Post-Colonial Critic. Interviews, Strategies, Dialogues*, ed. Sarah Harasym, New York and London, Routledge, 1990, and other works in bibliography.
81 San Francisco, Calif., Spinsters/Aunt Lute, 1987 and 1990.
82 Boston, Mass., Beacon Press, 1986.
83 Edited by Margot Badran and Miriam Cooke, Bloomington, Ind., Indiana University Press, 1990.
84 London, Zed Press, 1987.
85 Bloomington, Ind., Indiana University Press, 1991.
86 London, The Women's Press, 1991.
87 *Feminist Art News*, 3, 10, 1992, back cover.

3 DECONSTRUCTING AFRICAN FEMALE SUBJECTIVITIES

1 "Writing Off Marginality, Minoring and Effacement," *Women's Studies International Forum*, 14, 4, 1991, pp. 249–263.
2 Lloyd Brown in *Women Writers in Black Africa*, Westport, Conn. and London, Greenwood Press, 1981, pp. 84–121 includes some thought-

ful discussion on *Anowa* and Aidoo's other works and, at that time, was one of the few early treatments of Aidoo's work. See, though, Vincent Odamtten's recent *The Art of Ama Ata Aidoo. Polylectics and Reading Against Neocolonialism*. Gainesville, University of Florida Press, 1994. Mildred Hill-Lubin has presented a number of papers on Ama Ata Aidoo's use of orality and storytelling modes at various conferences. See bibliography in Carole Boyce Davies and Anne Adams Graves, eds, *Ngambika. Studies of Women in African Literature*, Trenton, NJ, Africa World Press, 1986, for some listings.

3 Mary Naana Nicholson's MA thesis, "The Affirmation of African Womanhood in the Works of Ama Ata Aidoo," University of Florida, Gainesville is one of a developing body of criticism on Aidoo. See also Chimalum Nwankwo's, "The Feminist Impulse and Social Realism in Ama Ata Aidoo's *No Sweetness Here* and *Our Sister Killjoy*," in Boyce Davies and Adams Graves, eds, *Ngambika*, pp. 151–160.

4 "GHANA: To Be a Woman," in Robin Morgan, ed., *Sisterhood is Global*, Garden City, NY, Anchor Press/Doubleday, 1984, pp. 258–265.

5 Urbana and Chicago, Ill., University of Illinois Press, 1978.

6 See Naana Banyiwa Horne's article, "The Mouth That Would Eat Salt and Pepper", ALA Conference paper, 1984.

7 In Dennis Duerden and Cosmo Pieterse, eds, *African Writers Talking*, London, Heinemann, 1972, p. 23. It is interesting how in the interview Maxine Lautre McGregor does not allow Aidoo to complete this thought or develop it further.

8 Aidoo said in discussions after a lecture at Binghamton, April 10, 1993, that were she writing the play now she could think of several different ways of having Anowa exit rather than the tragic ending. This in a way speaks to the issue of re-oralization, historical location, political and social movements and literary creativity.

9 Modupe Olaogun, "The Poetics of Transformation," in Modupe Olaogun, ed., *When Anowa Meets Ogun. The Politics and Poetics of Writing in Africa and the Diaspora*, Toronto, forthcoming.

10 See Ato Sekyi-Otu, "Lesbos and Anowa. Versions of Feminist Ontology and Politics," in Olaogun, ed., *When Anowa Meets Ogun*.

11 See "Foriwa" as short story, "New Life at Kyerefaso," in Charlotte Bruner's collection, *Unwinding Threads*, London, Heinemann, 1983, pp. 17–23.

12 See Dick Hebdige, "Redeeming Witness. In the Tracks of the Homeless Vehicle Project," *Cultural Studies*, 7, 2, May, 1993, pp. 173–223, an interesting article which discusses some of the contemporary issues of homelessness.

13 See Teresa L. Ebert's "Political Semiosis in/of American Cultural Studies," *American Journal of Semiotics*, 8, 1–2, 1991, pp. 113–135; and Rosemary Hennessy's "Feminist Standpoint, Discourse, and Authority. From Women's Lives to Ideology Critique," in her *Materialist Feminism and the Politics of Discourse*, London, Routledge, 1993, which she made available to me before its publication.

14 Ama Ata Aidoo, *Anowa*, Washington, DC, Three Continents Press and London, Longman, Drumbeat, 1970, pp. 29–30. Although the play was first produced in the late 1960s, it remained out of print for a number of years and was recently reissued with *Dilemma of a Ghost*, London, Longman, 1985.

15 Ibid., p. 36.

16 Ibid.

17 Vincent Odamtten's work on Aidoo (see note 2) offers a great deal of historical information which aids in understanding some of the social transitions that were taking place during the time in which this play was located.

18 Chandra Talpade Mohanty and Biddy Martin, "Feminist Politics. What's Home Got To Do With It?" in Teresa de Lauretis, ed., *Feminist Studies/Critical Studies*, Bloomington, Ind., Indiana University Press, 1986, p. 196.

19 *Simians, Cyborgs, and Women. The Reinvention of Nature*, New York, Routledge, 1991, p. 201.

20 Aidoo, *Anowa*, p. 17.

21 Ibid., p. 19.

22 Ibid., p. 61.

23 Aidoo says in discussion that she sees that as a valid possible alternative ending.

24 "To Be a Woman," p. 259.

25 Aidoo, *Anowa*, p. 52.

26 In *Sisterhood is Global*, p. 501.

27 See Gayatri Spivak, "The Political Economy of Women as Seen by a Literary Critic," in Elizabeth Weed, ed., *Coming to Terms: Feminism, Theory, Politics*, New York, Routledge, 1989, and a number of pieces like her "Scattered Speculations on the Question of Value," in *In Other Worlds. Essays in Cultural Politics*, New York, Methuen, 1987, pp. 154–175 which begins some of the questions she addresses in "Can the Subaltern Speak?" in Cary Nelson and Martin Grossberg, eds, *Marxism and the Interpretation of Culture*, Urbana and Chicago, Ill., University of Illinois Press, 1988, pp. 271–313. See also Maria Mies, Veronika Berholdt-Thomsen and Claudia von Werlhof, *Women. The Last Colony*, London and Atlantic Highlands, NJ, Zed Press, 1988.

28 *Africa Quarterly*, 15, 1975, pp. 35–47.

29 Mary Russo in "Female Grotesques. Carnival and Theory," in de Lauretis, ed., *Feminist Studies/Critical Studies*, suggests that "carnival and carnival laughter remain on the horizon with a new social subjectivity" (p. 226).

30 Aidoo, *Anowa*, p. 53.

31 Filomina Chioma Steady, "The Black Woman Cross-Culturally. An Overview," introduction to her *The Black Woman Cross-Culturally*, Cambridge, Mass., Schenkman, 1981, pp. 1–41.

32 Aidoo, *Anowa*, pp. 12–13.

33 Naana Banyiwa-Horne makes this point, personal communication July 1, 1993.

34 Ebert, "Political Semiosis," pp. 118–119.

35 Julia Kristeva, "Woman Can Never Be Defined," in Elaine Marks and Isabelle de Courtivron, eds, *New French Feminisms*, New York, Schocken Books, 1981, p. 137.

36 See, for example, Marilyn Strathern's *The Gender of the Gift*, Berkeley, Calif., California University Press, 1988.

37 Brown, *Women Writers in Black Africa*, p. 98.

38 Gayle Rubin, "The Traffic in Women. Notes on the Political Economy of Sex," in Rayna Rapp Reiter, ed., *Toward an Anthropology of Women*, New York, Monthly Review Press, 1975, pp. 157–210, which can be said to have begun a lot of this discussion.

39 Brown, *Women Writers in Black Africa*, p. 97.

40 *Sociological Review*, 4, November, 1987, pp. 721–743.

41 Ed. by Essex Hemphill and conceived by Joseph Beam, Boston, Mass., Alyson Publications Inc., 1992.

42 New York and London, Routledge, 1990.

43 Ibid., p. 148.

44 In Marks and de Courtivron, eds, *New French Feminisms*, pp. 199–203.

45 Ibid., p. 203.

46 I interviewed Aidoo on this subject on April 10, 1993, in Binghamton, New York and she also spoke to the multiple meanings of the word "witch" in this text and as it circulates culturally.

47 A number of these pieces were anthropological and carried all the marks of the colonial/anthropological project. For example, the special *Africa* issue on witchcraft, edited by E. Evans-Pritchard, 8, 4, October, 1935, had pieces like S.F. Nadel, "Witchcraft and Anti-Witchcraft in Nupe Society," pp. 423–447, C. Clifton Roberts, "Witchcraft and Colonial Legislation," pp. 488–503 and Audrey I. Richards, "A Modern Movement of Witch-Finders," pp. 448–461. But it also had a section from which I was able to get the most information, entitled, "The African Explains Witchcraft," pp. 504–559, which, though sometimes in translation, had a number of African peoples speaking to their definitions and understandings of witchcraft. But see also, Barbara E. Wards, "Some Observations on Religious Cults in Ashanti," *Africa*, 26, 1956, pp. 47–61, which speaks about the "persistence of witchcraft beliefs," in the face of Christianity. M.J. Field, *Religion and Medicine of the Ga People*, London, Oxford University Press and Accra, Presbyterian Book Depot, 1937, has a chapter on witchcraft but I found her conclusions very much located in Western, Christian assumptions such as witchcraft as "bad medicine directed destructively against other people" (p. 135). Monica Hunter Wilson, "Witch Beliefs and Social Structure," *American Journal of Sociology*, 51, 4, January, 1951, pp. 307–313, was helpful as was Frank Melland, "Ethical and Political Aspects of African Witchcraft," *Africa*, 8, pp. 495–503, as they spoke of structures. Both were also very colonial and full of all the assumptions and associations. S.F. Nadel, "Witchcraft in Four African Societies. An Essay in Comparison," in Simon and Phoebe Ottenberg, eds, *Cultures and Societies of Africa*,

New York, Random House, 1960, pp. 407–420 provided interesting leads.

48 In private conversation, June 30, 1993, with Abena P.A. Busia, she would identify the issue of studied powers, the ability to think in a context of power, either to harm or to help, and activate it as the principal distinguishing factor. She would also argue that even the African people commenting on witchcraft would have only peripheral information since much of that resides with the initiates.

49 Personal communication, July 1, 1993.

50 See Tess Onwueme's "Bodies in Silence. The Missing Diaspora in African Literature," *Drum Voices*, 2, Fall/Winter, 1992/93, nos. 1 and 2, pp. 157–169.

51 Henry John Drewal and Margaret Thompson Drewal, *Gẹlẹdẹ. Art and Female Power Among the Yoruba*, Bloomington, Ind., Indiana University Press, 1990, pp. 74–75. Conversation with Ronke Oyewumi, whose forthcoming book, to be published by University of Minnesota Press, deals with Yoruba women within the context of gender discourses, helped to clarify this point.

52 Hélène Cixous and Catherine Clément, *The Newly Born Woman*, Minneapolis, Minn., University of Minnesota Press, 1986.

53 Sandra Gilbert and Susan Gubar, *The Madwoman in the Attic. The Woman Writer and the Nineteenth Century Literary Imagination*, New Haven, Conn., Yale University Press, 1979.

54 See Jeanne Snitgen Garane, "History, Identity and the Constitution of the Female Subject," in Carole Boyce Davies, ed., "Black Women's Writing. Crossing the Boundaries," *Matatu*, Heft 6, 3, Jahrgang, 1989, pp. 55–71, for discussion.

55 Marjorie Garber, *Vested Interests*, London, Routledge, 1991, also panel discussion following interview with the writer at the ICA, London, May, 1992.

56 From conversation with Naana Banyiwa Horne, personal communication, July 1, 1993.

57 "Mothering and Healing in Recent Black Women's Fiction," *Sage*, 2, 1, Spring, 1985, pp. 41–43.

58 See Lene Dresen-Coenders, "Witches as Devils' Concubines. On the Origin of Fear of Witches and Protection Against Witchcraft," in *Saints and She-Devils*, London, The Rubicon Press, 1987, pp. 59–82; also Irene Silverblatt, *Moon, Sun and Witches. Gender Ideologies and Class in Inca and Colonial Peru*, Princeton, NJ, Princeton University Press, 1987.

59 New York, The Feminist Press, 1973.

60 The work of Juana Elbin Dos Santos, such as *Os Nago e a Morte* (*Nago and Death*), Petropolis, Brazil, Editora Vozes Ltd, 1976 and other work on African religions in Brazil, for example, identifies this connection between women and power in African religions.

61 "The African Woman Today," *Dissent*, Summer, 1992, pp. 319–325.

62 "Mama's Baby, Papa's Maybe. An American Grammar Book," *Diacritics*, 17, 2, Summer, 1987, pp. 65–81.

4 FROM "POST-COLONIALITY" TO UPRISING TEXTUALITIES

1 An early and preliminary version of this chapter was first presented at the MLA Annual Convention in New York City, December, 1992.
2 Bloomington and Indianapolis, Ind., Indiana University Press, 1989. See also her "Not You/Like You. Post-Colonial Women and the Interlocking Questions of Identity and Difference," in Gloria Anzaldua, ed., *Making Face, Making Soul/Haciendo Caras: Creative and Critical Perspectives by Feminists of Color*, Francisco, Calif., Spinsters/ Aunt Lute Foundation, 1990, pp. 371–375.
3 "Tsitsi Dangarembga's *Nervous Conditions* At The Crossroads of Feminism and Post-Colonialism," *World Literature Written in English*, 31,1, 1991, pp. 102–103.
4 I discuss this point substantially in an unpublished conference paper.
5 McWilliams, "Tsitsi Dangarembga's," p. 105
6 See *Cultural Critique*, Spring and Fall, 1987.
7 Bill Ashcroft, Gareth Griffiths and Helen Tiffin, *The Empire Writes Back. Theory and Practice in Post-Colonial Literatures*, London and New York, Routledge, 1989, p. 2.
8 Ama Ata Aidoo, "That Capacious Topic. Gender Politics," in Philomena Mariani, ed., *Critical Fictions. The Politics of Imaginative Writing*, Seattle, Wash., Bay Press, 1991, p. 152.
9 Ruth Frankenberg and Lata Mani, "Crosscurrents, Crosstalk. Race, 'Postcoloniality' and the Politics of Location," in *Cultural Studies*, 7, 2, May, 1993, pp. 299, 301, 302.
10 A number of works have begun the process of deconstructing "post-coloniality." These include, Arun Mukherjee, "Whose Post-Colonialism and Whose Postmodernism?", *World Literature Written in English*, 30, 2, 1990, pp. 1–9; Benita Parry, "Problems in Current Theories of Colonial Discourse," *Oxford Literary Review*, 9, 1–2, 1987, pp. 27–57; Linda Hutcheon, "Circling the Downspout of Empire," in Ian Adam and Helen Tiffin, eds, *Past the Last POST. Theorizing Post-Colonialism and Post-Modernism*, Calgary, University of Calgary Press, 1990, pp. 167–189; Biodun Jeyifo, "The Nature of Things. Arrested Decolonization and Critical Theory," *Research in African Literatures*, 21, 1990, pp. 33–47; Anne McClintock, "The Angel of Progress. Pitfalls of the Term 'Post-Colonialism,'" *Social Text*, 31–32, 1992, pp. 84–98; Ella Shohat, "Notes on the 'Post-Colonial'," *Social Text*, 31–32, 1992, pp. 99–113; Anthony Appiah, "Is the Post-in Postmodernism the Post- in Postcolonial?" *Critical Inquiry*, 17, Winter, 1991, pp. 336–357; Frank Shulze-Engler, "Beyond Post-Colonialism. Multiple Identities in East African Literature," in Gordon Collier, ed., *Us/Them. Translation, Transcription and Identity in Post-Colonial Literary Cultures*, Amsterdam and Atlanta, Ga., Rodopi, 1992, pp. 319–328; Stephen Slemon, "Unsettling the Empire. Resistance Theory for the Second World," *World Literature Written in English*, 30, 2, 1990, pp. 30–41.
11 Carlos Fuentes, "The End of Ideologies?" *Transition. An International*

Review, 51, 1991, pp. 26–31, argues that "the most serious social problems have not vanished" but have brought many of the confrontations with the Other to an urban unit which will have to create new models to deal with the polycultural nature of itself.

12 Calgary, Alberta, University of Calgary Press, 1990. There is debate between some of the essays which grew out of a special issue of *World Literature Written in English*. Linda Hutcheon's contribution, "Circling the Downspout of Empire," mounts a good challenge of the post-colonial/postmodern imperative. But see Diana Brydon's "The White Inuit Speaks: Contamination as Literary Strategy," pp. 191–203. I am nevertheless troubled by Simon Gikandi's essay, "Narration in the Post-Colonial Moment. Merle Hodge's *Crick Crack Monkey*," which has transformed Hodge's critique of coloniality and the personal exploration of Tee's growth to post-colonialist textualities.

13 In Michèle Barrett and Anne Phillips, eds, *Destabilizing Theory. Contemporary Feminist Debates*, Stanford, Calif., Stanford University Press, 1992, pp. 31–52.

14 *Research in African Literatures*, 21, 1990, pp. 33–47. Another unpublished manuscript, "Literary Theory and Theories of Decolonization," supplied by the author takes this discussion further. A combined version of both papers was delivered at the "Decentering Discourses" Conference, SUNY Binghamton, 1990.

15 "Literary Theory and Theories of Decolonization," p. 5.

16 *Oxford Literary Review*, 9, 1–2, 1987, p. 34. Anne Maxwell's "The Debate on Current Theories of Colonial Discourse," *Kunapipi*, 13, 3, 1991, pp. 70–84, offers an interesting summary of some of the key points of this discussion.

17 See note 10.

18 In Judith Butler and Joan Scott, eds, *Feminists Theorize the Political*, New York and London, Routledge, 1992, pp. 426–441.

19 See, for example, Handel Kashope Wright and Rinaldo Walcott, "How Esu's Children Signify at the Zoo. The Praxis of Being Black and Afrocentric in the Academy," unpublished manuscript of paper presented at African Studies Association Conference, supplied by authors (Ontario Institute for Studies in Education, 1992).

20 London, Heinemann, 1993.

21 London, Hutchinson, 1982.

22 Title of a collection published by Dangaroo Press, 1989.

23 A number of works have engaged this question of the link between post-coloniality and postmodernism. See, for example, the essays in Adam and Tiffin, eds, *Past the Last Post*. See also Simon During, "Postmodernism or Post-Colonialism Today," *Textual Practice*, 1, 1, 1987, pp. 32–47; Gerald Raulet, "From Modernity as One-Way Street to Postmodernity as Dead End," *New German Critique*, 11, 33, Fall, 1984, pp. 155–177; Walby, "Post-Post-Modernism?" pp. 31–52.

24 *Modern Fiction Studies*, 35, 1, Spring, 1989, pp. 157–179.

25 Ibid., p. 158.

26 Stephen Greenblatt and Giles Gunn, eds, *Redrawing the Boundaries*, New York, MLA, 1992.

27 Kumkum Sangari, "The Politics of the Possible," *Cultural Critique*, 7, Fall, 1987, pp. 157–186, raises some interesting questions on this issue in the closing section of her essay after offering a reading of the narrative structures of Gabriel Garcia Marquez and Salman Rushdie.

28 *Transition*, 51, 1991, pp. 32–40.

29 Ibid., p. 40.

30 A much more developed reading of Spivak's work is needed. This is not this chapter's concern. However, in trying to make space for the discussion of Black women's writing, and the theoretical explorations of women of color, it is necessary to identify how discourses of "postcoloniality" are located in relation to, and challenged by, these writings of Black women in Britain.

31 "Words and Things. Materialism and Method in Contemporary Feminist Analysis," in Barrett and Phillips, eds, *Destabilizing Theory*, pp. 218–219.

32 See, for example, a note to Homi Bhabha's paper "Of Mimicry and Man. The Ambivalence of Colonial Discourse," *October*, 28, 1984, p. 126, describes the paper as a contribution to a panel on "Colonialist and Post-Colonialist Discourse," organized by Gayatri Spivak for the MLA in New York, 1983.

33 *Social Text*, 31–32, 1992, pp. 8–19.

34 Robert Gooding-Willams, ed., *Reading Rodney King. Reading Urban Uprising*, New York and London, Routledge, 1993, uses Rodney King's words to analyze their meanings, in his introduction, "On Being Stuck," p. 3.

35 *Socialist Review*, 20, 3, July–September, 1990, pp. 81–97.

36 I surveyed all that was available of the *Subaltern Studies* collection, edited by Ranajit Guha (Oxford and Delhi, Oxford University Press, in this case vols 1, 4, 5, 1983, 1985, 1987), and found the contributions helpful, particularly Ranajit Guha, "The Prose of Counter-Insurgency," pp. 1–40, and contributions like those on protests and uprisings against coloniality and for struggles which predate coloniality. What concerns me, however, is the acceptance of the language of subalternization as a naming, even though of Gramscian origin. I was unable to see a definition of post-coloniality there as an originary point. Dipesh Chakrabarty in the discussion to volume 4 defines the "Subaltern Studies Project" as trying to "understand the consciousness that informed and still informs political actions taken by subaltern classes on their own, independently of any elite initiatives" (p. 374). Further "subalternity" refers to the "composite culture of resistance to and acceptance of domination and hierarchy – is a characteristic of class relations in our society, where the veneer of bourgeois equality barely masks the violent, feudal nature of much of our systems of power and authority" (p. 376). It therefore "opens up once more the thorny question of 'consciousness' and how Marxists might study it" (p. 376).

37 See, for example, conversations with Trinh Minh-ha and others, "If Upon Leaving What We Have to Say We Speak. A Conversation Piece," in Russell Ferguson, William Olander, Marcia Tucker and

Karen Fiss, eds, *Discourses. Conversations in Postmodern Art and Culture*, New York, The New Museum of Contemporary Art, and Cambridge, Mass. and London, MIT Press, 1990, pp. 44–66, and my earlier work, "Collaboration and the Ordering Imperative in Life Story Production," in Sidonie Smith and Julia Watson, eds, *De/Colonizing the Subject. The Politics of Gender in Women's Autobiography*, Minneapolis, Minn., University of Minnesota Press, 1992, pp. 3–19, for discussion of some of the imperatives of interviewing and voicing ourselves.

38 "Poststructuralism, Marginality, Postcoloniality and Value," in P. Collier and Gaya Ryan, eds, *Literary Theory Today*, Cambridge, Polity, 1990, p. 227.

39 Edited by Sarah Harasym, New York and London, Routledge, 1990.

40 Her work such as "Can the Subaltern Speak?" in Cary Nelson and Lawrence Grossberg, eds, *Marxism and the Interpretation of Culture*, Urbana and Chicago, Ill., University of Illinois Press, 1988, pp. 271–313, and other essays on women have advanced the discussion by non-Western feminists in many ways. See also her discussion, "Subaltern Studies. Deconstructing Historiography," in Guha, ed., *Subaltern Studies*, 4, pp. 330–363 which links the question of woman to "notions of territoriality and the communal mode of power" (p. 358). But in this particular encounter, the ideas which have been developed in written work remained outside the pales of the discussion.

41 Spivak, "Can the Subaltern Speak?" I find this one of the most haunting and critical interrogatives in contemporary feminist/gender discourses.

42 New York and London, Routledge, 1988 (first published by Methuen, 1987).

43 As, for example, in Gayatri Spivak, "Three Women's Texts and a Critique of Imperialism," *Critical Inquiry*, 12, 1, Autumn, 1985, and "Displacement and the Discourse of Woman," in Mark Krupnick, ed., *Displacement. Derrida and After*, Bloomington, Ind., Indiana University Press, 1983, and some of the essays in her *In Other Worlds*. Spivak in the concluding words to a presentation at SUNY Binghamton in 1991, "Teaching Multiculture," spoke of the need to "give the woman to the other woman" as a mode of advancing some of the stalled discourses. Spivak had earlier constructed discourses as interrupting strands where, for example, the discourse of race must necessarily interrupt the discourse of gender, etc. This formulation rather than a holding together of a variety of theoretical positions, as I see it, creates this approach, useful nevertheless in some contexts, where one pursues one line of analysis.

44 See, for example, her *Outside in the Teaching Machine*, London and New York, Routledge, 1993.

45 Kumkum Sangari and Sudesh Vaid, eds, *Recasting Women in India. Essays in Colonial History in India*, New Brunswick, NJ, Rutgers University Press, 1990, pp. 1–2, which is in many ways the unaccounted for "other" in the "subaltern" project which Spivak alluded to.

46 In surveying library holdings on this topic, I observed an interesting shift from "Commonwealth literatures," to "New English literatures," to "New literatures in English," to "Post-colonial literatures," the most recent being Feroza Jussawalla and Reed Way Dasenbrock, eds, *Interviews with Writers of the Post-Colonial World*, Jackson, Miss. and London, University Press of Mississippi, 1992.

47 "Conference Presentation," p. 152.

48 Personal conversation, London, August, 10, 1992.

49 Discussions during dialogue as part of the ALA Women's Caucus Luncheon, African Literature Association Conference, April, 19, 1993. These and similar positions have been consistently raised by a number of writers who resent being defined within a discourse like post-coloniality. A writer like Werewere Liking can hardly be defined within any post-colonial context. See Anne Adams, "To W/Rite in a New Language," *Callaloo*, 16, 1, Winter, 1993, pp. 153–168.

50 London, Sheba Feminist Publishers, 1988. But see also Pratibha Parmar's earlier piece, "Gender, Race and Class: Asian Women in Resistance," in Centre for Contemporary Cultural Studies, *The Empire Strikes Back*, pp. 236–275.

51 Grewal *et al.*, *Charting the Journey*, p. 10.

52 Ibid., p. 11.

53 *Feminist Review*, 17, July, 1984, p. 17.

54 Grewal *et al.*, *Charting the Journey*, p. 118.

55 Edited by the Black Womantalk Collective (Da Choong, Olivette Wilson Cole, Bernardine Evaristo, Gabriela Pearse), London, Black Womantalk, 1987. See also their *Don't Ask Me Why. An Anthology of Short Stories by Black Women*, London, Black Womantalk, 1991.

56 London, Hutchinson, 1987.

57 London, Karnak House, 1987.

58 London, Hansib Publishing Ltd, 1988. This offers an annotated bibliography with introductory discussions of a variety of texts of Black British literature.

59 Ibid., p. 134.

60 London, Paladin, 1992.

61 Institute of Race Relations, *Policing Against Black People*, London, Institute of Race Relations, 1987.

62 Beverley Bryan, Stella Dadzie and Suzanne Scafe, *The Heart of the Race. Black Women's Lives in Britain*, London, Virago, 1985.

63 Selma James, ed., *Strangers and Sisters. Women, Race and Immigration*, Bristol, Falling Wall Press, 1985.

64 Bristol, Falling Wall Press, 1980/1986.

65 Heidi Safia Mirza, *Young, Female and Black*, London and New York, Routledge, 1992.

66 Ibid., p. 199.

67 London, Virago, 1978.

68 See my "Collaboration and the Ordering Imperative in Life Story Production," pp. 3–19, for further discussion of this mode.

69 London, Cassell & Co., 1976.

70 Ibid., p. 43.

71 Edited by Lauretta Ngcobo, London, Virago, 1988.

72 This has its benefit but may relate to the marked absence of Black women at the university level where the production of intellectual analysis often takes place. Susheila Nasta who is employed at the university level has produced a great deal of work such as is represented in *Motherlands*, London, The Women's Press, 1991, and New Brunswick, NJ, Rutgers University Press, 1992, and her editing of the journal *Wasafiri* has given scholarly attention to a variety of literary works.

73 See Janice Liddell's review, "Pain and Pathology," *Caribbean Commentary*, 1, 3, April–May, 1990, pp. 33–34.

74 Joan Riley, *The Unbelonging*, London, The Women's Press, 1985, p. 13.

75 Ibid., p. 74.

76 In Rhonda Cobham and Merle Collins, eds, *Watchers and Seekers*, London, The Women's Press, 1987, pp. 40–49.

77 London, The Women's Press, 1987. Another novel, *Romance*, was also published in 1988 (London, The Women's Press), and *A Kindness to the Children*, her most recent novel, was published in 1992 (London, The Women's Press).

78 See frontispiece of *Waiting in the Twilight*.

79 London, The Women's Press, 1992.

80 In Grewal *et al.*, *Charting the Journey*, pp. 145–156.

81 Interview with Claudette Williams in London, April, 1993.

82 London, Heinemann, 1989.

83 In Cobham and Collins, eds, *Watchers and Seekers*, p. 88.

84 *Feminist Art News*, 3, 10, 1992, p. 23.

85 In *Inside Ant's Belly*, ed. Merle Collins, London, National Association for the Teaching of English, 1994, pp. 79–90.

86 3, 10, 1991, p. 1.

87 Ibid., p. 24.

88 Ibid., p. 26.

89 Ibid., p. 22.

90 London, The Women's Press, 1992. Also author of *Angel*, Seattle, Wash., Seal Press, 1987, and *Because the Dawn Breaks*, London, Karia Press, 1985, and other works identified in the bibliography.

91 In Cobham and Collins, eds, *Watchers and Seekers*, pp. 103–107.

92 In Cobham and Collins, eds, *Watchers and Seekers*, pp. 123–126. See also her collection, *Gifts from My Grandmother*, London, Sheba Feminist Publishers, n.d.

93 In Cobham and Collins, eds, *Watchers and Seekers*, pp. 118–119.

94 *Cultural Critique*, 7, Fall, 1987, pp. 157–186.

95 London, Verso, 1988, pp. 271–282.

96 Boston, Mass., Beacon Press, 1986.

97 There is some debate about the designation Black British, with suggestions that these two conjoined are contradictions in terms. A number of these writers may not refer to themselves as Black British but as Afro-Caribbean, Guyanese, Trinidadian, Black Scottish, Asian and so on. Some feel they have no particular sets of identifications they

need to claim. Dorothea Smartt would suggest that Black British often refers to the generation born in England as opposed to the ones who migrate. What many of these writers have in common, however, is that they define themselves as Black women writers. Discussion with Dorothea Smartt, in London, May, 1993. Janice Shinebourne and other writers I talked to on several occasions would help clarify this point, particularly about making distinctions and not approaching this group as monolithic, but there are of course a variety of perspectives on this issue of naming.

98 See Velma Pollard's work such as "Innovation in Jamaican Creole. The Speech of Rastafari," in Manfred Gorlach and John A. Holm, eds, *Varieties of English Around the World*, vol. 8, Amsterdam and Philadelphia, John Benjamins, 1986, pp. 157–166.

99 Grewal *et al.*, *Charting the Journey*, p. 280.

100 From Grace Nichols, *I Is a Long Memoried Woman*, London, Karnak House, 1983/1990, p. 65.

101 London, Virago, 1989.

102 London, Virago, 1984.

103 London, Leda Serene/YOD video, 1990; available from New York, Women Make Movies.

104 Hebden Bridge, West Yorkshire, Urban Fox Press, 1985.

105 An installation at the Foyer Galleries, Royal Festival Hall, in London, 7 April to 10 May, 1992.

106 Hebden Bridge, West Yorkshire, Urban Fox Press, 1990.

107 In Grewal *et al.*, *Charting the Journey*, p. 205.

108 Black Womantalk, ed., *Black Women Talk*, p. 111.

109 London, Sheba Feminist Publishers, 1986.

110 London, The Women's Press, 1987.

111 Some of the creative energy is expressed in Centerprise Black Women's Poetry space and in Apples and Snakes, *The Popular Front of Contemporary Poetry Anthology*, London, Apples and Snakes/Angel Press, 1992, which allows some space for Black women poets. There are a number of collections, poets and other writers that I could not identify here because of space and the nature of this present undertaking. There is room for a much more extended examination of this literature which is still in process and still "to be continued."

112 Sister Netifa, *A Woman Determined*, London, Research Associates, 1987. Netifa has two albums of poetry and a new collection forthcoming.

113 Much of the energy has been directed towards producing collections. See, for example, the recent *Daughters of Africa*, ed. Margaret Busby, London, Jonathan Cape and New York, Pantheon, 1992. It seems it is more important for the women to document their creativity and their presence in as many ways as possible. But see the recent Gina Wisker, *Black Women's Writing*, New York, St Martin's Press, 1993, which brings Black British women writers under the same critical attention as Black American women writers.

114 Published jointly as *Adah's Story*, London, Allison & Busby, 1983, and New York, Fontana, 1988. See also her *Gwendolen* also published as

The Family, London, Collins, 1989 and New York, Braziller, 1990, which attempts to deal with incest in a migrant Caribbean family in a similar way as had Joan Riley's earlier work. My review, "You Big 'Oman Nuh, June-June," in *Belles Lettres*, 6, 1, Fall, 1990, pp. 20–21, discusses this further.

5 WRITING HOME

1 This chapter appeared in an earlier version in Carole Boyce Davies and Elaine Savory Fido, eds, *Out of the Kumbla. Caribbean Women and Literature*, Trenton, NJ, Africa World Press, 1990, pp. 59–73, and has been rewritten here for the purposes of this book.
2 June Jordan, "Notes Towards Home," in her *Living Room*, New York, Thunder's Mouth Press, 1985.
3 Peter Nobel, "Refugees and Other Migrants Viewed with the Legal Eye – or how to Fight Confusion," in Kirsten Holst Petersen and Anna Rutherford, eds, *Displaced Persons*, Sydney, Coventry and Mundelstrup, Denmark, Dangaroo Press, 1988, pp. 18–31, has interesting discussion of this issue.
4 Shabnam Grewal *et al.*, *Charting the Journey. Writings by Black and Third World Women*, London, Sheba Feminist Publishers, 1988, p. 10.
5 Ibid., p. 11.
6 Stuart Hall, "Signification, Althusser and the Post-Structuralist Debates," *Critical Studies in Mass Communication*, 2, 2, June, 1985, p. 109.
7 New York, Pantheon, 1992.
8 Ibid., pp. 135–138.
9 This point was repeatedly made at the "Dreaming of the Homeland. African Writers in Exile Conference," Bethnal Green, London, April, 1991.
10 *Research in African Literatures*, 22, 4, Winter, 1991, pp. 5–27.
11 Ibid., p. 22.
12 Barbara Christian has a useful discussion of this point in "Trajectories of Self-Definition. Placing Contemporary Afro-American Women's Fiction," in Marjorie Pryse and Hortense Spillers, eds, *Conjuring*, Bloomington, Ind., Indiana University Press, 1985, pp. 233–248.
13 Paule Marshall's novels discussed here include: *Brown Girl, Brownstones*, New York, Random House, 1959; *The Chosen Place, The Timeless People*, New York, Harcourt Brace, 1969; *Praisesong for the Widow*, New York, G.P. Putnam's Sons, 1983; *Daughters*, New York, Plume, 1991.
14 Freedom, Calif., The Crossing Press, 1982.
15 See Caren Kaplan's "Deterritorializations. The Rewriting of Home and Exile in Western Feminist Discourse," *Cultural Critique*, 6, Spring 1987, pp. 187–198, for some discussion of Cliff's first work.
16 I have seen comprehensive anthologies and critical studies of, for example, African-American writers which did not include Marshall or Lorde, critical studies of Caribbean writers which did not include Cliff or Lorde or Marshall.

17 Makeda Silvera has recently edited *Piece of My Heart. A Lesbian of Color Anthology*, Toronto, Sister Vision Press, 1992, which develops in much better fashion some of these questions.
18 *Reena and Other Stories*, New York, The Feminist Press, 1983, pp. 95–106.
19 New York, G.P. Putnam's Sons, 1983.
20 In Mari Evans, ed., *Black Women Writers (1950–1980). A Critical Evaluation*, New York, Doubleday, 1984, pp. 295–315.
21 Julie Dash, with Toni Cade Bambara and bell hooks, *The Making of an African American Woman's Film. Daughters of the Dust*, New York, The New Press, 1992. My unpublished interview with Frances Anne Solomon took place in London in May, 1992.
22 Edward Brathwaite, "The African Presence in Caribbean Literature," *Daedalus*, 103, 2, Spring, 1974, pp. 73–109.
23 Carole Boyce Davies, "Black Woman's Journey Into Self. A Womanist Reading of Paule Marshall's *Praisesong for the Widow*," *Matatu*, Heft 1, 1, 1987, pp. 19–34.
24 New York, Plume, 1991.
25 See Marshall's interview with Della Scott in *Abafazi*, 3, 2 (Spring/ Summer, 1993), pp. 34–38. See also Peter Erickson's review, "Hard Work. Paule Marshall's *Daughters*," *Callaloo*, 16, 1, pp. 268–271. This issue also has the most extensive bibliography of works on Marshall.
26 "Grenada Revisited. An Interim Report," in *Sister Outsider. Essays and Speeches*, Freedom, Calif., The Crossing Press, 1984, pp. 176–190.
27 I am indebted to Maya Chowdhry for a discussion of this latter point in personal conversation, London, April 22, 1992. See also Gloria Anzaldua's "To(o) Queer the Writer – Loca, escritora y chicana," in Betsy Warland, ed., *Inversions*, Vancouver, Press Gang Publishers, 1991, pp. 249–263, which spends a great deal of time talking about naming and situatedness.
28 Watertown, Mass., Persephone Press, 1980. But see also her other works like *Abeng*, Freedom, Calif., The Crossing Press, 1984, *No Telephone to Heaven*, New York, Random House, 1989, *The Land of Look Behind*, Ithaca, NY, Firebrand Books, 1985, *Bodies of Water*, New York, Pantheon, 1990.
29 Jean Rhys, *Wide Sargasso Sea*, London, Penguin, 1966.
30 In *The Land of Look Behind*, pp. 57–76.
31 New York, Alfred A. Knopf, 1974.
32 *Our Sister Killjoy or Reflections from a Black-Eyed Squint*, London, Longman, 1977.
33 See Lemuel Johnson, "A-beng. (Re)Calling the Body In(to) Question," in Boyce Davies and Savory Fido, eds, *Out of the Kumbla*, pp. 111–142. More recently, Belinda Edmondson's "Race, Privilege, and the Politics of (Re)Writing History. An Analysis of the Novels of Michelle Cliff," *Callaloo*, 16, 1, 1993, pp. 180–191.
34 Jamaica Kincaid, *At the Bottom of the River*, New York, Vintage Books, 1985, are stories published between 1978 and 1983, *Annie John*, New York, Farrar, Strauss, Giroux, 1985, *Lucy*, New York, Farrar,

Strauss, Giroux, 1991, *A Small Place*, New York, Farrar, Strauss, Giroux, 1988.

35 George Lamming, *In The Castle of My Skin*, New York, McGraw Hill, 1953; Merle Hodge, *Crick Crack Monkey*, London, André Deutsch, 1970.

36 "My Mother," in *At the Bottom of the River*, p. 60.

37 Delores M. Mortimer and Roy S. Bryce Laporte, *Female Immigrants to the United States: Caribbean, Latin American and African Experiences*, and *Caribbean Immigration to the United States*, Washington, DC, The Smithsonian Institution, RIIES Occasional Papers, nos 1 and 2, 1981 and 1983.

38 Saskia Sassen, "Capital Mobility and Labor Migration," in her *The Mobility of Labor and Capital*, London and New York, Cambridge University Press, 1988.

39 Paule Marshall's "From the Poets in the Kitchen," in *Reena and Other Stories*, pp. 3–12.

6 MOBILITY, EMBODIMENT AND RESISTANCE IN BLACK WOMEN'S WRITING IN THE US

1 Clara Smith, "Freight Train Blues," *Women's Railroad Blues*, Rosetta Records, RR 1301, 1980, cited in Hazel Carby, "It Just Be's Dat Way Sometime. The Sexual Politics of Women's Blues," in Robyn R. Warhol and Diane Price Herndl, eds, *Feminisms. An Anthology of Literary Theory and Criticism*, New Brunswick, NJ, Rutgers University Press, 1991, pp. 746–758; and Daphne Duval Harrison's *Black Pearls. Blues Queens of the 1920's*, New Brunswick, NJ, Rutgers University Press, 1990.

2 See Mary Helen Washington's discussion of this issue in her introduction to "Incidents," *Invented Lives. Narratives of Black Women, 1860–1960*, New York, Anchor Press/Doubleday, 1987. See also the work of Valerie Smith such as " 'Loopholes of Retreat.' Architecture and Ideology in Harriet Jacobs's *Incidents in the Life of a Slave Girl*", in Henry Louis Gates Jr, ed., *Reading Black. Reading Feminist. A Critical Anthology*, New York, Meridian, 1990, pp. 212–226; and Sherley Anne Williams in her essay, "Some Implications of Womanist Theory," *Callaloo*, 9, 2, Spring, 1986, pp. 303–308 which examines some of the pathways through which Black males pursued the "heroic quest".

3 Smith, " 'Loopholes of Retreat,' "p. 217.

4 *Black American Literature Forum*, 14, 4, Winter, 1986, p. 157.

5 Ibid., p. 157. See Claudia Tate's introduction to her *Black Women Writers at Work*, New York, Continuum, pp. xx–xxi.

6 Tate, *Black Women Writers at Work*.

7 For example, Henry Louis Gates Jr, Black Fiction Project which has been engaged in the process of uncovering missing works. Gates has constantly asserted that the discovery of these works will change radically some of our accepted truisms of Black literature. His edition of *The Schomburg Library of 19th Century Black Women Writers*, Oxford

University Press, 1988; and Deborah McDowell's series of reprints of out of print Black women writers for Beacon Press, Boston.

8 *Cultural Studies*, 7, 2, May, 1993, pp. 224–239.

9 Ibid., p. 234.

10 In Alain Locke, ed., *The New Negro*, New York, Atheneum, 1980, p. 147 (originally published in 1925).

11 Cited in Harrison, *Black Pearls*, p. 90.

12 Chicago, Ill., and London, University of Chicago Press, 1984.

13 Ibid., p. 202.

14 In Warhol and Price Herndl, eds, *Feminisms*.

15 Ibid., p. 752.

16 New York and Oxford, Oxford University Press, 1988.

17 Smith, " 'Loopholes of Retreat,' " pp. 212, 213.

18 As, for example, Hazel Carby's *Reconstructing Womanhood. The Emergence of the Afro-American Woman Novelist*, New York and Oxford, Oxford University Press, 1987 and several other works on Black women would indicate.

19 Contradictory descriptor taken from Barbadian oral discourse as reported in Paule Marshall's "From the Poets in the Kitchen," in her *Reena and Other Stories*, New York, The Feminist Press, 1983.

20 New York, Alfred A. Knopf Inc., 1987.

21 New York, William Morrow Inc., 1986.

22 In her *Common Differences. Conflicts in Black and White Feminist Perspectives*, Garden City, NY, Anchor Books, 1981.

23 *Sage*, 4, 2, 1987, pp. 3–10.

24 Carby, *Reconstructing Womanhood*.

25 See version in Erlene Stetson's *Black Sister*, Bloomington and Indianapolis, Ind., Indiana University Press, 1981, p. 24.

26 Ibid. Nell Painter is engaged in work on Sojourner Truth which she claims will change many of our accepted mythologies surrounding Sojourner Truth: lecture at Women's History Seminar, University of London, April, 1992.

27 *Sage*, 2, 1, Spring, 1985, pp. 41–43.

28 *Our Nig. Sketches from the Life of a Free Black*, New York, Random House, 1983.

29 New York, Harcourt Brace Jovanovich, 1989.

30 Gloria Naylor, "A Conversation with Toni Morrison," *Southern Review*, 21, 3, July, 1985, pp. 567–593.

31 Lecture at Cornell University, May 10, 1988.

32 Susan Suleiman, "On Maternal Splitting. A Propos of Mary Gordon's *Men and Angels*," *Signs*, 14, 1, Autumn, 1988, pp. 25–41; Sara Ruddick, *Maternal Thinking. Towards a Politics of Peace*, Boston, Mass., Beacon, 1989; Nancy Chodorow and Susan Contratto, "The Fantasy of the Perfect Mother," in Barrie Thorne and Marilyn Yalom, eds, *Rethinking the Family*, New York, Longman, 1982, pp. 54–73.

33 In Joyce Trebilcot, ed., *Mothering. Essays in Feminist Theory*, Totowa, NJ, Rowan and Allenheld, 1984, pp. 315–330.

34 *Diacritics* 17, 2, Summer, 1987, pp. 65–81.

35 Morrison, *Beloved*, p. 79.

36 Ibid., p. 61.

37 The repeated manifestation of a single child in the life of a woman who loses infant children after they are born. Once this situation attains some repetitiveness, the child has to be marked so that it may be identified upon return. E. Bolaji Idowu in *Oludumare. God in Yoruba Belief*, London, Longman, 1962, describes the *abiku*. Wole Soyinka uses it symbolically in some of his work. Chinua Achebe's *Things Fall Apart* (1959), New York, Fawcett, 1988, explored the Igbo version, the *ogbanje*: "one of those wicked children who, when they died, entered their mother's wombs to be born again" (p. 70). See also Ben Okri, *The Famished Road*, London, Cape, 1991.

38 Morrison, *Beloved*, p. 120.

39 Ibid., p. 164.

40 Spillers, "Mama's Baby, Papa's Maybe," p. 80.

41 In Deborah McDowell and Arnold Rampersad, eds, *Slavery and the Literary Imagination*, Baltimore Md, and London, The Johns Hopkins University Press, 1989, pp. 144–163.

42 Angelita Reyes's research in this area is pursuing the historical record of the Margaret Garner story. See also the account in Middleton Harris *et al.*, eds, *The Black Book*, New York, Random House, 1974, p. 10. See also Linda Krumholz, "The Ghosts of Slavery. Historical Recovery in Toni Morrison's *Beloved*," *African-American Review*, 26, 3, 1992, pp. 395–408.

43 Cited in the Author's Note to Williams, *Dessa Rose*, pp. 5–6.

44 "The Meaning of Motherhood in Black Culture and Black Mother-Daughter Relationships."

45 In *Sister Outsider*, Freedom, Calif., The Crossing Press, 1984, pp. 72–80.

46 *History Workshop: A Journal of Socialist Historians*, 5, Spring, 1978, pp. 9–66.

47 In *In Other Worlds. Essays in Cultural Politics.* New York and London, Routledge, 1988, pp. 222–240 (first published by Methuen, 1987).

48 Ibid., pp. 241–268.

49 Ibid., p. 248.

50 "The Black Woman's Role in the Community of Slaves," *Black Scholar*, 2, 4, December, 1971, p. 5.

51 Notes taken at a lecture at Syracuse University, June, 1986. Deborah McDowell, "Reading Family Matters," in Cheryl Wall, ed., *Changing Our Own Words*, New Brunswick, NJ and London, Rutgers University Press, 1989, pp. 75–97.

52 *The Mother/Daughter Plot. Narrative, Psychoanalysis, Feminism*, Bloomington, Ind., Indiana University Press, 1989.

53 New York, Random House, 1969.

54 The notion of the "outraged mother" is offered by Joanne Braxton in "Ancestral Presence. The Outraged Mother Figure in Contemporary Afra-American Writing," in Joanne Braxton and Andree Nicola McLaughlin, eds, *Wild Women in the Whirlwind*, New Brunswick, NJ, Rutgers University Press, 1989, pp. 75–97.

55 Lectures at Cornell and Syracuse Universities, 1988, 1989.

55 Lectures at Cornell and Syracuse Universities, 1988, 1989.

56 Marita Golden, *Long Distance Life*, New York, Bantam, 1990, p. 47.

57 *Meridian*, Harcourt Brace Jovanovich, 1976. See also Christine Hall, "Art, Action and the Ancestors. Alice Walker's *Meridian* in its Context," in Gina Wisker, ed., *Black Women's Writing*, New York, St Martin's Press, 1993, pp. 96–110.

58 New York, Anchor Press, 1983.

59 By Francophone Caribbean writer, Myriam Warner-Vieyra, London, Heinemann, 1987 (trans. Betty Wilson).

60 Carole Boyce Davies, "Black Woman's Journey Into Self. A Womanist Reading of Paule Marshall's *Praisesong for the Widow*," *Matatu*, Heft 1, 1, Jahrgang, 1987, pp. 19–34.

61 See also Abena P.A. Busia, "What is Your Nation? Reconnecting Africa and Her Diaspora through Paule Marshall's *Praisesong for the Widow*," in Wall, ed., *Changing Our Own Words*, pp. 196–211.

62 Toni Morrison, *Sula*, New York, Alfred A. Knopf, 1974.

63 New York, Alfred A. Knopf, 1981.

64 Zora Neale Hurston, *Their Eyes Were Watching God*, Urbana and Chicago, Ill., University of Illinois Press, 1978, p. 36.

65 Ibid., p. 44.

66 "Zora Neale Hurston. A Subversive Reading," in Carole Boyce Davies, ed., "Black Women's Writing. Crossing the Boundaries," *Matatu*, Heft 6, 3, Jahrgang, 1989, pp. 5–23.

67 Ibid., p. 22.

68 New York, Kitchen Table: Women of Color Press, 1983, pp. xix–lvi.

69 *Technical Difficulties. African-American Notes on the State of the Union*, New York, Pantheon, 1992.

70 Boston, Mass., Beacon Press, 1979.

71 See also Donna Haraway's discussion of Butler's work within the context of "Biopolitics of Postmodern Bodies," in her *Simians, Cyborgs, and Women. The Reinvention of Nature*, New York, Routledge, 1991, pp. 225–230.

72 I believe Hazel Carby's conclusion, "The Quicksands of Representation," in her *Reconstructing Womanhood*, pp. 163–175, is such a beginning even as it concludes her book, speaking as it does to the issues of representation and the dismantling of singular conceptions of the self.

73 "Commercial Deportation as Rite of Passage in Black Women's Novels," in Carole Boyce Davies, ed., "Black Women's Writing," pp. 127–154.

74 In Braxton and McLaughlin, eds, *Wild Women in the Whirlwind*, pp. 379–394.

75 Ibid., p. 379.

76 Cheryl Keyes, " 'We're More Than a Novelty, Boys.' Strategies of Female Rappers in the Rap Music Tradition," in Joan Newton Radner, ed., *Feminist Messages. Coding in Women's Folk Culture*, Urbana and Chicago, Ill., University of Illinois Press, 1993, p. 214.

77 Cited in Dominique de Prima, "Beat the Rap," *Mother Jones*, September/October, 1990, pp. 32–36, 80–82.

7 OTHER TONGUES. GENDER, LANGUAGE, SEXUALITY AND THE POLITICS OF LOCATION

1 French based patois for my co-mother (*ma commère*).
2 Gayatri Spivak, "Can the Subaltern Speak?" in Cary Nelson and Lawrence Grossberg, eds, *Marxism and the Interpretation of Culture*, Urbana and Chicago, Ill., University of Illinois Press, 1988, pp. 271–313.
3 Stuart Hall, "Cultural Identity and Cinematic Representation," *Framework*, special issue on Theory and the Politics of Location, 36, 1989, p. 74.
4 Audre Lorde, "Age, Race, Class, and Sex. Women Redefining Difference," in *Sister Outsider*, Freedom, Calif., The Crossing Press, 1984, p. 116.
5 Spivak, "Can the Subaltern Speak?" p. 273.
6 Trinh T. Minh-ha, "Cotton and Iron," in Russell Ferguson, Martha Gever, Trinh T. Minh-ha and Cornel West, eds, *Out There. Marginalization and Contemporary Cultures*, Cambridge, Mass. and London, MIT Press, 1990, p. 328.
7 Hall, "Cultural Identity and Cinematic Representation," p. 73.
8 Ibid.
9 Joan Borsa, "Frida Kahlo. Marginalization and the Critical Female Subject," *Third Text*, 12, Autumn, 1990, p. 37.
10 "Choosing the Margin as a Space of Radical Openness," *Framework*, 36, 1990, p. 15.
11 Urbana and Chicago, Ill., University of Illinois Press, 1978 (first pub. 1937), p. 17.
12 New York, Farrar, Strauss, Giroux, 1991, p. 43.
13 Ibid., p. 72.
14 Ibid., p. 65.
15 Ibid., p. 83.
16 New York, Farrar, Strauss, Giroux, 1985.
17 Kincaid, *Lucy*, p. 102.
18 *Cultural Critique*, Winter, 1990, pp. 81–104.
19 Afterword to Carole Boyce Davies and Elaine Savory Fido, eds, *Out of the Kumbla. Caribbean Women and Literature*, Trenton, NJ, Africa World Press, 1990, pp. 355–372.
20 London, James Currey, Nairobi and Portsmouth, NH, Heinemann, Harare, Zimbabwe Publishing House, 1986.
21 Edward Kamau Brathwaite, *History of the Voice. The Development of Nation Language in Anglophone Caribbean Poetry*, London and Port-of-Spain, New Beacon Books, 1984.
22 *She Tries Her Tongue. Her Silence Softly Breaks*, Charlottetown, Prince Edward Island, Canada, Ragweed Press, 1989.
23 Ibid., p. 58.
24 In *Testimonies of Exile*, Trenton, NJ, Africa World Press, 1990, p. 3.
25 Toronto, Sister Vision Press, 1992.
26 London, Karnak House, 1983, p. 87.
27 Trinidad and Tobago, New Voices, 1992. This poet's work came to my attention at the Caribbean Women Writers' Conference in

Curaçao in August 1992, after much of this chapter had been written and where a version of this chapter was presented.

28 "'I Is a Long-Memoried Woman'. A 50-minute Drama and Dance Video Based on the Collection of Poems by Grace Nichols." London: Leda Serene/YOD Video, 1990.

29 Alette Olin Hill, *Mother Tongue, Father Time. A Decade of Linguistic Revolt*, Bloomington and Indianapolis, Ind., Indiana University Press, 1986.

30 In Boyce Davies and Savory Fido, eds, *Out of the Kumbla*, p. 276.

31 Kincaid, *Lucy*, p. 90.

32 In Gayle Greene and Coppelia Kahn, eds, *Making a Difference. Feminist Literary Criticism*, London, Methuen, 1985, pp. 59–79.

33 Ibid., p. 69.

34 *Bearing the Word. Women Writers and Poetic Identity*, Princeton, NJ, Princeton University Press, 1980.

35 Ibid., p. 13.

36 In Brenda O. Daly and Maureen T. Reddy, eds, *Narrating Mothers. Theorizing Maternal Subjectivities*, Knoxville, Tenn., University of Tennessee Press, 1991, pp. 94–108. But see chapters on language and subjectivity by Cathy Urwin, "Power Relations and the Emergence of Language," in Julian Henriques *et al.*, *Changing the Subject. Psychology, Social Regulation and Subjectivity*, London and New York, Methuen, 1984, pp. 264–322.

37 In Philomena Mariani, ed., *Critical Fictions. The Politics of Imaginative Writing*, Seattle, Wash., Bay Press, 1991, p. 83.

38 Kincaid, *Lucy*, p. 91.

39 In Cheryl Wall, ed., *Changing Our Own Words. Essays on Criticism, Theory, and Writing by Black Women*, New Brunswick, NJ and London, Rutgers University Press, 1989, pp. 16–37.

40 bell hooks, *Talking Back. Thinking Feminist. Thinking Black*, Boston, Mass., South End Press, 1989.

41 Philip, *She Tries Her Tongue*, p. 67.

42 See Chris Weedon, Andrew Tolson and Frank Mort, "Theories of Language and Subjectivity," in Stuart Hall, ed., *Culture, Media, Language: Working Papers in Cultural Studies, 1972–79*, London, Hutchinson, 1980, for a review of some of the theoretical movements on the question of language.

43 Philip, *She Tries Her Tongue*, p. 71.

44 Ibid., p. 67. A number of similar issues are raised in Gloria Anzaldua, ed., *Making Face, Making Soul/Haciendo Caras*, San Francisco, Calif., Spinsters/Aunt Lute Foundation, 1990, particularly the introduction section "In Which Voice/With Which Voice", pp. xxii–xxiv as well as section 4, "In Silence, Giving Tongue. The Transformation of Silence into (An)Other Alphabet," in which women from different language communities speak to the issue of silence and voice. See also Gloria Anzaldua's "Speaking in Tongues. A Letter to Third World Women Writers" and other pieces in Cherrie Moraga and Gloria Anzaldua, eds, *This Bridge Called My Back. Writings by Radical Women of Color*, Watertown, Mass., Persephone Press, 1981.

BIBLIOGRAPHY

Adam, Ian and Helen Tiffin, eds. *Past the Last Post. Theorizing Post-Colonialism and Post-Modernism.* Calgary, University of Calgary Press, 1990.

—— "To W/Rite in a New Language. Werewere Liking's Adaptation of Ritual to the Novel." *Callaloo*, 16, 1, 1983, pp. 153–168.

Adams, Anne. ed. *Seventy African and Caribbean Women Writers.* New York, Greenwood Press, forthcoming.

"African Explains Witchcraft, The." *Africa.* 8, 4, October, 1935, pp. 504–599.

Aidoo, Ama Ata. Interview with Maxine Lautre McGregor. In Dennis Duerden and Cosmo Pieterse, eds, *African Writers Talking.* London, Heinemann, 1972, pp. 19–27.

—— *Our Sister Killjoy or Reflections from a Black-Eyed Squint.* London, Longman, 1977.

—— "GHANA: To Be a Woman." In Robin Morgan, ed., *Sisterhood is Global.* New York, Anchor Press/Doubleday, 1984, pp. 258–265.

—— *Anowa and Dilemma of a Ghost.* London, Longman, 1985.

—— *Changes.* London, The Women's Press, 1990.

—— "That Capacious Topic. Gender Politics." In Philomena Mariani, ed., *Critical Fictions. The Politics of Imaginative Writing.* Seattle, Wash., Bay Press, 1991, p. 152.

—— "The African Woman Today." *Dissent*, Summer, 1992, pp. 319–325.

Alcoff, Linda. "Cultural Feminism Versus Post-Structuralism. The Identity Question in Feminist Theory." *Signs*, 13, 3, 1988, pp. 419–436.

—— "The Problem of Speaking for Others." *Cultural Critique*, 20, Winter, 1991–1992, pp. 5–32.

Allen, Jeffner. "Motherhood. The Annihilation of Women." In Joyce Trebilcot, ed., *Mothering. Essays in Feminist Theory.* Totowa, NJ, Rowan & Allenheld, 1984, pp. 315–330.

Allen, Paula Gunn. *The Sacred Hoop. Recovering the Feminine in American Indian Traditions.* Boston, Mass., Beacon Press, 1986.

Alves, Miriam. *Momentos de Busca.* São Paulo, Copidart Ltd, 1983.

—— "Discurso Temerario." *Criacao Crioula, nu Elefante Branco.* São Paulo, Cadernos Negros, 1987, pp. 83–87.

—— ed. *Enfim, Todas Negras Brasileras Contemporaneas.* São Paulo, 1991. Washington, DC, Three Continents Press, forthcoming.

Amadiume, Ifi. *Male Daughters. Female Husbands.* London, Zed Press, 1987.

Amin, Samir. *Delinking. Towards a Polycentric World.* London and New Jersey, Zed Books, 1990.

Amos, Valerie and Pratibha Parmar. "Challenging Imperial Feminism." *Feminist Review*, 17, July, 1984, pp. 3–19.

Anderson, Benedict. *Imagined Communities. Reflections on the Spread of Nationalism.* London, Verso, 1983.

Angelou, Maya. *I Know Why the Caged Bird Sings.* New York, Random House, 1969.

—— *The Heart of a Woman.* New York, Random House, 1981.

Anzaldua, Gloria. "Speaking in Tongues. A Letter to Third World Women Writers." In Cherrie Moraga and Gloria Anzaldua, eds, *This Bridge Called My Back. Writings by Radical Women of Color.* Watertown, Mass., Persephone Press, 1981, pp. 165ff.

—— *Borderlands/La Frontera. The New Mestiza.* San Francisco, Calif., Spinsters/Aunt Lute, 1987.

—— ed. *Making Face, Making Soul/Haciendo Caras. Creative and Critical Perspectives by Feminists of Color.* San Francisco, Calif., Spinsters/Aunt Lute, 1990.

—— "To(o) Queer the Writer – Loca, escritora y chicana." In Betsy Warland, ed., *Inversions. Writings By Dykes, Queers and Lesbians.* Vancouver, Press Gang Publishers, 1991, pp. 249–263.

Appiah, Anthony. "Is the Post- in Postmodernism the Post- in Postcolonial?" *Critical Inquiry*, 17, Winter, 1991, pp. 336–357.

Arnold, A. James. *Modernism and Negritude. The Poetry and Poetics of Aimé Césaire.* Cambridge, Mass. and London, Harvard University Press, 1981.

Ashcroft, Bill, Gareth Griffiths and Helen Tiffin. *The Empire Writes Back. Theory and Practice in Post-Colonial Literatures.* London and New York, Routledge, 1989.

Badran, Margot and Miriam Cooke, eds. *Opening the Gates. A Century of Arab Feminist Writing.* Bloomington, Ind., Indiana University Press, 1990.

Baker, Houston. *Blues, Ideology and Afro-American Literature. A Vernacular Theory.* Chicago, Ill. and London, University of Chicago Press, 1984.

Barbotin, Maurice. *Archéologie Antillaise. Arawaks et Caraïbes.* Parc Naturel de Guadeloupe, 1987.

Barkley Brown, Elsa. "Polyrhythms and Improvisation. Lessons for Women's History." *History Workshop. A Journal of Socialist Historians*, 31, Spring, 1991, pp. 85–90.

Barrett, Michèle. "Words and Things. Materialism and Method in Contemporary Feminist Analysis." In Michèle Barrett and Anne Phillips, eds, *Destabilizing Theory. Contemporary Feminist Debates.* Stanford, Calif., Stanford University Press, 1992, pp. 201–219.

Barrett, Michèle and Anne Phillips. *Destabilizing Theory. Contemporary Feminist Debates.* Stanford, Calif., Stanford University Press, 1992.

Barzilai, Shuli. "Borders of Language. Kristeva's Critique of Lacan." *Publications of the Modern Language Association*, 106, 2, March, 1991, pp. 294–305.

Baucom, Ian. "Dreams of Home. Colonialism and Postmodernism." *Research in African Literatures*, 22, 4, Winter, 1991, pp. 5–27.

Becquer, Marcos and Jose Gatti. "Elements of Vogue." *Third Text*, 16–17, Autumn–Winter, 1991, pp. 65–81.

Bell, Roseann P., Bettye J. Parker and Beverly Guy-Sheftall. *Sturdy Black Bridges*. New York, Doubleday, 1979.

Benitez Rojo, Antonio. "The Repeating Island." *New England Review and Bread Loaf Quarterly*, 7, 1, Autumn, 1984, pp. 430–452.

—— *The Repeating Island. The Caribbean and the Postmodern Perspective*. Trans. by James E. Maraniss. Durham, NC and London, Duke University Press, 1992.

Bennett, Tony. *Outside Literature*. London and New York, Routledge, 1990.

Bernabé, Jean, Patrick Chamoiseau and Raphael Confiant. "In Praise of Creoleness." *Callaloo*, 13, 1990, pp. 886–909.

Bernal, Martin. *Black Athena*. New Brunswick, NJ, Rutgers University Press, vol. 1, 1987; vol. 2, 1991.

Bhabha, Homi K. "Of Mimicry and Man. The Ambivalence of Colonial Discourse." *October*, 28, 1984, pp. 125–133.

—— "Foreword. Remembering Fanon – Self, Psyche and the Colonial Condition." Introduction to Frantz Fanon, *Black Skin, White Masks*. London, Pluto Press, 1986.

—— "The Other Question. Difference, Discrimination and the Discourse of Colonialism." In Francis Barker, Peter Hulme, Margaret Iversen and Diana Loxley, eds, *Literature, Politics and Theory*. London and New York, Methuen, 1986, pp. 147–172.

—— "The Commitment to Theory." In Jim Pines and Paul Willemen, eds, *Questions of Third Cinema*. London, British Film Institute, 1989, pp. 111–132.

Bhabha, Homi, K., ed. *Nation and Narration*. London and New York, Routledge, 1990.

Bhabha, Homi, K. "Postcolonial Criticism." In Stephen Greenblatt and Giles Gunn, eds, *Redrawing the Boundaries*. New York, The Modern Language Association of America, 1992, pp. 437–465.

Black Womantalk Collective (Da Choong, Olivette Wilson Cole, Bernardine Evaristo, Gabriela Pearse), eds. *Black Women Talk Poetry*. London, Black Womantalk, 1987.

Blum, Linda N. "Mothers, Babies, and Breastfeeding in Late Capitalist America. The Shifting Contexts of Feminist Theory." *Feminist Studies*, 19, 2, Summer, 1993, pp. 291–312.

Bordo, Susan. "Feminism, Postmodernism, and Gender-Scepticism." In Linda Nicholson, ed., *Feminism/Postmodernism*. London, Routledge, 1990, pp. 133–156.

Borsa, Joan. "Frida Kahlo. Marginalization and the Critical Female Subject." *Third Text*, 12, Autumn, 1990.

Bové, Paul. *In the Wake of Theory*. Hanover, NH and London, Wesleyan University Press, 1992.

Boyce Davies, Carole. "Mothering and Healing in Recent Black Women's Fiction." *Sage*, 2, 1, Spring, 1985, pp. 41–43.

—— "Feminist Consciousness and African Literary Criticism." In Carole Boyce Davies and Anne Adams Graves, eds, *Ngambika. Studies of Women in African Literature*. Trenton, NJ, Africa World Press, 1986, pp. 1–23.

—— "Finding Some Space. South African Women Writers." *A Current Bibliography of African Affairs*, 19, 1, 1986–1987, pp. 31–45.

—— "Black Woman's Journey Into Self. A Womanist Reading of Paule Marshall's *Praisesong for the Widow*." *Matatu*, Heft 1, 1, Jahrgang, 1987, pp. 19–34.

Boyce Davies, Carole, ed. "Black Women's Writing. Crossing the Boundaries." *Matatu*, Heft 6, 3, Jahrgang, 1989.

Boyce Davies, Carole. "Private Selves and Public Spaces. Autobiography and the African Woman Writer." *College Language Association Journal*, 34, 3, 1991, pp. 267–289.

—— "Writing Off Marginality, Minoring and Effacement." *Women's Studies International Forum*, 14, 4, 1991, pp. 249–263.

—— "Collaboration and the Ordering Imperative in Life Story Production." In Sidonie Smith and Julia Watson, eds, *De/Colonizing the Subject. The Politics of Gender in Women's Autobiography*. Minneapolis, Minn., University of Minnesota Press, 1992, pp. 3–19.

Boyce Davies, Carole and Anne Adams Graves, eds. *Ngambika. Studies of Women in African Literature*. Trenton, NJ, Africa World Press, 1986.

—— and 'Molara Ogundipe-Leslie eds. *Black Women's Diasporas. Writing New Worlds*. London, Pluto Press, 1994.

Boyce Davies, Carole and Elaine Savory Fido, eds. *Out of the Kumbla. Caribbean Women and Literature*. Trenton, NJ, Africa World Press, 1990.

Boyce Davies, Carole and Elaine Savory Fido. "African Women Writers. Towards a Literary History." In Oyekan Owomoyela, ed., *Twentieth-Century African Literatures*, Lincoln, Nebr., University of Nebraska Press, 1993, pp. 311–346.

Braga, Julio. "Candomble. Força e Resistencia." *Afro-Asia*. (Salvador da Bahia, Brazil), April, 1992, pp. 13–17.

Braidotti, Rosi. *Patterns of Dissonance*. London and New York, Routledge, 1991.

Brathwaite, Edward Kamau. "The African Presence in Caribbean Literature." *Daedalus*, 103, 2, Spring, 1974, pp. 73–109.

—— "Caliban, Ariel, and Unprospero in the Conflict of Creolization. A Study of the Slave Revolt in Jamaica." *New York Academy of Sciences*, 292, 1977, pp. 41–62.

—— *History of the Voice. The Development of Nation Language in Anglophone Caribbean Poetry*. London and Port-of-Spain, New Beacon Books, 1984.

Bratlinger, Patrick. *Crusoe's Footprints. Cultural Studies in Britain and America*. New York and London, Routledge, 1990.

Braxton, Joanne. "Ancestral Presence. The Outraged Mother Figure in Contemporary Afra-American Writing." In Joanne Braxton and Andrée Nicola McLaughlin, eds, *Wild Women in the Whirlwind. Afra-American*

Culture and the Contemporary Literary Renaissance. New Brunswick, NJ, Rutgers University Press, 1989, pp. 75–97.

—— *Black Women Writing Autobiography. A Tradition Within a Tradition.* Philadelphia, Temple University Press, 1989.

Britzman, Deborah. *Practice Makes Practice.* Albany, NY, SUNY Press, 1991.

Brown, Lloyd. *Women Writers in Black Africa.* Westport, Conn., Greenwood Press, 1981.

Bruner, Charlotte. *Unwinding Threads.* London, Heinemann, 1983.

Bryan, Beverley, Stella Dadzie and Suzanne Scafe. *The Heart of the Race. Black Women's Lives in Britain.* London, Virago Press, 1985.

Brydon, Diana. "The White Inuit Speaks. Contamination as Literary Strategy." In Ian Adam and Helen Tiffin, eds, *Past the Last POST. Theorizing Post-Colonialism and Post-Modernism,* Calgary, University of Calgary Press, 1990, pp.191–203.

Brydon, Lynne and Sylvia Chant. *Women in the Third World. Gender Issues in Rural and Urban Areas.* Hampshire, England, Edward Elgar Publishing Limited, 1989.

Buffong, Jean and Nellie Payne. *Jump-Up-and-Kiss-Me.* London, The Women's Press, 1990.

Burford, Barbara. *The Threshing Floor.* London, Sheba Feminist Publishers, 1986.

Burford, Barbara, Lindsay Mac Rae and Sylvia Paskin, eds. *Dancing the Tightrope. New Love Poems by Women.* London, The Women's Press, 1987.

Busby, Margaret, ed. *Daughters of Africa. An International Anthology of Words and Writings by Women of African Descent from the Ancient Egyptian to the Present.* London, Jonathan Cape and New York, Pantheon, 1992.

Busia, Abena P.A. "Words Whispered Over Voids. A Context for Black Women's Rebellious Voices in the Novel of the African Diaspora." In Joe Weixlmann and Houston A. Baker Jr, eds, *Studies in Black American Literature III* (Black Feminist Criticism and Critical Theory). Greenwood, Fla., Penkevill Publishing Company, 1988, pp. 1–41.

—— "What is Your Nation? Reconnecting Africa and Her Diaspora through Paule Marshall's *Praisesong for the Widow.*" In Cheryl Wall, ed., *Changing Our Own Words. Essays on Criticism, Theory, and Writing by Black Women.* New Brunswick, NJ and London, Rutgers University Press, 1989, pp. 196–211.

—— "Silencing Sycorax. On African Colonial Discourse and the Unvoiced Female." *Cultural Critique,* Winter, 1990, pp. 81–104.

—— *Testimonies of Exile.* Trenton, NJ, Africa World Press, 1990.

Butler, Judith. *Gender Trouble. Feminism and the Subversion of Identity.* New York and London, Routledge, 1990.

Butler, Octavia. *Kindred.* Boston, Mass., Beacon Press, 1979.

Cade Bambara, Toni. *The Black Woman. An Anthology.* New York, New American Library, 1970.

Campbell, Mavis. *The Maroons of Jamaica, 1655–1796. A History of Resistance, Collaboration and Betrayal.* Trenton, NJ, Africa World Press, 1990.

Carby, Hazel. "White Woman Listen! Black Feminism and the Boundaries of Sisterhood." In Centre for Contemporary Cultural Studies. *The Empire Strikes Back. Race and Racism in 70's Britain.* London, Hutchinson, 1982, pp. 212–235.
—— *Reconstructing Womanhood: The Emergence of the Afro-American Woman Novelist.* New York and Oxford, Oxford University Press, 1987.
—— "It Just Be's Dat Way Sometime. The Sexual Politics of Women's Blues." In Robyn R. Warhol and Diane Price Herndl, eds, *Feminisms. An Anthology of Literary Theory and Criticism,* New Brunswick, NJ, Rutgers University Press, 1991, pp. 746–758.
Carmichael, Stokeley and Charles Hamilton. *Black Power. The Politics of Liberation in America.* New York, Vintage, 1981.
Centre for Contemporary Cultural Studies. *The Empire Strikes Back. Race and Racism in 70's Britain.* London, Hutchinson, 1982.
Césaire, Aimé. *Discourse on Colonialism.* New York, Monthly Review Press, 1972 (first published, Présence Africaine, 1955).
Cham, Mbye. *Ex-iles. Essays on Caribbean Cinema.* Trenton, NJ, Africa World Press, 1991.
Chinosole, "Audre Lorde and the Matrilineal Diaspora. Moving History Beyond Nightmare Into Structures for the Future." In Joanne Braxton and Andrée Nicola McLaughlin, eds, *Wild Women in the Whirlwind, Afra-American Culture and the Contemporary Literary Renaissance.* New Brunswick, NJ, Rutgers University Press, 1990, pp. 379–394.
Chinweizu, Jemie Onwuchekwa and Ikechukwu Madubuike. *Toward the Decolonization of African Literature.* Washington, DC, Howard University Press, 1983.
Chodorow, Nancy and Susan Contratto. "The Fantasy of the Perfect Mother." In Barrie Thorne and Marilyn Yalom, eds, *Rethinking the Family.* New York, Longman, 1982, pp. 54–73.
Choong, Da, Olivette Wilson Cole, Sylvia Parker and Gabriela Pearse, eds. *Don't Ask Me Why. An Anthology of Short Stories by Black Women.* London, Black Womantalk, 1991.
Chowdhry, Maya. "Diary of Home." In *Inside Ant's Belly.* London, National Association for the Teaching of English, 1994, pp. 79–90.
—— "Birth Certificate." *Feminist Art News,* 3, 10, 1992, p. 23.
Christian, Barbara. *Black Feminist Criticism.* New York, Pergamon, 1985.
—— "Trajectories of Self-Definition. Placing Contemporary Afro-American Women's Fiction." In Marjorie Pryse and Hortense Spillers, eds, *Conjuring.* Bloomington, Ind., Indiana University Press, 1985, pp. 233–248.
—— "The Race for Theory." *Cultural Critique,* 6, Spring, 1987, pp. 51–63.
—— "Fixing Methodologies. Beloved." *Cultural Critique,* 24, Spring, 1993, pp. 5–15.
Churchill, Ward. *Struggle for The Land. Indigenous Resistance to Genocide, Ecocide and Expropriation in Contemporary North America.* Monroe, ME., Common Courage Press, 1993.
Cixous, Hélène and Catherine Clément. *The Newly Born Woman.* Minneapolis, Minn., University of Minnesota Press, 1986.
Clark, Vèvè. "Developing Diaspora Literacy. Allusion in Maryse Condé's

Heremakhonon." In Carole Boyce Davies and Elaine Savory Fido, eds, *Out of the Kumbla. Caribbean Women and Literature.* Trenton, NJ, Africa World Press, 1990, pp. 303–320.

Clarke, Cheryl. *Living as a Lesbian.* Freedom, Calif., The Crossing Press, 1986.

Cliff, Michelle. *Claiming an Identity They Taught Me to Despise.* Watertown, Mass., Persephone Press, 1980.

—— *Abeng.* Freedom, Calif., The Crossing Press, 1984.

—— *The Land of Look Behind.* Ithaca, NY, Firebrand Books, 1985, pp. 57–76.

—— *No Telephone to Heaven.* New York, Random House, 1989.

—— *Bodies of Water.* New York, Pantheon, 1990.

Clifford, James. "Notes on Travel and Theory." *Inscriptions*, 5, 1989, pp. 177–188.

Cobham, Rhonda. "Introduction." *Research in African Literatures*, 19, 2, Summer, 1988, pp. 137–142.

Cobham, Rhonda and Merle Collins, eds. *Watchers and Seekers. Creative Writing by Black Women in Britain.* London, The Women's Press, 1987.

Cocks, Joan E. *The Oppositional Imagination. Feminism, Critique and Political Theory.* London, Routledge, Chapman and Hall, 1989.

Collier, Eugenia. "The Closing of the Circle. Movement from Division to Wholeness in Paule Marshall's Fiction." In Mari Evans, ed., *Black Women Writers (1950–1980). A Critical Evaluation.* New York, Doubleday, 1984, pp. 295–315.

Collins, Merle. *Because the Dawn Breaks.* London, Karia Press, 1985.

—— *Angel.* Seattle, Wash., Seal Press, 1987.

—— *Rotten Pomerack.* London, The Women's Press, 1992.

Collins, Patricia Hill. "Learning from the Outsider Within. The Social Significance of Black Feminist Thought." *Social Problems*, 33, 6, 1986, pp. 14–32.

—— "The Meaning of Motherhood in Black Culture and Black Mother-Daughter Relationships." *Sage*, 4, 2, 1987, pp. 3–10.

—— *Black Feminist Thought. Knowledge, Consciousness and the Politics of Empowerment.* London and New York, Routledge, 1991.

Condé, Maryse. *I, Tituba. Black Witch of Salem.* Charlottesville, Va., and London, University Press of Virginia, 1992.

Connolly, William. *The Terms of Political Discourse.* Martin Robertson, 1983.

Cooper, Afua. *Memories Have Tongue.* Toronto, Sister Vision Press, 1992.

Craib, Ian. "Masculinity and Male Dominance." *Sociological Review*, 4, November, 1987, pp. 721–743.

Cudjoe, Selwyn R., ed. *Caribbean Women Writers. Essays from the First International Conference.* Massachusetts, Calaloux, 1990.

Dabydeen, David and Nana Wilson Tagoe. *A Reader's Guide to West Indian and Black British Literature.* London, Hansib Publishing Limited, 1988.

Dangarembga, Tsitsi. *Nervous Conditions.* London, The Women's Press and Seattle, Wash., Seal Press, 1989.

Dash, Julie. With Toni Cade Bambara and bell hooks. *The Making of an*

African-American Woman's Film. Daughters of the Dust. New York, The New Press, 1992.

Davin, Anna. "Imperialism and Motherhood." *History Workshop. A Journal of Socialist Historians*, 5, Spring, 1978, pp. 9–66.

Davis, Angela. "The Black Woman's Role in the Community of Slaves." *Black Scholar*, 2, 4, December, 1971, pp. 3–15.

Davis, James. *Who is Black? One Nation's Definition.* Philadelphia, Pa., Pennsylvania State University Press, 1991.

de Chungara, Domitilia Barrios. With Moema Viezzer. *Let Me Speak. Testimony of Domitilia, A Woman of the Bolivian Mines.* Trans. by Victoria Ortiz. New York, Monthly Review Press, 1978.

de Lauretis, Teresa. *Feminist Studies/Critical Studies.* Bloomington, Ind., Indiana University Press, 1986.

—— *Technologies of Gender. Essays on Theory, Film and Fiction.* Bloomington, Ind., Indiana University Press, 1987.

De Prima, Dominique. "Beat the Rap." *Mother Jones*, September–October, 1990, pp. 32–36, 80–82.

de Veaux, Alexis. *Blue Heat.* New York, self-published, 1985.

Deleuze, Giles. "Nomad Thought." In David B. Allison, ed., *The New Nietzche.* New York, Dell, 1977, pp. 142–149.

Deleuze, Giles and Felix Guattari. "What is a Minor Literature?" In Giles Deleuze and Felix Guattari, *Kafka. Toward a Minor Literature.* Minneapolis, Minn., University of Minnesota Press, 1986, pp. 16–27.

Diallo, Nafissatou. *A Dakar Childhood.* London, Longman, 1982.

Diawara, Manthia. "Englishness and Blackness. Cricket as Discourse on Colonialism." *Callaloo*, 13, 1990, pp. 886–909.

—— "The Nature of Mother in *Dreaming Rivers.*" *Third Text*, 13, Winter, 1991, pp. 73–84.

Diaz-Diocaretz, Myriam. *Translating Poetic Discourse: Questions on Feminist Strategies in Adrienne Rich.* Philadelphia, Pa., John Benjamins Pub. Co., 1985.

Diop, Cheikh Anta. *Precolonial Black Africa.* Connecticut, Lawrence Hill & Co., 1987.

Doane, Mary Ann. "Dark Continents. Epistemologies of Racial and Sexual Difference in Psychoanalysis and Cinema." *Femmes Fatales: Feminism, Film Theory and Psychoanalysis*, London and New York, Routledge, forthcoming.

Donaldson, Laura E. "(ex)Changing (wo)Man. Towards a Materialist-Feminist Semiotics." *Cultural Critique*, Winter, 1988–1989, pp. 5–23.

Dos Santos, Juana Elbin. *Os Nago e a Morte. (Nago and Death).* Petropolis, Brazil, Editora Vozes Ltd, 1976.

Dresen-Coenders, Lene. "Witches as Devils' Concubines. On the Origin of Fear of Witches and Protection Against Witchcraft." In *Saints and She-Devils.* London, The Rubicon Press, 1987, pp. 59–82.

Drewal, Henry John and Margaret Thompson. *Gẹlẹdẹ. Art and Female Power Among the Yoruba.* Bloomington, Ind., Indiana University Press, 1990.

Duggan, Lisa. "Making it Perfectly Queer." *Socialist Review*, 22, 1, January–March, 1992, pp. 11–31.

Duley, Margot I. and Mary Edwards. *The Cross-Cultural Study of Women: A Comprehensive Guide.* New York, The Feminist Press, 1986.

Durham, Carolyn Richardson. "Sonia Fatima da Conceiçao's Literature for Social Change." *Afro-Hispanic Review*, 11, 1–3, 1992, pp. 21–25.

During, Simon. "Postmodernism or Post-Colonialism Today." *Textual Practice*, 1, 1, 1987, pp. 32–47.

Ebert, Teresa L. "Political Semiosis in/of American Cultural Studies." *American Journal of Semiotics*, 8, 1–2, 1991, pp. 113–135.

—— "Ludic Feminism, the Body, Performance and Labor. Bringing Materialism Back Into Feminist Cultural Studies." *Cultural Critique*, Winter, 1993, pp. 5–50.

Ehrenreich, Barbara and Deirdre English. *Witches, Midwives, and Nurses. A History of Women Healers.* New York, The Feminist Press, 1973.

el Saadawi, Nawal. *The Hidden Face of Eve.* London, Zed Press, 1979.

Emecheta, Buchi. *Adah's Story.* London, Allison & Busby, 1983, and New York, Fontana, 1988.

—— *Head Above Water.* London, Fontana, 1986.

—— *Gwendolen.* New York, George Braziller, 1990. (Also published as *The Family*, London, Collins, 1989.)

Enloe, Cynthia. *Bananas, Beaches & Bases. Making Sense of International Politics.* Berkeley, Calif., University of California Press, 1990.

Evans-Pritchard, E.E. "Witchcraft." *Africa*, 8, 4 (special issue), October, 1935.

Fanon, Frantz. "Algeria Unveiled." In Ibrahim and Hopkins, eds, *Arab Society in Transition*. Cairo, American University in Cairo, 1977, pp. 149–172.

Farr, Cecilia Konchar. "Her Mother's Language." In Brenda O. Daly and Maureen T. Reddy, eds, *Narrating Mothers. Theorizing Maternal Subjectivities*. Knoxville, Tenn., University of Tennessee Press, 1991, pp. 94–108.

Feminist Art News. 3, 10, 1991 and 4, 1, 1992.

Ferguson, Russell, William Olander, Marcia Tucker and Karen Fiss, eds. *Discourses. Conversations in Postmodern Art and Culture.* New York, The New Museum of Contemporary Art and Cambridge, Mass., and London, MIT Press, 1990.

Field, M.J. *Religion and Medicine of the Ga People.* London, Oxford University Press and Accra, Presbyterian Book Depot, 1937.

Flores, Juan and George Yudice. "Living Borders/Buscando America. Languages of Latino Self-Formation." *Social Text*, 24, 1990, pp. 57–84.

Forbes, Jack D. *Africans and Native Americans. The Language of Race and the Evolution of Red-Black Peoples.* Urbana and Chicago, Ill., University of Illinois Press, 1993.

Frankenberg, Ruth and Lata Mani. "Crosscurrents, Crosstalk. Race, 'Post-coloniality' and the Politics of Location." *Cultural Studies*, 7, 2, May, 1993, pp. 292–310.

Fryer, Peter. *Staying Power. The History of Black People in Britain.* London, Pluto Press, 1984.

Fuentes, Carlos. "The End of Ideologies?" *Transition. An International Review*, 51, 1991, pp. 26–31.

Fuller, Vernella. *Going Back Home*. London, The Women's Press, 1992.

Furman, Nelly. "The Politics of Language. Beyond the Gender Principle." In Gayle Greene and Coppelia Kahn, eds, *Making a Difference. Feminist Literary Criticism*. London and New York, Methuen, 1985, pp. 59–79.

Fuss, Diana. *Essentially Speaking. Feminism, Nature and Difference*. New York and London, Routledge, 1989.

Gabriel, Teshome H. "Thoughts on Nomadic Aesthetics and the Black Independent Cinema. Traces of a Journey." In Mbye B. Cham and Claire Andrade-Watkins, eds, *Blackframes. Critical Perspectives on Black Independent Cinema*. Cambridge, Mass., and London, MIT Press, 1988, pp. 62–79.

Gallie, William Bryce. "Essentially Contested Concepts." In Max Black, ed., *The Importance of Language*. Prentice-Hall, 1963.

Ganguly, Keya. "Migrant Identities. Personal Memory and the Construction of Selfhood." *Cultural Studies*, 6, 1, January, 1992, pp. 27–50.

Garane, Jeanne Snitgen. "History, Identity, and the Constitution of the Female Subject." In Carole Boyce Davies, ed., "Black Women's Writing. Crossing the Boundaries." *Matatu*, Heft 6, 3, Jahrgang, 1989, pp. 55–71.

Garber, Marjorie. *Vested Interests*. London, Routledge, 1991.

Gates Jr, Henry Louis, ed. *"Race," Writing and Difference*. Chicago, Ill., and London, University of Chicago Press, 1985.

Gates Jr, Henry Louis. *The Signifying Monkey. A Theory of African-American Literary Criticism*. New York and Oxford, Oxford University Press, 1988.

Gates Jr, Henry Louis, ed. *Reading Black. Reading Feminist*. New York, Penguin, 1990.

Giddings, Paula. *When and Where I Enter. The Impact of Black Women on Race and Sex in America*. New York, Bantam, 1984.

Gilroy, Beryl. *Black Teacher*. London, Cassell & Company, 1976.

—— *Frangipani House*. London, Heinemann, 1986.

—— *Boy-Sandwich*. London, Heinemann, 1989.

—— *Echoes and Voices, (Open-Heart Poetry)*. New York, Vantage Press, 1991.

Gilroy, Paul. *There Ain't No Black in the Union Jack*. London, Hutchinson, 1987.

—— "Nothing but Sweat Inside my Hand. Diaspora Aesthetics and Black Arts in Britain." *Black Film. British Cinema*, ICA Document 7. London, Institute of Contemporary Arts, 1988, pp. 44–46.

—— "Cruciality and the Frog's Perspective. An Agenda of Difficulties for the Black Arts Movement in Britain." *Third Text*, 5, Winter, 1988–1989.

—— "Art of Darkness. Black Art and the Problem of Belonging to England." *Third Text*, 10, Spring, 1990, pp. 45–52.

—— "Nationalism, History and Ethnic Absolutism." *History Workshop Journal*, 30, Autumn, 1990, pp. 114–120.

—— "It Ain't Where You're From, It's Where You're At. The Dialectics of Diasporic Identification." *Third Text*, 13, Winter, 1991, pp. 3–16.

Glissant, Edouard. *Caribbean Discourse. Selected Essays.* Charlottesville, Va., University Press of Virginia, 1989.

Golden, Marita. *Migrations of the Heart.* New York, Anchor Press, 1983.

—— *Long Distance Life.* New York, Bantam, 1990.

Gooding-Williams, Robert, ed. *Reading Rodney King. Reading Urban Uprising.* London and New York, Routledge, 1993.

Grech, Joyoti. "In Answer to Some Questions." *Feminist Art News,* 3, 10, 1992, back cover.

Greene, Gayle and Coppelia Kahn. *Making a Difference. Feminist Literary Criticism.* London, Methuen, 1985.

Grewal, Shabnam, Jackie Kay, Liliane Landor, Gail Lewis and Pratibha Parmar, eds. *Charting the Journey. Writings by Black and Third World Women.* London, Sheba Feminist Publishers, 1988.

Grossberg, Lawrence. "Wandering Audiences, Nomadic Critics." *Cultural Studies,* 2, 3, 1988, pp. 377–391.

Gunn Allen, Paula. *The Sacred Hoop. Recovering the Feminine in American Indian Traditions.* Boston, Mass., Beacon Press, 1986.

Hall, Stuart. "Signification. Althusser and the Post-Structuralist Debates." *Critical Studies in Mass Communication,* 2, 2, June, 1985, pp. 91–114.

—— "On Postmodernism and Articulation. An Interview." *Journal of Communication Inquiry,* 10, Summer, 1986, pp. 45–60.

—— "Popular Culture and the State." In Tony Bennett *et al.,* eds, *Popular Culture and Social Relations.* Milton Keynes, Open University Press, 1986.

—— "New Ethnicities." *Black Film. British Cinema.* ICA Document 7. London, Institute of Contemporary Arts, 1988, pp. 27–30.

—— *The Road to Renewal.* London, Verso, 1988.

—— "Cultural Identity and Cinematic Representation." *Framework,* 36, (issue on Theory and the Politics of Location), 1989, pp. 65–81. (Also in Mbye Cham, ed., *Ex-iles,* Trenton NJ, Africa World Press, 1992, pp. 220–236.)

—— "Old and New Ethnicities." Unpublished ms., Binghamton, Department of Art History, 1990.

—— "The Local and the Global. Globalization and Ethnicity." Unpublished ms., Binghamton, Department of Art History, 1990.

Hanchard, Michael. "Identity, Meaning and the African-American." *Social Text,* 24, 1990, pp. 31–42.

—— "Racial Consciousness and Afro-Diasporic Experiences. Antonio Gramsci Reconsidered." *Socialism and Democracy,* 3, Fall, 1991, pp. 83–106.

—— "A Notion of Afro-Diasporic Time." A paper prepared for the workshop, "The World the Diaspora Makes. Social Science and the Reinvention of Africa," University of Michigan, 1992 and African Literature Association, Guadeloupe, 1993 on panel "Afro-Brazilian Cultural and Literary Connections."

Haraway, Donna J. *Simians, Cyborgs, and Women. The Reinvention of Nature.* New York, Routledge, 1991.

Harlow, Barbara. *Resistance Literature.* New York and London, Methuen, 1987.

Harrison, Alferdteen, ed. *Black Exodus. The Great Migration from the American South*. Jackson, Miss., and London, University Press of Mississippi, 1991.

Harrison, Daphne Duval. *Black Pearls. Blues Queens of the 1920's*. New Brunswick, NJ, Rutgers University Press, 1990.

Head, Bessie. *A Question of Power*. London, Heinemann, 1974.

Hebdige, Dick. "Redeeming Witness. In the Tracks of the Homeless Vehicle Project." *Cultural Studies*, 7, 2, May, 1993, pp. 173–223.

Hekman, Susan. "Reconstituting the Subject. Feminism, Modernism, and Postmodernism." *Hypatia*, 6, 2, Summer, 1991, pp. 44–63.

Hemphill, Essex, ed. (conceived by Joseph Beam). *Brother to Brother. New Writings by Black Gay Men*. Boston, Mass., Alyson Publications Inc., 1992.

Henderson, Mae Gwendolyn. "Speaking in Tongues. Dialogics, Dialectics and the Black Woman Writer's Literary Tradition." In Cheryl Wall, ed., *Changing Our Own Words. Essays on Criticism, Theory, and Writing by Black Women*. New Brunswick, NJ, and London, Rutgers University Press, 1989, pp. 16–37.

Hennessy, Rosemary. *Materialist Feminism and the Politics of Discourse*. London, Routledge, 1993.

Henriques, Julian, Wendy Hollway, Cathy Urwin, Couze Venn and Valerie Walkerdine. *Changing the Subject. Psychology, Social Regulation and Subjectivity*. London and New York, Methuen, 1984.

Hicks, Diane Emily. *Border Writing. The Multi-Dimensional Text*. Minneapolis, Minn., University of Minnesota Press, 1991.

Hill, Alette Olin. *Mother Tongue, Father Time. A Decade of Linguistic Revolt*. Bloomington and Indianapolis, Ind., Indiana University Press, 1986.

Hiro, Dilip. *Black British, White British. A History of Race Relations in Britain*. London, Paladin, 1992.

Hirsch, Marianne. *The Mother/Daughter Plot. Narrative, Psychoanalysis, Feminism*. Bloomington, Ind., Indiana University Press, 1989.

Hitchcock, Peter. *Dialogics of the Oppressed*. Minneapolis, Minn., and London, University of Minnesota Press, 1993.

Homans, Margaret. *Bearing the Word. Women Writers and Poetic Identity*. Princeton, NJ, Princeton University Press. 1980.

hooks, bell. *Ain't I A Woman. Black Women and Feminism*. Boston, Mass., South End Press, 1981.

—— *Feminist Theory. From Margin to Center*. Boston, Mass., South End Press, 1984.

—— *Talking Back. Thinking Feminist. Thinking Black*. Boston, Mass., South End Press, 1989.

—— "Choosing the Margin as a Space of Radical Openness." *Framework*, 36: "Third Scenario. Theory and the Politics of Location," 1990, pp. 15–23.

—— *Yearning. Race, Gender and Cultural Politics*. Boston, Mass., South End Press, 1990.

—— *Black Looks. Race and Representation*, Boston, Mass., South End Press, 1992.

Hope Scott, Joyce. "Commercial Deportation as Rite of Passage in Black

Women's Novels." In Carole Boyce Davies, ed., "Black Women's Writing. Crossing the Boundaries." *Matatu*, Heft 6, 3, Jahrgang, 1989, pp. 127–154.

Horno-Delgado, Asunción, Eliana Ortega, Nina M. Scott and Nancy Saporta Sternbach. *Breaking Boundaries. Latina Writing and Critical Readings.* Amherst, Mass., University of Massachusetts, 1989.

Hull, Gloria, Patricia Bell Scott and Barbara Smith, eds. *All the Women are White, All the Blacks are Men, But Some of Us Are Brave.* New York, The Feminist Press, 1982.

Hurston, Zora Neale. *Their Eyes Were Watching God.* Urbana and Chicago, Ill., University of Illinois Press, 1978 (first published 1937).

—— "How It Feels to Be Colored Me." In Alice Walker, ed., *I Love Myself When I am Laughing . . . A Zora Neale Hurston Reader.* New York, The Feminist Press, 1979, pp. 151–155.

Hutcheon, Linda. *The Politics of Postmodernism.* London and New York, Routledge, 1989.

—— "Circling the Downspout of Empire." In Ian Adam and Helen Tiffin, eds, *Past the Last POST. Theorizing Post-Colonialism and Post-Modernism.* Calgary, University of Calgary Press, 1990, pp. 167–189.

Idowu, E. Bolaji. *Oludumare. God in Yoruba Belief.* London, Longman, 1962.

Institute of Race Relations. *Policing Against Black People.* London, Institute of Race Relations, 1987.

Irigaray, Luce. *je, tu, nous. Toward a Culture of Difference.* New York and London, Routledge, 1993.

Jacobs, Harriet. *Incidents in the Life of a Slave Girl.* New York and Oxford, Oxford University Press, 1988 (first published 1861).

Jama, Zainab. "Finding a Voice. Somali Nationalist Women's Songs." In Theodora Ezeigbo and Liz Gunner, eds, *African Languages and Cultures.* London, SOAS, Department of African Languages and Cultures Publications, June, 1991.

James, Adeola. *African Women Writers Talk. In Their Own Voices.* London, James Currey, 1991.

James, Selma, ed. *Strangers and Sisters. Women, Race and Immigration.* Bristol, Falling Wall Press, 1985.

James, Stanlie and Abena P.A. Busia. *Theorizing Black Feminisms.* London, Routledge, 1993.

Jameson, Frederic. "Postmodernism, or the Cultural Logic of Late Capitalism." *New Left Review*, 146, July-August, 1984, pp. 53–91.

JanMohamed, Abdul R. and David Lloyd, eds. *The Nature and Context of Minority Discourse.* New York, Oxford University Press, 1991; or *Cultural Critique*, 6 and 7, 1987.

Jayamanne, Laleen, Leslie Thornton and Trinh Minh-ha. "If Upon Leaving What We Have to Say We Speak. A Conversation Piece." In Russell Ferguson, William Olander and Marcia Tucker, eds, *Discourses. Conversations in Postmodern Art and Culture.* New York, The New Museum of Contemporary Art and Cambridge, Mass., and London, MIT Press, 1990, pp. 44–66.

Jayawardena, Kumari. *Feminism and Nationalism in the Third World*. London and Atlantic Highlands, NJ, Zed Books, 1986.

Jeyifo, Biodun. "Literary Theory and Theories of Decolonization." Unpublished ms., 1990, supplied by author.

—— "The Nature of Things. Arrested Decolonization and Critical Theory." *Research in African Literatures*, 21, 1990, pp. 33–47.

Jin, Meiling. *Gifts from My Grandmother*. London, Sheba Feminist Publishers, n.d.

Johnson, Amryl. *Tread Carefully in Paradise*. Coventry, Cofa Press, 1991.

Johnson, Georgia Douglas. "Escape." In Alain Locke, ed., *The New Negro*. New York, Atheneum, 1980, p. 147 (first published 1925).

Johnson, Paul. "Colonialism's Back – and Not a Moment Too Soon." *New York Times Magazine*, April 18, 1993.

Jordan, June. *Living Room*. New York, Thunder's Mouth Press, 1985.

—— *Technical Difficulties. African-American Notes on the State of the Union*. New York, Pantheon, 1992.

Joseph, Gloria. "Black Mothers and Daughters. Their Roles and Functions in American Society." In her *Common Differences. Conflicts in Black and White Feminist Perspectives*. Garden City, NY, Anchor Books, 1981.

Jussawalla, Feroza and Reed Way Dasenbrock, eds. *Interviews With Writers of the Post-Colonial World*. Jackson, Miss., and London, University of Mississippi Press, 1992.

Kaplan, Caren. "Deterritorializations. The Rewriting of Home and Exile in Western Feminist Discourse." *Cultural Critique*, 6, Spring, 1987, pp. 187–198.

Katrak, Ketu H. "Decolonizing Culture. Toward a Theory for Postcolonial Women's Texts." *Modern Fiction Studies*, 35, 1, Spring, 1989, pp. 157–179.

Katz, Jonathan Ned. "The Invention of Heterosexuality." *Socialist Review*, 20, 1, 1990, pp. 7–34.

Kennedy, Ellen Conroy (ed.). *The Negritude Poets*. New York, Thunder's Mouth Press, 1989.

Kenny, Lorraine. "Travelling Theory. The Cultural Politics of Race and Representation. An Interview with Kobena Mercer." *Afterimages: A Publication of the Visual Studies Workshop*, 18, 2, 1990, pp. 7–9.

Keyes, Cheryl. " 'We're More Than a Novelty, Boys.' Strategies of Female Rappers in the Rap Music Tradition." In Joan Newton Radner, ed., *Feminist Messages. Coding in Women's Folk Culture*. Urbana and Chicago, Ill., University of Illinois Press, 1993, pp. 203–220.

Kibreab, Gaim. *Refugees and Development in Africa*. Trenton, NJ, Red Sea Press, 1987.

Kincaid, Jamaica. *At the Bottom of the River*. New York, Farrar, Strauss, Giroux, 1983.

—— *Annie John*. New York, Farrar, Strauss, Giroux, 1985.

—— *A Small Place*. New York, Farrar, Strauss, Giroux, 1988.

—— *Lucy*. New York, Farrar, Strauss, Giroux, 1991.

—— "On Seeing England for the First Time." *Transition*, 51, 1991, pp. 32–40.

Kippax, Susan, June Crawford, Cathy Waldby and Pam Benton. "Women

Negotiating Heterosex. Implications for AIDS Prevention." *Women's Studies International Forum*, 13, 6, 1990, pp. 533–542.

Kristeva, Julia. *Revolution in Poetic Language*. New York, Columbia University Press, 1984.

—— "Woman Can Never Be Defined." In Elaine Marks and Isabelle de Courtivron, eds, *New French Feminisms*. New York, Schocken Books, 1981.

Krumholz, Linda. "The Ghosts of Slavery. Historical Recovery in Toni Morrison's *Beloved*." *African-American Review*, 26, 3, 1992, pp. 395–408.

Krupat, Arnold. "Criticism and the Canon. Cross Relations." *Diacritics*, 17, 1987, pp. 3–20.

—— "Post-Structuralism and Oral Literature." In Brian Swann and Arnold Krupat, eds, *Recovering the Word: Essays on Native American Literature*. Berkeley, Calif., University of California Press, 1987, pp. 113–148.

Kubayanda, Josaphat B. "Minority Discourse and the African Collective. Some Examples from Latin America and the Caribbean." *Cultural Critique*, 6, Spring, 1987, pp. 113–130.

—— "On Colonial/Imperial Discourse and Contemporary Critical Theory." Lecture Series. Working Papers 10. Department of Spanish and Portuguese, University of Maryland, College Park, 1990.

—— *The Poet's Africa. Africanness in the Poetry of Nicolas Guillen and Aimé Césaire*. New York, Greenwood Press, 1990.

Kulkarni, Harihar. "Paule Marshall. A Bibliography." *Callaloo*, 16, 1, Winter, 1993, pp. 243–271.

Laclau, Ernesto and Chantal Mouffe. *Hegemony and Socialist Strategy. Toward a Radical Democratic Politics*. London, Verso, 1985.

Lamming, George. *The Pleasures of Exile*. London, Michael Joseph, 1960.

Larsen, Nella. *Quicksand and Passing*. New Brunswick, NJ, Rutgers University Press, 1986.

Liddell, Janice Lee. "Pain and Pathology. A Review of THE UNBELONGING." *Caribbean Commentary*, 1, 3, April–May, 1990, pp. 33–34.

Lindfors, Bernth. "The Teaching of African Literature in the African Universities. An Instructive Canon." *Wasafiri*, 11, Spring, 1990, pp. 13–16.

Linthwaite, Illona. *Ain't I a Woman. Poems By Black and White Women*, London, Virago Press, 1987.

Lippard, Lucy. *Mixed Blessings. New Art in a Multicultural America*. New York, Pantheon, 1990.

Longmore, Zenga. *Tip-Taps to Trinidad. A Journey Through the Caribbean*. London, Arrow Books, 1989.

Lorde, Audre. *Zami. A New Spelling of My Name*. Freedom, Calif., The Crossing Press, 1982.

—— *Sister Outsider. Essays and Speeches*. Freedom, Calif., The Crossing Press, 1984.

—— "I Am Your Sister. Black Women Organizing Across Sexualities." Albany, NY, Kitchen Table: Women of Color Press, Freedom Organizing Series, no. 3, 1985.

—— *Our Dead Behind Us.* New York and London, W.W. Norton, 1986, pp. 16–18.

Lutz, Catherine. "The Gender of Theory." Unpublished ms., SUNY, Binghamton, 1990.

McClintock, Anne. "The Angel of Progress. Pitfalls of the Term 'Post-Colonialism'." *Social Text*, 31–32, 1992, pp. 84–98.

McDowell, Deborah. "New Directions for Black Feminist Criticism." *Black American Literature Forum*, 14, 4, Winter, 1986.

—— "Negotiating Between Tenses. Witnessing Slavery After Freedom – Dessa Rose." In Deborah McDowell and Arnold Rampersad, eds, *Slavery and the Literary Imagination.* Baltimore, Md., and London, Johns Hopkins University Press, 1989, pp. 144–163.

—— "Reading Family Matters." In Cheryl Wall, ed., *Changing Our Own Words*, New Brunswick, NJ, Rutgers University Press, 1989, pp. 75–97.

McWilliams, Sally. "Tsitsi Dangarembga's *Nervous Conditions* At The Crossroads of Feminism and Post-Colonialism." *World Literature Written in English*, 31, 1, 1991, pp. 103–112.

Mani, Lata. "Multiple Mediations. Feminist Scholarship in the Age of Multinational Reception." *Inscriptions*, 5, 1989, pp. 1–23; and *Feminist Review*, 35, Summer, 1990, pp. 24–41.

"Many Voices, One Chant. Black Feminist Perspectives." A special issue of *Feminist Review*, 17, July, 1984.

Marks, Elaine and Isabelle de Courtivron, eds. *New French Feminisms. An Anthology.* New York, Schocken Books, 1981.

Marshall, Paule. *Brown Girl, Brownstones.* New York, Random House, 1959.

—— *The Chosen Place, The Timeless People.* New York, Harcourt Brace & World, 1969.

—— *Praisesong for the Widow.* New York, G.P. Putnam & Sons, 1983.

—— *Reena and Other Stories.* New York, The Feminist Press, 1983.

—— *Daughters.* New York, Plume, 1991.

Martin, Biddy and Chandra Talpade Mohanty. "Feminist Politics. What's Home Got to Do With It?" In Teresa de Lauretis, ed., *Feminist Studies/ Critical Studies.* Bloomington, Ind., Indiana University Press, 1986, pp. 191–212.

Mavinga, Isha McKenzie and Thelma Perkins. *In Search of Mr. McKenzie. Two Sisters' Quest for an Unknown Father.* London, The Women's Press, 1991.

Maxwell, Anne. "The Debate on Current Theories of Colonial Discourse." *Kunapipi*, 13, 3, 1991, pp. 70–84.

Meese, Elizabeth A. *(Ex)Tensions. Re-Figuring Feminist Criticism.* Urbana and Chicago, Ill., University of Illinois Press, 1990.

Melendez, Edwin and Edgardo, eds. *Colonial Dilemma. Critical Perspectives on Contemporary Puerto Rico*, Boston, Mass., South End Press, 1993.

Menchu, Rigoberta. *I . . . Rigoberta Menchu: An Indian Woman in Guatemala.* Ed. by Elisabeth Burgos-Debray, trans. by Ann Wright. London, Verso, 1984.

Menchu, Rigoberta and Jim Stephens. "Women are Raising Their Voices."

We Continue Forever. Sorrow and Strength of Guatemalan Women. New York, Women's International Resource Exchange, 1983, pp. 50–52.

Mercer, Kobena. "Diaspora Culture and the Dialogic Imagination. The Aesthetics of Black Independent Film in Britain." In Mbye Cham and Claire Andrade-Watkins, eds, *Black Frames: Critical Perspectives on Black Independent Cinema.* Cambridge, Mass. and London, MIT Press, 1988, pp. 50–61.

—— "Black Art and the Burden of Representation." *Third Text*, 10, Spring, 1990, pp. 61–78.

Mercer, Kobena and Isaac Julien. "Race, Sexual Politics and Black Masculinity. A Dossier." In Jonathan Rutherford and Rowena Chapman, eds, *Male Order. Unwrapping Masculinity.* London, Lawrence & Wishart, 1988.

—— "True Confessions. A Discourse on Images of Black Male Sexuality." In Essex Hemphill, ed. (conceived by Joseph Beam), *Brother to Brother. New Writings by Gay Men.* Boston, Mass., Alyson Publications Inc., 1992, pp. 167–173.

Merini, Rafika. "The Subversion of the Culture of Voyeurism in The Works of Leila Sebbar and Assia Djebar." Unpublished Ph.D. dissertation, SUNY, Binghamton, 1992.

Mies, Maria, Veronika Bennholdt-Thomsen and Claudia von Werlhof. *Women: The Last Colony.* London and Atlantic Highlands, NJ, Zed Press, Ltd., 1988.

Miller, Christopher. *Blank Darkness. Africanist Discourse in French.* Chicago, Ill., University of Chicago Press, 1985.

—— "Theories of Africans." In Henry Louis Gates Jr, ed., *"Race," Writing and Difference.* Chicago, Ill. and London, University of Chicago Press, 1985, pp. 281–300.

Miller, Nancy. "Changing the Subject. Authorship, Writing and the Reader." In Teresa de Lauretis, ed., *Feminist Studies/Critical Studies.* Bloomington, Ind., Indiana University Press, 1986, pp. 102–120.

Minh-ha, Trinh T. *Woman Native Other. Writing Postcoloniality and Feminism.* Bloomington and Indianapolis, Ind., Indiana University Press, 1989.

—— "Cotton and Iron." In Russell Ferguson, Martha Gever, Trinh T. Minh-ha and Cornel West, eds, *Out There. Marginalization and Contemporary Cultures.* New York, The New Museum of Contemporary Art, and Cambridge, Mass. and London, MIT Press, 1990, pp. 327–336.

—— "Not You/Like You. Post-Colonial Women and the Interlocking Questions of Identity and Difference." In Gloria Anzaldua, ed., *Making Face, Making Soul/Haciendo Caras.* San Francisco, Calif., Spinsters/Aunt Lute, 1990, pp. 371–375.

—— *When the Moon Waxes Red. Representation, Gender and Cultural Politics.* London, Routledge, 1991.

—— *Framer Framed.* New York and London, Routledge, 1992.

Mirza, Heidi Safia. *Young, Female and Black.* London and New York, Routledge, 1992.

Mohanty, Chandra Talpade. "Under Western Eyes. Feminist Scholarship and Colonial Discourse." *Boundary 2*, XII, 3 and XIII, 1, Spring–Fall, 1984, pp. 333–358.

—— "Feminist Encounters. Locating the Politics of Experience." In Michèle Barrett and Anne Phillips, eds, *Destabilizing Theory. Contemporary Feminist Debates*. Stanford, Calif., Stanford University Press, 1992, pp. 74–92.

Mohanty, Chandra Talpade and Biddy Martin. "Feminist Politics. What's Home Got To Do With It?" In Teresa de Lauretis, ed., *Feminist Studies/ Critical Studies*. Bloomington, Ind., Indiana University Press, 1986, pp. 191–212.

Mohanty, Chandra Talpade, Ann Russo and Lourdes Torres, eds. *Third World Women and the Politics of Feminism*. Bloomington, Ind., Indiana University Press, 1991.

Mohanty, Satya P. "Us and Them. On the Philosophical Bases of Political Criticism." *Yale Journal of Criticism*, 2, 2, Spring, 1989, pp. 1–31.

—— "The Epistemic Status of Cultural Identity." *Cultural Critique*, 24, Spring, 1993, pp. 41–80.

Moi, Toril. *Sexual/Textual Politics: Feminist Literary Theory*. London and New York, Routledge, 1985.

—— *The Kristeva Reader*. New York, Columbia University Press, 1986.

Mora, Pat. *Borders*. Houston, Tex., Arte Publico Press, 1986.

Morejon, Nancy. "The Invisible Afro-America." Lecture SUNY, Binghamton, April, 1993.

Morrison, Toni. *Sula*. New York, Alfred A. Knopf Inc., 1974.

—— *Song of Solomon*. New York, Alfred A. Knopf Inc., 1977.

—— *Tar Baby*. New York, Alfred A. Knopf Inc., 1981.

—— *Beloved*. New York, Alfred A. Knopf Inc., 1987.

—— "Unspeakable Things Unspoken. The Afro-American Presence in American Literature." *Michigan Quarterly Review*, 28, 1, Winter, 1989, pp. 1–34.

—— *Jazz*. New York, Alfred A. Knopf Inc., 1992.

Mortimer, Delores M. and Roy S. Bryce-Laporte. *Female Immigrants to the United States: Caribbean, Latin American and African Experiences*, and *Caribbean Immigration to the United States*. Washington, DC, The Smithsonian Institution, RIIES Occasional Papers, nos 1 and 2, 1981 and 1983.

Mukherjee, Arun. "Whose Post-Colonialism and Whose Postmodernism?" *World Literature Written in English*, 30, 2, 1990, pp. 1–9.

Nadel, S.F. "Witchcraft and Anti-Witchcraft." *Nupe Religion*. London, Routledge & Kegan Paul Ltd, 1954.

—— "Witchcraft in Four African Societies. An Essay in Comparison." In Simon and Phoebe Ottenberg, eds, *Cultures and Societies of Africa*. New York, Random House, 1960, pp. 407–420.

Nasta, Susheila, ed. *Motherlands. Black Women's Writing from Africa, the Caribbean and South Asia*. London, The Women's Press, 1991, and New Brunswick, NJ, Rutgers University Press, 1992.

Naylor, Gloria. "A Conversation with Toni Morrison." *Southern Review*, 21, 3, July, 1985, pp. 567–593.

Nelson Garner, Shirley, Claire Kahane and Madelon Sprengnether. *The*

Mother Tongue: Essays in Feminist Psychoanalytic Interpretation. Ithaca, NY, Cornell University Press, 1985.

Nero, Charles I. "Toward a Black Gay Aesthetic. Signifying in Contemporary Black Gay Literature." In Essex Hemphill, ed. (conceived by Joseph Beam), *Brother to Brother. New Writings by Gay Black Men.* Boston, Mass., Alyson Publications Inc., 1992.

Netifa. *A Woman Determined.* London, Research Associates, 1987.

Newton, Judith and Deborah Rosenfelt, eds. *Feminist Criticism and Social Change: Sex, Class and Race in Literature and Culture.* New York, Methuen, 1985.

Ng, Siu Won. "Just Another Woman." *Feminist Art News,* 4, 2, p. 29.

Ngcobo, Lauretta, ed. *Let It Be Told. Black Women Writers in Britain.* London, Virago Press, 1988.

Ngugi wa Thiong'o. *Decolonising the Mind. The Politics of Language in African Literature.* London, James Currey; Portsmouth, NH and Nairobi, Heinemann; Harare, Zimbabwe Publishing House, 1986.

—— *Moving the Centre. The Struggle for Cultural Freedoms.* London, Heinemann, 1993.

Ngugi wa Thiong'o, Henry Owuor-Anyumba and Taban Lo Liyong. "On the Abolition of the English Department." In Ngugi wa Thiong'o, ed., *Homecoming. Essays on African and Caribbean Literature, Culture and Politics.* London, Heinemann, 1972, pp. 145–150.

Nichols, Grace. *I Is a Long Memoried Woman,* London, Karnak House, 1983.

—— *The Fat Black Woman's Poems.* London, Virago Press, 1984.

—— *Lazy Thoughts of a Lazy Woman.* London, Virago Press, 1989.

Nobel, Peter. "Refugees and Other Migrants Viewed with the Legal Eye – or how to Fight Confusion." In Kirsten Holst Petersen and Anna Rutherford, eds, *Displaced Persons.* Sydney, Mundelstrup, Denmark and Coventry, Dangaroo Press, 1988, pp. 18–31.

Nothing But the Same Old Story. The Roots of Anti-Irish Racism. London, Information on Ireland, 1984.

Odeh, Lama Abu. "Post-Colonial Feminism and the Veil. Thinking the Difference." *Feminist Review,* 43, Spring, 1993, pp. 26–37.

Offen, Karen. "Defining Feminism. A Comparative Historical Approach." *Signs,* 14, 1, 1988, pp. 119–262.

Ogundipe-Leslie, 'Molara. "Not Spinning on the Axis of Maleness." In Robin Morgan, ed., *Sisterhood is Global.* New York, Anchor Press/Doubleday, 1984, pp. 498–504.

—— *African Women and Critical Transformations. Theory and Practice.* Trenton, NJ, Africa World Press, 1994.

Ong, Aihwa. "Colonialism and Modernity. Feminist Representations of Women in Non-Western Societies." *Inscriptions,* 3, 4, pp. 79–93.

Onoge, Omafume. "The Crisis of Consciousness in Modern African Literature." In Georg M. Gugelberger, ed., *Marxism and African Literature.* Trenton, NJ, Africa World Press, 1986.

Onwueme, Tess. "Bodies in Silence. The Missing Diaspora in African Literature." *Drum Voices,* 2, Fall/Winter, 1992/93, nos 1 and 2, pp. 157–169.

Other Story, The. Exhibition Catalogue. London, Hayward Gallery, 1989.

Parker, Andrew, Mary Russo, Doris Sommer and Patricia Yaeger, eds. *Nationalisms and Sexualities.* New York and London, Routledge, 1992.

Parmar, Pratibha. "Gender, Race and Class. Asian Women in Resistance." In Centre for Contemporary Cultural Studies, *The Empire Strikes Back. Race and Racism in 70's Britain.* London, Hutchinson, 1982, pp. 236–275.

Parry, Benita. "Problems in Current Theories of Colonial Discourse." *Oxford Literary Review,* 9, 1–2, 1987, pp. 27–57.

Pathak, Zakia. "A Pedagogy for Postcolonial Feminists." In Judith Butler and Joan Scott, eds, *Feminists Theorize the Political.* New York and London, Routledge, 1992, pp. 426–441.

Philip, Marlene Nourbese. *She Tries Her Tongue. Her Silence Softly Breaks.* Charlottetown, Prince Edward Island, Canada, Ragweed Press, 1989.

—— *Looking for Livingstone. An Odyssey of Silence.* Stratford, Ontario, Mercury Press, 1991.

—— "The White Soul of Canada." *Third Text,* 14, Spring, 1991, pp. 63–77.

—— *Frontiers. Essays and Writings in Racism and Culture, 1984–1992.* Stratford, Ontario, Mercury Press, 1992.

Phizacklea, Annie, ed. *One Way Ticket. Migration and Female Labour.* London, Routledge, 1983.

Pines, Jan and Paul Willeman, eds. *Questions of Third Cinema.* London, British Film Institute Publishing, 1989.

Pollard, Velma. "Innovation in Jamaican Creole. The Speech of Rastafari." In Manfred Gorlach and John A. Holm, eds. *Varieties of English Around the World,* vol. 8. Amsterdam and Philadelphia, Pa., John Benjamins, 1986, pp. 157–166.

—— "Mothertongue Voices in the Writing of Olive Senior and Lorna Goodison." In Susheila Nasta, ed., *Motherlands. Black Women's Writing from Africa, the Caribbean and South East Asia.* London, The Women's Press, 1991, pp. 238–253.

Prakash, Gyan. "Postcolonial Criticism and Indian Historiography." *Social Text,* 31–32, 1992, pp. 8–19.

Prescod, Margaret. *Black Women: Bringing It All Back Home.* Bristol, Falling Wall Press, 1980.

Radhakrishnan, R. "Ethnic Identity and Post-Structuralist Difference." *Cultural Critique,* 6, 1987, pp. 199–220.

—— "Negotiating Subject Positions in an Uneven World." In Linda Kaufmann, ed., *Feminism and Institutions: Dialogues on Feminist Theory.* Oxford and New York, Basil Blackwell, 1989, pp. 276–290.

Radway, Janice. "Reception Study. Ethnography and the Problems of Dispersed Audiences and Nomadic Subjects." *Cultural Studies,* 2, 3, 1988, pp. 359–376.

Rahim, Jennifer. *Mothers are not the Only Linguists and Other Poems.* Diego Martin, Trinidad, The New Voices, 1992.

Ramos, Juanita, ed. *Compañeras. Latina Lesbians.* New York, Latina Lesbian History Project, 1987.

Randall, Margaret. *Walking to the Edge. Essays of Resistance.* Boston, Mass., South End Press, 1990.

Reagon, Bernice Johnson. "Coalition Politics. Turning the Century." In

Barbara Smith, ed., *Homegirls: A Black Feminist Anthology*. New York, Kitchen Table: Women of Color Press, 1983, pp. 356–368.

Retamar, Roberto. "Caliban. Notes Towards a Discussion of Culture in Our America." *Massachusetts Review*, Winter–Spring, 1974.

— *Caliban and Other Essays*. Trans. by Edward Baker. Minneapolis, Minn., University of Minnesota Press, 1989.

Rhys, Jean. *Wide Sargasso Sea*. London, Penguin, 1966.

Riley, Joan, *The Unbelonging*. London, The Women's Press, 1985.

— *Waiting in the Twilight*. London, The Women's Press, 1987.

— *Romance*. London, The Women's Press, 1988.

— *A Kindness to the Children*. London, The Women's Press, 1992.

Rubin, Gayle. "The Traffic in Women. Notes on the Political Economy of Sex." In Rayna Rapp Reiter, ed., *Toward an Anthropology of Women*. New York, Monthly Review Press, 1975, pp. 157–210.

Ruddick, Sara. *Maternal Thinking. Towards a Politics of Peace*, Boston, Mass., Beacon, 1989.

Rutherford, Jonathan and Rowena Chapman, eds. *Male Order. Unwrapping Masculinity*. London, Lawrence & Wishart, 1988.

Saakana, Amon Saba. *The Colonial Legacy in Caribbean Literature*. London, Karnak House, 1987.

Said, Edward. "Opponents, Audiences, Constituencies, and Community." *Critical Inquiry*, 9, 1982, pp. 1–26.

— *The World, The Text and The Critic*. London, Vintage, 1991.

Sandoval, Chela. "U.S. Third World Feminism. The Theory and Method of Oppositional Consciousness in the Postmodern World." *Genders*, 10, Spring, 1991, pp. 1–24.

Sangari, Kumkum. "The Politics of the Possible." *Cultural Critique*, 7, Fall, 1987, pp. 157–186.

Sangari, Kumkum and Sudesh Vaid, eds. *Recasting Women in India. Essays in Colonial History in India*. New Brunswick, NJ, Rutgers University Press, 1990.

Santiago-Vallès, Kelvin. *Subject Peoples and Colonial Discourses. Economic Transformation and Social Disorder in Puerto Rico, 1898–1947*. Albany, NY, SUNY Press, 1994.

Sassen, Saskia. *The Mobility of Labor and Capital. A Study in International Investment and Labor Flow*. London and New York, Cambridge University Press, 1988.

Schulze-Engler, Frank. "Beyond Post-Colonialism. Multiple Identities in East African Literature." In Gordon Collier, ed., *Us/Them. Translation, Transcription and Identity in Post-Colonial Literary Cultures*. Amsterdam and Atlanta, Ga., Rodopi, 1992, pp. 319–328.

Scott, Della. Interview with Paule Marshall. *Abafazi*, 3, 3, Spring–Summer, 1993, pp. 34–38.

Shohat, Ella. "Notes on the 'Post-Colonial'." *Social Text*, 31–32, 1992, pp. 99–113.

Silko, Leslie Marmon. "Language and Literature from a Pueblo Indian Perspective." In Philomena Mariani, ed., *Critical Fictions. The Politics of Imaginative Writing*. Seattle, Wash., Bay Press, 1991, pp. 83–93.

Silvera, Makeda, ed. *Piece of My Heart. A Lesbian of Color Anthology.* Toronto, Sister Vision Press, 1992.

Silverblatt, Irene Marsha. *Moon, Sun and Witches. Gender Ideologies and Class in Inca and Colonial Peru.* Princeton, NJ, Princeton University Press, 1987.

Slemon, Stephen. "Unsettling the Empire. Resistance Theory for the Second World." *World Literature Written in English,* 30, 2, 1990, pp. 30–41.

Slemon, Stephen and Helen Tiffin, eds. "Special Issue on Post-Colonial Criticism." *Kunapipi,* XI, 1, 1989.

Smith, Barbara, ed. *Homegirls,* New York, Kitchen Table: Women of Color Press, 1983.

Smith, Paul. *Discerning the Subject.* Minneapolis, Minn., University of Minnesota Press, 1988.

Smith, Sidonie. *A Poetics of Women's Autobiography. Marginality and the Fictions of Self Representation.* Bloomington, Ind., Indiana University Press, 1987.

Smith, Valerie. " 'Loopholes of Retreat'. Architecture and Ideology in Harriet Jacobs's *Incidents in the Life of a Slave Girl.*" In Henry Louis Gates Jr, ed., *Reading Black. Reading Feminist. A Critical Anthology.* New York, Penguin, 1990, pp. 212–226.

Solomon, Frances Anne. *I Is a Long Memoried Woman.* London, Leda Serene/YOD Video, 1990.

Spillers, Hortense J. "Cross-Currents, Discontinuities. Black Women's Fiction." In Marjorie Pryse and Hortense Spillers, eds, *Conjuring. Black Women, Fiction and Literary Tradition.* Bloomington, Ind., Indiana University Press, 1985, pp. 249–261.

—— "Mama's Baby, Papa's Maybe. An American Grammar Book." *Diacritics,* 17, 2, Summer, 1987, pp. 65–81.

Spivak, Gayatri Chakravorty. "French Feminism in an International Frame." *Yale French Studies,* 62, 1981, pp. 154–188.

—— "Displacement and the Discourse of Woman." In Mark Krupnick, ed., *Displacement. Derrida and After.* Bloomington, Ind., Indiana University Press, 1983, pp. 169–195.

—— "Subaltern Studies. Deconstructing Historiography." In Ranajit Guha, ed., *Subaltern Studies,* vol. 4. London, Oxford University Press, 1985, pp. 330–363.

—— "Three Women's Texts and a Critique of Imperialism." *Critical Inquiry,* 12, 1, Autumn, 1985, pp. 243–262.

—— *In Other Worlds. Essays in Cultural Politics.* New York, Methuen, 1987/New York and London, Routledge, 1988.

—— "Can the Subaltern Speak?" In Cary Nelson and Lawrence Grossberg, eds, *Marxism and the Interpretation of Culture.* Urbana and Chicago, Ill., University of Illinois Press, 1988, pp. 271–313.

—— "The Political Economy of Women as Seen by a Literary Critic." In Elizabeth Weed, ed., *Coming to Terms: Feminism, Theory, Politics.* New York, Routledge, 1989, pp. 218–229.

—— Poststructuralism, Marginality, Postcoloniality and Value." In P.

Collier and Gaya Ryan, eds, *Literary Theory Today*. Cambridge, Polity, 1990, pp. 219–244.

—— *The Post-Colonial Critic. Interviews, Strategies, Dialogues*. Ed. by Sarah Harasym. New York and London, Routledge, 1990.

—— "The Politics of Translation." In Michèle Barrett and Anne Phillips, eds, *Destabilizing Theory. Contemporary Feminist Debates*. Stanford, Calif., Stanford University Press, 1992, pp. 177–200.

—— *Outside in the Teaching Machine*. New York and London, Routledge, 1993.

Stam, Robert. *Subversive Pleasures. Bakhtin, Cultural Criticism and Film*. Baltimore, Md., Johns Hopkins University Press, 1989.

Stam, Robert and Louise Spence. "Colonialism, Racism, and Representation. An Introduction." *Screen*, 24, 2, March–April, 1983, pp. 632–649.

Steady, Filomina Chioma. *The Black Woman Cross-Culturally*. Cambridge, Mass., Schenckman, 1981.

Stetson, Erlene, ed. *Black Sister. Poetry by Black American Women 1746–1980*. Bloomington and Indianapolis, Ind., Indiana University Press, 1981.

Strathern, Marilyn. *The Gender of the Gift*. Berkeley, Calif., University of California Press, 1988.

Suleiman, Susan. "On Maternal Splitting. A Propos of Mary Gordon's *Men and Angels*." *Signs*, 14, 1, Autumn, 1988, pp. 25–41.

Sulter, Maud. *As a Blackwoman. Poems 1982–1985*. Hebden Bridge, West Yorkshire, Urban Fox Press, 1985.

Sulter, Maud, ed. *Passion. Discourses on Blackwomen's Creativity*. Hebden Bridge, West Yorkshire, Urban Fox Press, 1990.

Sutherland, Efua. "New Life at Kyerefaso." In Charlotte Bruner, ed., *Unwinding Threads*. London, Heinemann, 1983, pp. 17–23.

Takaki, Ronald, ed. *From Different Shores. Perspectives on Race and Ethnicity in America*. London, Oxford University Press, 1987.

Talkers Through Dream Doors. Poetry and Short Stories by Black Women. Manchester, Crocus, 1989.

Taylor, Clyde. "Eurocentrics vs. New Thought at Edinburgh." *Framework*, 34, 1987, pp. 140–148.

—— "Black Cinema in the Post-Aesthetic Era." In Jim Pines and Paul Willemen, eds, *Questions of Third Cinema*. London, British Film Institute, 1989, pp. 90–110.

Thiam, Awa. *Black Sisters, Speak Out. Feminism and Oppression in Black Africa*. London, Pluto Press, 1986.

"Thinking Through Ethnicities." A special issue of *Feminist Review*, 45, Autumn, 1993.

Todorov, Tzvetan. *The Conquest of America: The Question of the Other*. Trans. by Richard Howard. New York, Harper & Row, 1984.

Truth, Sojourner. "Ain't I A Woman." In Erlene Stetson, ed., *Black Sister*. Bloomington, Ind., Indiana University Press, 1981, p. 24.

Van den Abbeele, Georges. "Sightseers. The Tourist as Theorist." *Diacritics*, Winter, 1980, pp. 2–14.

Walby, Sylvia. "Post-Post-Modernism? Theorizing Social Complexity." In Michèle Barrett and Anne Phillips, eds, *Destabilizing Theory*.

Contemporary Feminist Debates. Stanford, Calif., Stanford University Press, 1992, pp. 31–52.

Wall, Cheryl, ed. *Changing Our Own Words. Essays on Criticism, Theory, and Writing by Black Women.* New Brunswick, NJ and London, Rutgers University Press, 1989.

Walker, D.J.R. *Columbus and the Golden World of the Island Arawaks. The Story of the First Americans and their Caribbean Environment.* Kingston, Jamaica, Ian Randle Publishers and Sussex, The Book Guild, 1992.

Walker, Alice. *Meridian.* Harcourt Brace Jovanovich, 1976.

—— *The Temple of My Familiar.* New York, Harcourt Brace Jovanovich, 1989.

—— "What Can the (White) Man . . .   . . . Say to the Black Woman." *Nation*, May 22, 1989, pp. 691–692.

Wallace, Michele. *Invisibility Blues. From Pop to Theory.* London, Verso, 1990.

Warner-Vieyra, Myriam. *Juletane.* Trans. by Betty Wilson. London, Heinemann, 1987.

Washington, Mary Helen. *Black Eyed Susans.* New York, Anchor Press/ Doubleday, 1975.

—— *Midnight Birds. Stories by Contemporary Black Women Writers.* New York, Anchor Press/Doubleday, 1980.

—— *Invented Lives. Narratives of Black Women 1860–1960*, New York, Anchor Press/Doubleday, 1987.

Weedon, Chris. *Feminist Practice and Poststructuralist Theory.* London, Basil Blackwell, 1987.

Weedon, Chris, Andrew Tolson and Frank Mort. "Theories of Language and Subjectivity." In Stuart Hall, ed., *Culture, Media, Language: Working Papers in Cultural Studies, 1972–79.* London, Hutchinson, 1980, pp. 195–216.

West, Cornel. "Decentring Europe. A Memorial Lecture for James Snead. Introduced by Colin MacCabe." *Critical Quarterly*, 33, 1, 1991, pp. 1–19.

Williams, Patricia. *The Alchemy of Race and Rights.* Cambridge, Mass., Harvard University Press, 1991.

Williams, Sherley Anne. *Dessa Rose.* New York, William and Morrow Inc., 1986.

—— "Some Implications of Womanist Theory." *Callaloo*, 9, 2, Spring, 1986, pp. 303–308.

Wilson, Amrit. *Finding a Voice. Asian Women in Britain.* London, Virago Press, 1978.

Wilson, Harriet. *Our Nig. Sketches from the Life of a Free Black.* New York, Random House, 1983.

Wilson, Monica Hunter. "Witch Beliefs and Social Structure." *American Journal of Sociology*, 51, 4, January, 1951, pp. 307–313.

Winant, Howard. Interview. "Gayatri Spivak on the Politics of the Subaltern." *Socialist Review*, 20, 3, July–September, 1990, pp. 81–97.

Wisker, Gina, ed. *Black Women's Writing.* New York, St Martin's Press, 1993.

Wolff, Janet. "On the Road Again. Metaphors of Travel in Cultural Criticism." *Cultural Studies*, 7, 2, May, 1993, pp. 224–239.

Wynter, Sylvia. "Beyond Miranda's Meanings. Un/Silencing the 'Demonic Ground' of Caliban's 'Woman'." In Carole Boyce Davies and Elaine Savory Fido, eds, *Out of the Kumbla. Caribbean Women and Literature.* Trenton, NJ, Africa World Press, 1990, pp. 355–372.

Yudice, George. "Marginality and the Ethics of Survival." In Andrew Ross, ed., *Universal Abandon.* Minneapolis, Minn., University of Minnesota Press, 1988, pp. 214–236.

Zahno, Kamila. "Ethnic Monitoring or a Geography Lesson." *Feminist Art News*, 3, 10, p. 24.

INDEX